PENGUIN CLASSICS

LIFE OF GALILEO

BERTOLT BRECHT was born in Augsburg, Bavaria, in 1898 and left Germany in 1933 when Hitler came to power. He lived in the United States for seven years, settling with his family in Santa Monica and New York, and continuing to work on plays and films. After the war, Brecht returned to Germany, where he founded the Berliner Ensemble. He died in 1956.

RICHARD FOREMAN has written, directed, and designed over fifty of his own plays both in New York City and abroad. Five of his plays have received OBIE Awards as best play of the year—and he has received five other OBIEs for directing and for "sustained achievement." He has received the annual Literature Award from the American Academy and Institute of Arts and Letters, a Lifetime Achievement in Theatre Award from the National Endowment for the Arts, the PEN Club Master American Dramatist Award, a MacArthur "Genius" Fellowship, and in 2004 was elected officer of the Order of Arts and Letters of France. Foreman is the founder and artistic director of the nonprofit Ontological-Hysteric Theater (1968–present). He has also directed and designed many classical productions with major theaters around the world. Seven collections of his plays have already been published, and books studying his work have been published in New York, Paris, Berlin, and Tokyo.

NORMAN ROESSLER, PhD, is editor of *Communications*, the performance journal of the International Brecht Society, and is a lecturer at Temple University in Philadelphia, Pennsylvania.

P9-DFS-171

BERTOLT BRECHT

Life of Galileo

Foreword by
RICHARD FOREMAN

Introduction to the Penguin Classics Edition by
NORMAN ROESSLER

Edited with an Introduction by
JOHN WILLETT *and* RALPH MANHEIM

Translated by
JOHN WILLETT

PENGUIN BOOKS

PENGUIN BOOKS
Published by the Penguin Group
Penguin Group (USA) Inc., 375 Hudson Street, New York, New York 10014, U.S.A.
Penguin Group (Canada), 90 Eglinton Avenue East, Suite 700, Toronto, Ontario, Canada M4P 2Y3
(a division of Pearson Penguin Canada Inc.) • Penguin Books Ltd, 80 Strand, London WC2R 0RL,
England • Penguin Ireland, 25 St Stephen's Green, Dublin 2, Ireland (a division of Penguin Books Ltd) •
Penguin Group (Australia), 250 Camberwell Road, Camberwell, Victoria 3124, Australia
(a division of Pearson Australia Group Pty Ltd) • Penguin Books India Pvt Ltd, 11 Community Centre,
Panchsheel Park, New Delhi–110 017, India • Penguin Group (NZ), 67 Apollo Drive, Rosedale, North
Shore 0632, New Zealand (a division of Pearson New Zealand Ltd) • Penguin Books (South Africa) (Pty)
Ltd, 24 Sturdee Avenue, Rosebank, Johannesburg 2196, South Africa

Penguin Books Ltd, Registered Offices:
80 Strand, London WC2R 0RL, England

First published in Great Britain by Eyre Methuen Ltd. 1980
First published in the United States of America by Arcade Publishing, Inc. 1994
Published by arrangement with Arcade Publishing, Inc.
This edition with a foreword by Richard Foreman and introductions by Norman Roessler published in
Penguin Books 2008

7 9 10 8

Copyright © Arvid Englind Teaterforlag, a.b., 1940
Copyright renewed Stefan S. Brecht, 1967
Copyright © Suhrkamp Verlag, Frankfurt am Main, 1955
Translation of play and texts by Brecht copyright © Stefan S. Brecht, 1980
Galileo translated by Charles Laughton copyright © Bertolt Brecht, 1952
Introduction by Ralph Manheim and John Willett and editorial notes copyright © Eyre Methuen Ltd., 1980
Foreword copyright © Richard Foreman, 2008
Introductions copyright © Norman Roessler, 2007, 2008
All rights reserved

Life of Galileo, originally published in German under the title Leben des Galilei,
was first published in this translation in 1980.

CAUTION: This play is fully protected by copyright. All inquiries concerning the rights for professional
or amateur stage production should be directed to Jerold L. Couture, Fitelson, Lasky, Aslan & Couture,
551 Fifth Avenue, New York, New York 10176. Inquiries concerning the rights for professional stage
production outside of the United States of America or the music for this play should be directed to the
International Copyright Bureau Ltd., 22a Aubrey House, Maida Avenue, London W2 1TQ, England, and
those for amateur stage production outside of the United States of America to Samuel French Ltd.,
52 Fitzroy Street, London W1T 5JR, England. Inquiries about use of any material other than in
performance should be directed to Arcade Publishing, Inc., 116 John Street, New York, New York 10038.

LIBRARY OF CONGRESS CATALOGING IN PUBLICATION DATA
Brecht, Bertolt, 1898–1956.
[Leben des Galilei. English]
Life of Galileo / Bertolt Brecht ; foreword by Richard Foreman ; introduction to the Penguin Classics edi-
tion by Norman Roessler ; edited with an introduction by John Willett and Ralph Manheim ; translated
by John Willett.
p. cm.
Includes bibliographical references.
ISBN 978-0-14-310538-1
1. Galilei, Galileo, 1564–1642—Drama. I. Foreman, Richard, 1937– II. Roessler, Norman. III. Willett,
John. IV. Manheim, Ralph, 1907–1992. V. Title.
PT2603.R397L415 2008
832'.912—dc22   2008009340

Printed in the United States of America
Set in Sabon

Contents

Foreword by RICHARD FOREMAN   vii

Introduction to the Penguin Classics Edition by
   NORMAN ROESSLER   xiii

Introduction by JOHN WILLETT *and* RALPH MANHEIM   xxvii

LIFE OF GALILEO

Notes and Variants
   Texts by Brecht   113
   Editorial Notes   157
   Appendix   195

Foreword

There is no question that my encounter with Brecht was the most important artistic event of my theatrical life. It was Brecht who "saved me" from normal theater!

It was the early 1950s, and I was a thirteen-year-old junior high school student in Scarsdale, New York—an enclave of upper-middle-class security and respectability. Even at that age I had begun acting in plays and designing scenery for both school productions and neighboring community theaters. Plus, each weekend I traveled to New York City to see every Broadway play I could fit into my schedule. But I regularly left those performances in anguish—turning to the schoolmate who accompanied me, exclaiming, "John—there's no hope for me! If what we just saw is what succeeds in the theater—I could never bring myself to make something that banal and obvious." (And this included all the big hits of the day.)

What depressed me was an "audience pandering" style that aimed for empathy between stage and spectator. Telegraphing at each moment what the audience was supposed to feel, instead of allowing a free spectator to discover what was at work onstage. I felt I was drowning in banalities.

But then I was thrown a life preserver! In 1952, I chanced upon Mordecai Gorelik's 1940 book *New Theaters for Old*, a history of progressive trends in twentieth-century theater, featuring a chapter on Brecht and director Erwin Piscator. Looking into the book for the first time in thirty years, I was surprised to discover Piscator discussed at greater length than Brecht. Nevertheless, it was the references to Brecht's rejection of both Aristotelian form and the normal theater's basis in empathy that struck me with the force of revelation.

After that initiation I eagerly sought more material on Brecht, but in 1952 America there wasn't much to find. Then, in 1953, Eric Bentley's *In Search of Theater* arrived, going into more detail concerning Brecht's theatrical practice and philosophy. That excited me; there seemed no hope of seeing an actual Brecht performance in New York. (I had been too young to see the poorly received 1947 Brecht–Charles Laughton production of *Galileo*.)

Throughout my theatrical youth, Brecht was looked upon as either misguided (in his condemnation of audience-involving plot and seductive Stanislavski-style "method" performance)—or as the enemy (i.e., a Communist!).

In fact, as a student at Brown University in 1958, when I persuaded the drama club to produce *The Caucasian Chalk Circle*, the dean of the college canceled it, announcing Brown would never present a play by a Communist!

Two years before, in 1956, I had had my one experience of seeing a rare New York production of a genuine Brecht play, *The Good Woman of Setzuan*, presented by the Phoenix Theater, translated and directed by Eric Bentley, starring Uta Hagen and Zero Mostel. It was a flop, of course. The critics dismissed it as being "without feeling"—but I loved its cold, clinical (Brechtian) nature. Brecht, however, was still a nonperson as far as America was concerned—though I followed reports from Europe claiming him as one of the greats of the twentieth century.

Ironically, that's not the whole story. Brecht did have one success in New York—due to what I considered a misrepresentation. The Mark Blitzstein version of the Brecht-Weill *Threepenny Opera* was a big hit in the Village in 1954. At that time I too loved the production—I believe it succeeded because of Weill's great score and, secondarily, because of the softening and popularizing of Brecht's text in Blitzstein's very free translation.

Indeed, when I directed my own version of *The Threepenny Opera* at Lincoln Center in 1976, I chose the more accurate Ralph Manheim translation, which was harsher and less raffishly "friendly"—just like my staging. While Brecht's original production had captured the mood of the devil-may-care, thuglike world of capitalistic prewar Germany, I was trying to reflect the mood of my own time and place—big business–driven Cold War America—inside a sterile Lincoln Center environment that for me evoked the Pentagon.

But even in my antiempathic production, Brecht (plus Weill) again pleased vast audiences in a way he never otherwise managed (minus Weill's music) in the professional New York Theater. It's true that in following years, many of his texts made their way onstage in America (mostly in colleges and universities). But rare indeed was the production that attempted to capture the full rigor of the "alienation effect" that Brecht made notorious in theory and on stage.

Remembering this sad fact makes me revisit certain curious theater experiences I had as a young man attending Broadway plays. Walking out after most productions thinking, "That was a mediocre text in a banal staging," I was shocked to realize the next day, thinking back on the performance, that it had somehow "crystallized" in my memory into a "strong and effective memory object," magically acquiring all the positive qualities critics and audiences had been applauding. Did that mean my initial reaction had been wrong? No, I concluded. It was simply that by watching the performance—moment by moment with alert and "detached" rigor (i.e., the Brechtian "alienation")—each small unit of the event displayed, so directly viewed, its truly pedestrian nature. A day later, however, the "play object"—no longer directly present before my conscious attention—had become a memory of the experience, softened and glazed over by the usual workings of time passing. And shockingly, the memory of the play had become stronger than the play as actually experienced!

To explain this to myself, I concluded that as a rule, most people watching a play do so by identifying with story and character, thereby transforming the onstage event as they are watching it, obscuring its reality with the distorting lens of personal involvement and emotional commitment to a breathlessly awaited outcome.

And it was Brecht who provided backup for this theory, justifying my obsession that to highlight the "art" of theater (or anything else) was to savor above all the "facts" of performance set before one in each perceived moment of presence onstage. Brecht's message was to believe in a kind of theater in which the viewer never abandons the lucid self in a wash of feeling. This approach is echoed, of course, in *Galileo*, where Galileo himself, under attack, urges men not to abandon themselves to established habits of tradition or seemingly "logical" thought when that logic is based on convention rather than freshly observed fact.

Reoriented by my total commitment to Brecht, I too believed the first requirement of any sophisticated theater should be to ask at each moment, "What's *really* going on here?" In Brecht, of course, the "here" was both the onstage reality and the fact of human beings seized by the pincers of the sociopolitical situation. My own interests, however, were to recenter my theater on that self-constituting physical and mental "impulse-network" of perception, which I see as totally shaping our relation to the external world.

But I understood that my own focus—psychological and spiritual where Brecht was political—was powerfully facilitated when Brecht, through example and theory, had opened the door to a theatrical world into which Western theater had not yet ventured. His theater seemed to function scientifically, much like a medical operating arena, in which the flesh of the "seductive body" is peeled off to reveal to observers the networks operating beneath. As opposed to the important American dramatists (O'Neill, Miller, Williams), I saw Brecht as creating not an American-style theater rooted in warm, human "compassion," but a more rigorous art dedicated to the scientific display of the manipulative mechanisms at work on every level of human life and society—this of course, being directly echoed by the methods of the scientist Galileo, who we see stripping away the "heart warming" belief in man as the center of the universe.

But Brecht has also written that of all his plays, *Galileo* is the least rigorous in employing his famous "alienation" effects. Was this because, in a world that had just created the atomic bomb, it was of overriding importance to Brecht to "get his message across" through a less radical and idiosyncratic style than usual? Was this a major compromise? Or was he perhaps influenced by his less-than-happy experience in America, as a refugee from Hitler who was trying to downplay his Communist affiliations, as he recrafted the text for the play's first production in tandem with the nonpolitical Charles Laughton? (He later rewrote it for his own theater, of course. But it remains his most atypical "humanistic" work.)

No doubt his motives were complex, because while Brecht was a great artist, he was also, according to reports on his personal life, a manipulative and exploitive human being. Perhaps the great scene of Galileo's recantation and following self-justification can be thought of in the context of Brecht's behavior in front of the House Un-American Activities Committee. Testifying before that lamentable tribunal (at the same time that he was working on *Galileo*), Brecht effectively played humble and innocent—which was of course justifiable under the circumstances. Yet it was a performance that could be thought of as echoing much of his real-life behavior. Just as he shows us Galileo abandoning his principles in order to save himself and thereby enabling him to continue his important work in secret, so Brecht, often aggressive and less than honest, strategized to make great theater in often difficult circumstances. Developing this line of thought, I would suggest that Brecht's work can be fruitfully understood not through reference to the "official" noble and heroic intellectual icons of Western tradition, but rather through the filter of that great seventeenth-century student of human duplicity and fallibility, Jesuit scholar Baltasar Gracian, who was in fact a contemporary of Galileo!

Gracian stripped away the facade of human pretense, and suggested methods by which one might navigate an ignoble world. Such also is Brecht's procedure. To read Brecht through the lens of Gracian (hero to both Nietzsche and Lacan, each of whom join Brecht—along with Galileo—in upsetting all apple carts of "normal" procedure) would, I suggest, open a fresh window upon Brecht's methodology. It presents us, surprisingly, with a detailed road map with which to chart the world of Brecht's *Galileo*, where Brecht manages to display both himself and his protagonist, each mirroring the other.

RICHARD FOREMAN

Introduction to the Penguin Classics Edition

BERTOLT BRECHT

First comes eating and then comes morality.

Staring is not seeing.

Thinking is one of the chief pleasures of the human race.

Whether reading or viewing the work of the German artist Bertolt Brecht (1898–1956), one is greeted by a series of titles, gestures, images, aphorisms—like those listed above—which may be written on placards lowered from the rafters, projected on film screens, expressed through the performative body, or delivered with a hammerlike thud on the written page. On a linguistic, aesthetic, and philosophical level these effects are meant to pull the reader out of a passive and unconscious state of mind and into a heightened condition of awareness that leads to an alternative way of thinking and acting in the world. Such devices were just one element of Brecht's notion of a dialectical theater—a performance experience that explored, examined, and challenged traditional ideas of Western aesthetic philosophy as well as confronted the most important political and historical issues of the day in an intensely intellectual, oftentimes contradictory, yet always pleasurable manner.

To be good, yet live.

War teaches people nothing.

Whoever empathizes with someone, and does so completely, relinquishes criticism both of the object of their empathy and of

xiv   INTRODUCTION TO THE PENGUIN CLASSICS EDITION

themselves. Instead of awakening, they sleepwalk. Instead of doing something, they let something be done with them.

At the dawn of the twenty-first century, as the terrible landmarks of the previous century (Holocaust, world wars, the nuclear age) lose their immediacy and power, and the new century brings new monuments to our world (9/11, ethnic cleansing, global warming), we find Brecht, who seemed so absolutely determined by the twentieth century and hence rendered null and void by its end, to be even more relevant. For Brecht, although a product of the "dark times" of the twentieth century, nevertheless was not imprisoned by the era that he lived in. Brecht mediated his times through the grander lens of Western history, philosophy, and aesthetics; hence, Brecht provides not just a conversation with the twentieth century, but a dialogue that reaches back through Nietzsche, Ibsen, Marx, Shakespeare, Aristotle, Sophocles, and Socrates and forward to our current postmodern epoch. Moreover, it is not a simple conversation Brecht provides, but rather an elegant puzzle that includes the constant sting of the irritating gadfly. At every moment when we experience theater, film, music, art, video games, we feel the jab of Brecht asking us to stay awake, retain our critical faculties, conceive our existence in an aesthetic way, and finally intervene and change the world that we have constructed—because our life depends on it.

The proof of the pudding lies in the eating.

The philosophers have in various ways only interpreted the world; the point, however, is to change it.

ORIGINS

I have always needed the spur of contradiction.

Brecht was born in Augsburg, Germany (southwestern Germany, near Munich), in 1898 to comfortable middle-class parents, and he enjoyed a fairly normal childhood. Often sickly, and an inattentive student at school, he found early inspiration in the work of writers such as Villon, Rimbaud, and Wedekind, and as a result, produced a number of poems, songs, and play fragments throughout his youth. One of his earliest school friends from this period, Caspar Neher, would later design many of the stages for Brecht's theatrical work. Neither military service (medical orderly) at the end of World War I nor university education (one semester) at the University of Munich decisively affected his life, but in the same year, 1918, he did finish his first play, *Baal*. Until 1924, he would be based largely in Munich (with several important trips to Berlin), a period in which he would establish important relationships with Herbert Ihering (Berlin theater critic) and Helene Weigel (Jewish-Austrian, Marxist actor, and future wife) and write plays that would define his early career: *Drums in the Night* (1919), *In the Jungle of the Cities* (1922), as well as work with the material that would become *A Man's a Man* (1926). *Drums in the Night* would be his first play to be produced on the stage in September 1922 at the Munich Kammerspiele; when it premiered in Berlin in December of the same year it proved to be a decisive impetus for his career.

Brecht moved to Berlin in 1924, where he would be based until 1933, and as the Golden Age of the Weimar Republic played out, he would elevate his career to an international level. The Weimar Republic (the Roaring Twenties for an American audience) was the collective name given to the political society of Germany between the end of World War I (1918) and the rise of Adolf Hitler (1933). The Weimar Republic, similar to the French Revolution of the eighteenth century, is both a primer and cautionary tale about a Western, democratic, and capitalist culture that extends itself too far and descends into decadence, chaos, hyperinflation, and ultimately totalitarian dictatorship. It was during this period that Brecht established a collaborative relationship with both Elisabeth Hauptmann and Kurt Weill, worked with two famous directors (Max Reinhardt at the Deutsches Theater and Erwin Piscator at his Dramaturgical Collective), turned intellectually and politically to Marxism, and published a groundbreaking book of poems, *Hauspostille* (*Domestic Breviary*). *The Threepenny Opera* premiered in August 1928 at the Theater am Schiffbauerdamm in Berlin, which would later become the home theater of Brecht's theater collective, the Berliner Ensemble (BE), after World War II. The premiere was a huge success, catapulting Brecht and Weill to national and international fame. *The Threepenny Opera* moment is often seen as both the high point and fall of the Weimar Republic. With the onset of the Great Depression in October 1929, the Weimar Republic quickly descended into political and cultural chaos, which would eventually see the rise of Hitler and the Nazi Party. In the last years of the Weimar Republic, Brecht would continue his collaborative work with Hauptmann and Weill and establish new collaborative relationships with Margarete Steffin, Hanns Eisler, and Slatan Dudow, which would produce works such as the opera *Mahagonny*, the film *Kuhle Wampe*, and didactic plays such as *The Measures Taken*. Hitler became chancellor on January 30, 1933, and consolidated power through numerous acts of political terror, including the infamous Reichstag fire of February 28, 1933. Brecht, as the writer of *The Threepenny Opera*, with announced Marxist leanings, was on the short list of Nazi enemies and, hence, a day after the Reichstag fire, wasted no time fleeing into exile.

In exile, Brecht would take up residence in various countries: Denmark, 1933–1939; Sweden, 1939–1940; Finland, 1940–1941; and the United States, 1941–1947. Operating without a native language, stage, culture, or audience, Brecht nevertheless was able to produce theoretical, theatrical, and poetic work that has come to define his later career. In Denmark he established a collaborative relationship with Ruth Berlau, thus completing (along with Helene Weigel, Elisabeth Hauptmann, and Margarete Steffin) what contemporary scholarship—based on John Fuegi's 1994 book, *Brecht & Co.: Sex, Politics, and the Making of the Modern Drama*—has come to understand as Brecht's inner circle. This inner circle, Brecht & Co., has been defined in various ways: at its best, as a free, fluid, and equal collaborative ensemble, which accepted the single designation of "Brecht" for collaborative work; at its worst, an exploitative/parasitic relationship, in which Brecht, through sex and charisma, rendered invisible the authorship and voice of his female collaborators. This conundrum of Brecht & Co. brings up the issue of authorship—whether the work of art is ever just the effort of one person, or whether single authorship ultimately is based on the necessity of granting authorship to one individual instead of a group. Brecht is an extreme version of this problem, because his aesthetic works are monuments to fluidity, i.e., constantly being written and rewritten and hence never stable.

Beginning in 1938/1939 (as the Holocaust was prefigured through Kristallnacht, November 9, 1938, and the beginning of World War II with the invasion of Poland, September 1, 1939) Brecht would produce his great, mature works: *Galileo, Good Person of Szechwan, Mother Courage and Her Children, The Messingkauf Dialogues, The Resistible Rise of Arturo Ui,* and *The Caucasian Chalk Circle.* After the end of World War II he stayed in the United States for an additional two years, waiting to see what would happen in Germany and whether he could make it in the American theater and film industry. In October 1947, he was called to testify before the House Un-American Activities Committee (HUAC), which was investigating Communist and anti-American activity. To the dismay of many, he did not invoke his right not to testify, and instead performed an ambivalent piece of political theater, which in the end left everyone confused. This was his swan song in America, and he embarked the following day for Switzerland.

With the successful premiere of *Mother Courage* (with his wife, Helene Weigel, in the lead role) at the Deutsches Theater in Berlin as well as the publication of *A Short Organum for the Theatre* (a distillation of the *Messingkauf Dialogues*) in January 1949, Brecht successfully reintroduced himself back into the European theater scene. Germany was now a divided country, the concrete and symbolic center of the Cold War conflict between the United States and the Soviet Union, a situation that would last until 1990 when Germany was reunified. Brecht settled in East Berlin (yet kept his Austrian passports and Swiss bank accounts), eventually founding, along with Helene Weigel, his own theater company, the Berliner Ensemble (BE), in 1949. In the last years of his life he worked to bring all his theatrical work to the postwar audience, and at the same time attempted to negotiate the ambivalences of the Cold War. Beginning in 1954, the BE undertook a series of guest residencies throughout Europe, and it was these tours that thrust the BE and Brecht's theatrical work back into the international scene. He died in August 1956.

Over the last fifty years, Brecht has continued to play the Socratic gadfly, fascinating and irritating us at the same time. Epic theater, alienation effects, gestus, anti-Aristotelian, mimesis, empathy, illusion, psychological/social, dissonance—all these terms (and more) comprise the aesthetic philosophy of Brecht, and are rendered in this edition (and increasingly in scholarship) through the summary term "dialectical theater," a term Brecht himself used more and more at the end of his career. In short, dialectical theater resists absolutes, essentials, and identifications, and instead seeks out contradictions, diversities, and multiplicities. Nothing is eternal, all is fluid, and so, ultimately, all is changeable. In dialectical theater, the writer, actor, and spectator are consciously and cognitively involved in the performance they are collectively creating. This position stands in contrast to the main tradition of Western performance, what Brecht referred to as the Aristotelian tradition, in which one is asked to identify, empathize, and lose oneself to the illusion and mystery of the performance. In his theatrical works, especially his theoretical writings, Brecht explored this idea of dialectical theater. Indeed, what distinguishes Brecht most is his philosophical-theoretical work that accompanies his performance work. Brecht left behind extensive aesthetic writings, contained in seven volumes in the standard edition of his complete works in German, yet these writings do not form a systematic or even consistent expression of an aesthetic theory. What Brecht gives us in his theoretical and theatrical writings are political and aesthetic puzzles, which are meant to stimulate awareness and critical thinking, and which Brecht believed were necessary and pleasurable endeavors within the human condition.

THE PROOF OF THE PUDDING:
READING BRECHT

"The proof of the pudding lies in the eating" was a favored motto of Brecht and constantly reminded him that performance was about actions and not about theories. In this introduction, much has been said about Brecht's art, but how does all this theoretical commentary translate into actually reading Brecht? The text as a work of art is never a destination, but a portal experience. This is especially true of the performance text and, above all, true of the Brechtian performance text. Here are some of the portals that the reader should consider when reading these editions of Brecht in translation: 1) the primary playscript and its variations; 2) the secondary material that accompanies the playscript—theoretical ruminations, dramaturgical explanations, and photo descriptions; 3) the musical "text" contained within the playscript—songs and compositions; 4) extension of the playscript into other genres—theoretical essay, novel, film adaptation; 5) the significant global theatrical productions over the last fifty years; 6) the translations and adaptations into different languages.

When reading Brecht, one should keep these portals in mind as accompaniment in the reading of the primary text. For example, when reading the primary playscript, one should not be afraid to use the secondary material located in the back of the text as part of the performance material. Stopping one's reading in midpiece to consult another text is Brechtian in itself, and perusing the theoretical material and the questions and contradictions that they bring up will expand the puzzle of the text. Also, keep in mind that the Willett/Manheim translations used in this edition are not the only translations, and others from Eric Bentley, Tony Kushner, and David Hare (to name just a few) will show different ways of rendering the text. The image, or the description of the image from a historical production (e.g., Helene Weigel's "silent scream" in *Mother Courage*, Martin Wuttke contorting himself into a human swastika in *Arturo Ui*), and the sound of a song in varying renditions (e.g., "Mac

xx INTRODUCTION TO THE PENGUIN CLASSICS EDITION

the Knife" from *The Threepenny Opera* sung by Kurt Gerron, Bertolt Brecht, Scott Merrill, Bobby Darin, Sting, or Cyndi Lauper, or the "Alabama Song" from *Mahagonny* sung by Lotte Lenya, Jim Morrison, or Marilyn Manson) are all methods of constructing a richer experience.

LIFE OF GALILEO

STARING IS NOT SEEING

Life of Galileo is considered by many as Brecht's greatest play, not the least in America, where due to its literary genesis as well as its content it is often seen as his most "American" play. Indeed, it is perhaps his greatest play, but not necessarily because of its lofty content (Galileo, science, truth, faith), its autobiographical aspects (Brecht vs. Hitler, Brecht vs. HUAC), or its American roots in Brecht's California exile (1941–1947); rather, it is perhaps his greatest play by mere fact that it is able to function as a performance at all. For, in effect, it is not a theatrical work, but rather a Socratic dialogue, more akin to Plato's *Republic* than to *Death of a Salesman*. This is not surprising given that Brecht read Galileo's *Discourse on the Two New Sciences* (1638), written in dialogue form and patterned on the Socratic dialogues, which helped to inspire him to write not only *Galileo*, but also *The Messingkauf Dialogues* (1939–1955), his ruminations on the meaning, nature, and potential of theater. Moreover, a great deal of the play was constructed through Brecht's dialogues with the actor Charles Laughton. The result is a work that *reads* extremely well in its presentation of philosophical meditations on the scientific revolution, science and faith, and science through performance, but that does not easily inspire the theatrical imagination. Added to this conundrum is the fact that *Life of Galileo* is one of the most conventional theater works that Brecht ever produced; besides the scene titles, music, and the masked ball and carnival scenes, very little of Brechtian theater practices are on display. Hence, the work rides a fine line between Dialogue and Theater, and this is the real dramatic tension throughout the play.

STORY

The play sketches episodes from the life of Galileo Galilei (1564–1642), from 1609 on through to 1637. Standard Western history presents Galileo as the quintessential Renaissance figure (born in the same year as Shakespeare) and the Father of Modern Science who risked life and career to stand up to the political authority of the day and usher in the Scientific Revolution. The first scene opens with Galileo at the University of Padua right before the publication of *The Starry Messenger* (1610) and its celestial observations based on the new technology of the telescope. *The Starry Messenger* would confirm in concise, accessible, scientific form Copernicus's theory (*On the Revolutions of the Celestial Spheres*, 1543) of a heliocentric rather than a geocentric universe, the latter of which was supported by the authority of Aristotle/Ptolemy and the Roman Catholic Church. Brecht traces Galileo's career from this groundbreaking moment through the main character's interactions with his intimate circle of family and friends (his daughter, Virginia; Andrea; the Little Monk; and Ludovico) as well as his encounters with papal and scholarly authorities. Galileo's new ideas and the political and cultural challenges they presented to the dominant authorities eventually led to what history has come to call the Galileo Affair. In 1616, Galileo was called to Rome to stand before papal authorities and defend his heliocentric model. The papal authorities accepted the heliocentric universe model, but asserted that the Church had the power of when and how to disseminate this knowledge to the broader public, and hence counseled Galileo to continue his work, but keep his ideas to himself. Galileo remained quiet for roughly eight years, until the ascension of a new, scientifically oriented pope inspired Galileo to once again publish his ideas beginning in 1623. In 1632, with official papal sanction, Galileo published his *Dialogue Concerning the Two*

Chief World Systems; yet the reception of the text led to a heresy trial in 1633 in which Galileo recanted his ideas. He was sentenced to house arrest, and his books were banned. In 1638, he reworked the material from the *Dialogue* and published it as *The Discourse on the Two New Sciences*.

ORIGINS

Although Brecht would not sit down to formally write *Life of Galileo* until the end of the 1930s, evidence suggests that he was already considering the *Galileo* material as early as 1933. Conversations Brecht had with colleagues during this period point to the three hundredth anniversary of Galileo's condemnation and the Reichstag Fire Trial of 1933 as influential for his later work on *Galileo*. While in Danish exile (1933–1939), Brecht would develop these original insights in essays such as "Five Difficulties in Writing the Truth" (1934) as well as in his play *Fear and Misery of the Third Reich*. In early 1938, Brecht began developing sketches of the *Galileo* material, producing a first draft in November 1938, and then with the collaboration of Margarete Steffin, a finished version in February 1939. This version, known as the Danish version, would serve as the playscript for the Zurich premiere in 1943.

During his American exile (1941–1947) in Santa Monica, California, Brecht would develop a second version of the play in collaboration with the English actor Charles Laughton, with whom he started working in 1944. Over the course of three years, Brecht and Laughton would meet and negotiate a new version of the play. In what still must be considered one of the most interesting artistic partnerships of all time, Laughton, who did not speak or read German, and Brecht, who despite years living in the United States claimed to have little ability in English, negotiated an American adaptation of the play through mime, gesture, a fractured pidgin language, dictionary work, and role playing. Brecht would detail some of this experience in the associated text, *Building Up a Part: Laughton's Galileo* (included in this volume), in which he described the experience as a personal encounter with Epic Theater, in which the play and the characters had to be developed through the action and presentation of gestures and behaviors, thus inhibiting attempts at deeper psychological characterization. The result of this collaboration (which in the end would include music from Hanns Eisler, and input from a number of others including Eric Bentley, George Tabori, and Joseph Losey) was a sharply reduced text with a tighter, more dynamic theater flow and an Americanized language idiom. Thematically, the tone had changed as well: whereas the Danish version had emphasized the pursuit of science as a means to speak the truth against power, enabling social progress, the American version concentrated more on the individual responsibility of the scientist—a responsibility that took on even greater weight with the onset of the nuclear age with the bombing of Hiroshima in August 1945. The American version served as the playscript for both the Beverly Hills and New York City premieres in 1947.

Brecht left America in October 1947 after testifying before the House Un-American Activities Committee, a "performance event" that has endlessly fascinated those interested in Brecht, and returned to Europe, which was transforming into the Cold War political battleground that would dominate the second half of the twentieth century. Mediating these new experiences, Brecht once again picked up the Galileo material, and collaborating with his longtime assistants Elisabeth Hauptmann and Ruth Berlau as well as the BE director Benno Besson, he set about constructing a new synthesis based on the Danish and American versions. The new playscript, known as the Berlin version would be premiered in Cologne, Germany, in April 1955.

PERFORMANCE HISTORY

The world premiere of *Galileo* in its Danish playscript version took place at the Zurich Schauspielhaus (site of the premieres of *Mother Courage* and *The Good Person of Szechwan*) on September 9, 1943, and was directed by Leonard Steckel (who

also played the lead) with stage design by Teo Otto. Steckel portrayed Galileo's fight for scientific truth as an obvious allusion
to fascist Germany. The production met with critical and popular success, but surprised those acquainted with Brecht's work
with its standard dramatic construction and characterization.
The premiere of the American version occurred on July 30,
1947, at the Coronet Theatre in Beverly Hills, California. Directed by Joseph Losey (although Brecht exerted a great deal of
directorial vision behind the scenes), starring Charles Laughton
and a cast of young, unknown actors, the production ran for
seventeen performances. It engendered an ambivalent reception:
on the one hand, Laughton's acting skill and character study
received positive notices, and Brecht's dramatization of a timely
historical metaphor as well as his non-Aristotelian theater practices received notice; on the other hand, the lack of a deep, psychological character study combined with implied religious and
political criticism caused some critics to dismiss the production. Yet the production did well enough to be transferred to
New York for a premiere at the Maxine Elliot Theater. By the
time it premiered on December 7, 1947, Brecht had already appeared before HUAC and subsequently left America for good,
and the production met with a negative reception, running for
only six shows.

The Berlin playscript version enjoyed its premiere in April
1955 in Cologne, Germany. In contrast to the American premieres, this production met with popular and critical success,
and this success was repeated in January 1957, when the
Berliner Ensemble premiered the play, with Erich Engel directing and Ernst Busch starring as Galileo. Over the next fifty
years, *Galileo* would enjoy notable global productions: the Actor's Workshop, San Francisco, 1962, directed by Herbert Blau;
Piccolo Teatro, Milan, 1963, directed by Giorgio Strehler; the
Abbey Theatre, Dublin, 1965, directed by Michael O'Hen-
nessy; Lincoln Center Repertory Theatre, New York, 1967, directed by John Hirsch and starring Anthony Quayle; a 1975
film adaptation, directed by Joseph Losey and starring Topol,
Tom Contin, and John Gielgud; the Berliner Ensemble, Berlin,
1978, directed by Manfred Wekwerth/Joachim Tenschart and

starring Ekkehard Schall; the Goodman Theatre, Chicago, 1986, directed by Robert Falls, adapted by Adrian Hall/James Schevill, and starring Brian Dennehy; the National Theatre, London, 2006, directed by Howard Davies, adapted by David Hare, and starring Simon Russell Beale.

THE PROOF OF THE PUDDING: READING *LIFE OF GALILEO*

At the reader's disposal are three main textual supplements: texts by Brecht, excerpts from *Building Up a Part: Laughton's Galileo*, and the 1947 American version by Laughton. Because *Galileo* is in many ways a conventional historical drama of ideas, the reader should try to emphasize supplementary texts that open up one's imagination to how the play can be acted onstage. *Building Up a Part: Laughton's Galileo* proves to be very helpful in this regard, as does Laughton's adaptation. In terms of the latter, the reader might want to compare the differences in adaptations through Scene 1. As for the play itself, the masked ball and carnival scenes are the most theatrically vibrant scenes, and in a play with so much concentration on the main character, they diffuse the centripetal force of the Galileo character. The heliocentric universe is hardly a surprising notion anymore, and so the revolutionary nature of it might fall on the deaf ears of the contemporary reader. To combat this familiarity, the reader must only consider the Galilean revolution as the first phase of a scientific revolution that has been ongoing since the seventeenth century. Exchange Galileo for Darwin or Einstein, and the heliocentric universe for evolution or relativity, and one will appreciate the unsettling, revolutionary nature of Galileo's theories.

NORMAN ROESSLER

Introduction

In all Brecht's work there is no more substantial and significant landmark than the first version of *Galileo*, which he wrote in three weeks of November 1938, not long after the Munich agreement. As is well known, it inaugurated the series of major plays whose writing occupied him until his return to Germany some ten years later: from *Mother Courage* to *The Days of the Commune*, those great works of his forties on which his reputation largely rests. At the same time it marks the virtual end of his efforts to write plays and poems of instant political relevance, such as the Spanish Civil War one-acter *Señora Carrar's Rifles* or the loose sequence of anti-Nazi scenes known variously as 99%, *The Private Life of the Master Race* and *Fear and Misery of the Third Reich*. Short satirical poems designed for the exiles' cabarets or for broadcasting (notably by the Communist-run German Freedom Radio) now give way to something at once more personal and more pessimistic. The *Lenin Cantata* set by Eisler for the twentieth anniversary of the October Revolution is followed during 1938 by "To Those Born Later" and the great Lao-Tse poem. All along the line Brecht appears to be backing away from the kind of close political engagement which had occupied him since the crisis year of 1929, as also from the didactic and agitational forms to which this gave rise. Walter Benjamin, who visited him in his Danish cottage that June and stayed till after Munich, found him at once more isolated and more mellow than he had been four years earlier. "It's a good thing," he notes Brecht as saying, "when someone who has taken up an extreme position then goes into a period of reaction. That way he arrives at a half-way house."

Though such a change might seem compatible with the new aesthetic traditionalism being preached from Moscow after the Writers' Congress of 1934—with *Galileo* itself as part of the same historicizing trend as led to Heinrich Mann's Henri IV novels and Friedrich Wolf's play *Beaumarchais*—it primarily relates to something very different: to Brecht's shuddering consciousness of what he called "the dark time." The phrase was first used by him in a poem of 1937 and from then on it overshadows much of his writing right up to the crucial German defeats at Stalingrad and El Alamein in the autumn of 1943. For it was a desperate period, and the despair could be felt on at least three different levels. First of all there was the relentless progress of Fascism (intervention in Spain, Japanese invasion of China, the Austrian Anschluss, the annexation of the German-speaking areas of Czechoslovakia) aided by British appeasement and the fall of the French Popular Front. Overlapping these events, and in many ways closer to Brecht personally, was the great Soviet purge which by the time of Benjamin's visit had already carried away such friends of theirs as Tretiakoff, Ottwalt, Carola Neher and the Reichs, as well as Brecht's two Comintern contacts Béla Kun and Vilis Knorin, to as yet unclear fates. Linked with the new Russian spy mania, itself shot through with xenophobia, was the increasingly strict imposition of the Socialist Realist aesthetic whose German-language spokesmen were Alfred Kurella and Georg Lukács. With Meyerhold deprived of his allegedly "alien" theater in January 1938, Brecht that summer wrote a number of answers to Lukács which he seemingly thought wiser not to publish, even in the Moscow magazine *Das Wort* of which he was a nominal editor. "They want to play the *apparatchik* and exercise control over other people," he told Benjamin. "Every one of their criticisms contains a threat."

In the "working diary" (*Arbeitsjournal*) which he now began keeping, the place of *Galileo* is very clear. In October a short entry reflects on the unwillingness of any of the major powers, including Russia, to risk war for Czechoslovakia. In January 1939 another reports the arrest in Moscow of *Das Wort*'s sponsor Mikhail Koltsov—"my last link with that place"—and concludes that the right Marxist attitude to Stalinism was that of

Marx himself to German social-democracy: "constructively critical." Between these two pages comes the entry of 23 November, recording that this hitherto unmentioned play has taken three weeks to write. Before and after come biting comments on Lukács and the "Realism controversy." It must already have been in Brecht's mind ("for some while," so his collaborator Margarete Steffin wrote to Benjamin in the letter cited on p. 158); and certainly he had done a good deal of preliminary reading: of the standard German biography by Emil Wohlwill, for instance, as well as of nineteenth-century translations of the *Discorsi* and Bacon's *Novum Organum* (from which a number of key ideas were derived) and works by modern physicists such as Eddington and Jeans. But an important contributing factor was his decision, evidently taken around this time, to follow Hanns Eisler's example and apply for a quota visa to the United States, where he hoped that a work about the great physicist would make him some money. This idea crystallised just after Munich as a result of a visit by his American friend Ferdinand Reyher, a Hollywood script writer whom he had first met in Berlin at the time of *The Threepenny Opera*. Arriving in Copenhagen on 28 October, Reyher suggested that Brecht should start by writing *Galileo* as a film story which he, Reyher, could market for him. Though Brecht in the event found himself writing the play instead, and never even embarked on the film project, he said from the outset that it was "really intended for New York."

This original *Galileo*, revised with some minor changes in the first few weeks of 1939, was initially called *The Earth Moves*. In February Reyher wrote from Hollywood to say that while he would discuss its screen possibilities with the director William Dieterle—himself an old acquaintance of Brecht's from the early 1920s—he felt some measure of adaptation was needed to fit it for the American stage. With Brecht's permission, accordingly, he proposed not just to do a straight translation but to introduce "a little more speed":

> a sharpened drive, because our mode of thinking and our interests are gaited to a more nervous tempo, and what induces us to think in this country is not ideas, but action.

Brecht never seems to have agreed to this; nor do we know how Dieterle reacted to the film idea. Meantime, however, copies of the script were going to a number of other recipients: among them Piscator, Hanns Eisler, and Fritz Lang in the United States, Brecht's publisher Wieland Herzfelde in Prague, his translator Desmond Vesey in London, the main German-language theatres in Basle and Zurich, and Pierre Abraham and Walter Benjamin in Paris. Not long before leaving Denmark that spring he began writing his *Messingkauf Dialogues* on the model of Galileo's *Dialogues Concerning the Two Chief World Systems*. Characteristically, he had already become dissatisfied with the play, which he saw as "far too opportunist" and conventionally atmospheric, like the deliberately Aristotelian "empathy drama" *Señora Carrar's Rifles*, for which he was still being praised by the Party aestheticians. He even thought of remodelling the whole thing in a more didactic form, based on the example of the big unfinished *Fatzer* and *Breadshop* schemes of the late 1920s. However, there is no evidence that he did this except a rough outline for a "version for workers"; and instead the project slumbered while he wrote the next four of the major plays. Only in Moscow was there some interest in publishing an illustrated edition for which his new friend Hans Tombrock was to make the etchings. This too never materialised, though it prompted the vivid description of Galileo's appearance which we cite on p. 117.

The Brechts eventually moved to the United States in the summer of 1941, leaving via Moscow and Vladivostock a matter of days before the German invasion of the USSR. By then France, Poland, Yugoslavia and Greece had all fallen to Hitler; Benjamin had committed suicide on the Franco-Spanish frontier; Margarete Steffin was left in Moscow to die of tuberculosis. Settling in California in the hope of finding work in the film industry, Brecht was soon seeing both Dieterle and Reyher, who had by now evidently completed a straight translation of the play. The idea of a film version seems not to have been resumed. That autumn he discussed the script with the physicist Hans Reichenbach, a pupil of Einstein's then teaching in Los

Angeles at the University of California, who congratulated him on the accuracy of its scientific and historical aspects. Then at the end of the year he tried to interest his old friend Oskar Homolka, and for a time Homolka toyed with the idea of playing the part, something that made Brecht feel

> as if I were recalling a strange sunken theatre of a bygone age on continents that had been submerged.

A similar sense of unreality must have seized him in September 1943, when the Zurich Schauspielhaus finally gave the play its world première some two and a half years after that of *Mother Courage*. How he reacted to the news of the production—or when, indeed, he heard it—remains unclear; he never even alludes to it in his diary. Soberly interpreted by Leonard Steckel, who not only played Galileo but was also the director, it was greatly applauded despite its lack of dramatic effects: "a *Lehrstück* or a play for reading," one critic called it. What was not clear, however, in a generally clear performance, was whether Galileo recanted out of cowardice or as part of a deliberate plan to complete his life's work on behalf of human reason and smuggle it out to the free world. This ambiguity (which led so experienced a critic as Bernhard Diebold to favour the second, more topically anti-Nazi interpretation) is of course built into the first version of the play, where Galileo has already been conspiring with the stove-fitter (symbol of the workers) to send his manuscript abroad in the penultimate scene even before Andrea appears. (In Zurich this was in fact the last scene, that at the frontier being, as usual, cut.)

It was only in the spring of 1944 that the play seems once more to have become a reality to Brecht. Wintering in New York, he had discussed the possibility of a production with Jed Harris, the backer of Thornton Wilder's *Our Town*, and on getting back to Santa Monica he looked at *Galileo* with a fresh eye, re-checking its moral content, so he noted in his diary,

> since it had always worried me. Just because i was trying to follow the historical story, without being morally concerned, a

moral content emerged and i'm not happy about it. g. can no more resist stating the truth than eating an appetising dish; to him it's a matter of sensual enjoyment. and he constructs his own personality as wisely and passionately as he does his image of the world. actually he fails twice. the first time is when he suppresses or recants the truth because he is in mortal danger, the second when despite the mortal danger he once again seeks out the truth and disseminates it. he is destroyed by his own productivity. and it upsets me to be told that i approve of his publicly recanting so as to be able to carry on his work in secret. that's too banal and too cheap. g., after all, destroyed not only himself as a person but also the most valuable part of his scientific work. the church (i.e. the authorities) defended the teachings of the bible purely as a way of defending itself, its authority and its power of oppression and exploitation. the sole reason why the people became interested in g.'s ideas about the planets was that they were chafing under church domination. g. threw all real progress to the wolves when he recanted. he abandoned the people, and astronomy once again became an affair for specialists, the exclusive concern of scholars, unpolitical, cut off. the church made a distinction between these celestial 'problems' and those of the earth, consolidated its rule and then cheerfully went on to acknowledge the new solutions.

It is not clear just when Brecht first met Charles Laughton, who was then living within walking distance in a street called Corona del Mar above the Pacific Coast Highway; but it could even have been before his departure for New York the previous November. Both were friends of Berthold Viertel's wife Salka (best known perhaps as Greta Garbo's preferred script writer), and it seems to have been through her that they learnt to appreciate one another's company. As Laughton's biographer Charles Higham has put it, they found they had certain likes and dislikes in common:

They both shared a sympathy and concern for ordinary people, a dislike of pomp and circumstance and the attitudes and actions of the European ruling class. They both disliked elaborate artifice in

the theatre, as exemplified by the spangles-and-tinsel of Max
Reinhardt's stage and film productions of *A Midsummer Night's
Dream* . . .

Laughton had last acted in the theatre in 1934, and since playing
Rembrandt in Alexander Korda's 1936 film of that name (for
which Brecht's old friend Carl Zuckmayer wrote the script) he
had had a surfeit of supporting roles in second- and third-rate
Hollywood films. During the spring and summer of 1949 he read
the rough translation of Brecht's *Schweik in the Second World
War* and greatly enjoyed it, while Brecht for his part wrote the
long poem "Garden in Progress" to commemorate, not without
irony, the landslide which sent part of the Laughtons' beautifully
tended garden sliding down the cliff face to the road below. By
then the actor had evidently learnt enough about *Galileo*,
whether through Brecht's description or from the Vesey and Reyher translations, to decide that it might well be the masterpiece to
carry him back to the live stage. With Brecht's agreement he now
commissioned a fresh translation by a young writer called Brainerd Duffield, who had been working with Alfred Döblin and
other German exiles employed by MGM. By the end of November Duffield and his contemporary Emerson Crocker had once
again translated Brecht's original script and produced a third text
which both Laughton and the Brechts evidently approved. A
fortnight later actor and playwright together were getting down
to what the former terms "systematic work on the translation
and stage version of the *Life of the Physicist Galileo*." Whatever
the original intention, it was in effect to be a new play.

————

Brecht later called the work with Laughton a "zweijähriger
Spass," a two-year escapade, and undoubtedly it covers more
paper than did any other of his writings, so that altogether it
represents a prodigal expenditure of both men's time. But he
also saw it as the classic collaboration between a great dramatist and a great actor, and the loving account which he gives in
Building Up a Part (p. 128ff.) seems to have been filtered
through a warm Californian haze rather than the wintry greys

of Berlin. Inevitably there were long interruptions before a first script was ready. From February to May 1945 Laughton was off playing in the pirate film *Captain Kidd* (Brecht meantime consoling himself by trying to put the *Communist Manifesto* into Lucretian hexameters); then in June and July Brecht was in New York for a none too successful production of *The Private Life of the Master Race* in Eric Bentley's translation, directed initially by Piscator and finally by Viertel on Brecht's intervention. Generally however they worked as described by Brecht, with him reshaping the play in a mixture of German and English—his typescript drafts contain many instances of this, of which one is cited on p. 160—and both men then trying to get the English wording right. This reshaping often followed Laughton's suggestions, which went much further than the basic cutting and streamlining which were his most obvious contribution. Thus it was he who proposed the elimination of the Doppone character (see p. 162), the "positive entry" of the iron founder in scene 2, the argument between Ludovico and Galileo in the sunspot scene and the shifting of the handing-over of the *Discorsi* so that Galileo's great speech of self-abasement should come after it and offset it. Brecht too worked to make this self-abasement seem more of a piece with Galileo's concern for his own comforts, which were now to include thinking. In this, as in the new emphasis on Galileo's sensuality, he was aided by Laughton's character, of which Eric Bentley has written that

> It is unlikely that anyone again will combine as he did every appearance of intellectual brilliance with every appearance of physical self-indulgence.

If the 1938 version derived its political relevance from the need to smuggle the truth out of Nazi Germany, this new version was given an extra edge of topicality by the dropping of the first atomic bomb on 6 August 1945. Not that any significant change was needed apart from the addition of the passage about "a universal cry of fear" in the penultimate scene. The notion of a Hippocratic oath for scientists had still to be worked in. So before leaving the U.S. Brecht drafted the relevant passage, which could indeed have been in his mind from the inception of the play, the idea itself having been put forward by Lancelot Law White in *Nature* in 1938 and discussed at the time in an editorial in the *New York Times*.

On 1 December 1945 the new, "American" text was complete enough for Laughton to read it to the Brechts, Eisler, Reichenbach, Salka Viertel and other friends. About a week later he also read it to Orson Welles, whom both he and Brecht seem already to have had in mind for some while as the right director for the production towards which they were working. Welles instantly accepted the job, and a few days after that the three men saw Laughton's agents Berg-Allenberg to discuss whether to open in the spring or the summer. This question was bound up with their choice of producer, which seems to have veered initially between Welles himself, the film impresario Mike Todd and Elisabeth Bergner's husband Paul Czinner, for whom Brecht was already working on the *Duchess of Malfi* adaptation. Czinner was not congenial to Laughton, and once the idea of a spring production was abandoned he dropped out. Welles for his part apparently disliked Brecht; nevertheless for a time the intention was that he and Todd should combine forces; then a mixture of uncertainty about dates and dislike of the kind of teamwork proposed by Laughton and Brecht made Welles drop out after the middle of 1946, leaving Todd as sole producer. After that various directors were suggested: Elia Kazan, who had a particular appeal for Brecht because he did not claim to know all the answers; Harold Clurman, whom Brecht respected as "an intelligent critic and interested in theoretical issues" but saw primarily as a "Stanislavsky man" unlikely to let him have any say. He even inquired about Alfred Lunt. Meantime a great deal of detailed revision of the new Brecht-Laughton text went on, with Brecht and Reyher totally overhauling it in New York, then Laughton and Brecht again reworking it in California. Versions of the ballad-singer's song were made by Reyher and by Abe Burrows (of *Guys and Dolls* fame) while the inter-scene verses seem to have involved a whole host of collaborators including Brecht himself and his daughter Barbara; the only programme credit, however, for the "lyrics" went to a Santa

Monica poet called Albert Brush. The eventual director chosen
was Joseph Losey, who had met Brecht in Moscow in 1935 and
thereafter made his name with the Living Newspaper pro-
grammes of the Federal Theatre. Finally Todd too dropped out
after offering (in Losey's words) to "dress the production in
Renaissance furniture from the Hollywood warehouses," an
idea that was unacceptable to Brecht, Laughton and Losey
alike. With this the hope of any kind of production in 1946 dis-
appeared.

Instead the three partners decided to turn to a new smaller
management headed by Norman Lloyd and John Houseman,
who were then about to take over the Coronet Theatre on La
Cienega Boulevard, Los Angeles. They agreed to put on *Galileo*
as their second production, with the "extremely decent" (said
Brecht) T. Edward Hambleton as its principal backer. Though
Brecht was unable to get his old collaborator Caspar Neher over
from Europe as he wished, the substitute designer Robert Davi-
son accepted his and Laughton's ideas for an unmonumental,
non-naturalistic setting; Helene Weigel helped with the costumes. Eisler (who actually preferred the first version of the
play) wrote the music in a fortnight; Lotte Goslar did the cho-
reography. Rehearsals were scheduled to start at the end of
May 1947, when Laughton would have finished a film; the
opening would be on 1 July. Though this had to be put off till
the last day of the month everything otherwise seems—
amazingly enough—to have gone according to plan. Losey not
only justified Reyher's recommendation of him—

> He knows casting, has the feel for it; he knows what to do with
> actors; he can get a crowd sense without numbers, and movement
> that isn't just confusion, and keep the whole of a play in mind.

—but worked so closely with Brecht that the latter ever afterwards treated the production as his own. Laughton, exceptionally nervous before the première, resisted any temptation to
overact, and concentrated on bringing out the contradictory elements with which they had enriched Galileo's character; the one
point that still resisted him, according to Brecht, being the logic

of the deep self-abasement manifested in his "Welcome to the gutter" speech near the end of the play. Not that such refinements would have been particularly appreciated by the critics, for both *Variety* and the *New York Times* complained that the production was too flat and colourless. Charlie Chaplin too—who never really knew what to make of Brecht—sat next to Eisler at the opening and dined with him afterwards; he found that the play was not theatrical enough and said it should have been mounted differently. "When I told him," said Eisler later,

> that Brecht never wants to 'mount' things, he simply couldn't understand."

For Brecht himself however it was certainly the most important and satisfying theatrical occasion since he first went into exile in 1933:

> The stage and the production were strongly reminiscent of the Schiffbauerdamm Theatre in Berlin; likewise the intellectual part of the audience.

So he wrote to Reyher. Whether or not it played to such full houses as he later claimed, the whole achievement was an astonishing tribute to the actor's courage and the writer's relentless perfectionism: one of the great events in Brecht's life.

In the long struggle to stage the "American" version it might seem that Brecht hardly noticed that the Second World War was over. Thus his poem to Laughton "concerning the work on the play *The Life of Galileo*" (*Poems 1913–1956*, p. 405):

> Still your people and mine were tearing each other to pieces
>   when we
> Pored over those tattered exercise books, looking
> Up words in dictionaries, and time after time
> Crossed out our texts and then
> Under the crossings-out excavated

The original turns of phrase. Bit by bit—
While the housefronts crashed down in our capitals—
The façades of language gave way. Between us
We began following what characters and actions dictated:
New text.

Again and again I turned actor, demonstrating
A character's gestures and tone of voice, and you
Turned writer. Yet neither I nor you
Stepped outside his profession.

In fact however he had begun to prepare his return to Germany as early as 1944 (when the FBI reported him visiting the Czech consulate for the purpose), and in December 1945 he wrote in his "working diary," "maybe I'll no longer be here, next autumn." The *Galileo* discussions apart, this was the beginning of a curiously blank year in Brecht's biography, by the end of which he had had some kind of invitation to work in the Soviet sector of Berlin, once again at the Theater am Schiffbauerdamm. Early in 1947 he was trying to organise a common front with Piscator and Friedrich Wolf (who was already back there) with a view to rehabilitating the Berlin theatre; by March he and Weigel had got their papers to go to Switzerland. The machinations of the House Un-American Activities Committee (from May onwards) thus had less effect on his movements than is sometimes thought. Hanns Eisler was interrogated by one of their subcommittees that month and the FBI file on Brecht reopened, while Eisler's brother Gerhart was on trial during much of the *Galileo* rehearsals; finally Brecht himself appeared before the committee a day or two before leaving for Switzerland in September. But these words did probably affect the fortunes of the New York production, which Hambleton had delayed (according to Higham) in order to add the "passion, excitement, colour" which the critics had felt to be lacking. Further cuts were made there to give us the text as we now print it (see the appendix, p. 195), the odd facetious line was worked in; the cast was entirely new. Again however the reviews were bad, Brooks Atkinson in the *New York Times* dismissing the production as "stuffed with hokum," and it only ran for three weeks. Higham blames the difficulty of finding another theatre to which to transfer. But Laughton's earlier biographer Kurt Singer gave a somewhat different interpretation, writing (with an exaggeration indicative of the temper of those times) that

> The trouble lay in the political affiliations of the playwright. Berthold Brecht was a dyed-in-the-wool Communist. On the point of being deported from the United States for his Communist activities, he escaped and turned up again in East Germany, where he became the Soviet's pet author, supervising the literary life of the Soviet-controlled zone and turning out odes to Stalin on the various state holidays. The musical score for the play on Galileo had been composed by Hanns Eisler, another convinced Communist who had composed many propaganda songs, including *The Comintern March*. Several actors in the cast turned out to be Communists too . . .

Whether or not this put Laughton himself off the play, as Singer suggests, Brecht continued to count on the actor's collaboration in a proposed film version to be made in Italy. The producer who had initiated this scheme was Rod E. Geiger, who apparently had funds in that country as a result of his earnings on Rossellini's *Open City*. Negotiations continued while Brecht was in Switzerland, and a scheme was worked out with the approval of Laughton and his agents by which the former would come to London for a production of the play around the end of 1948, after which work on the film would follow. Brecht and Reyher would write the script, which Geiger felt must give more emphasis to the relationship between Virginia and her fiancé Ludovico. However, everything was conditional on Laughton's involvement, and he blew hot and cold, his own nervousness of Communist associations being no doubt aggravated by the warnings of his agent. So it all fell through—possibly prompting Brecht to the satirical

"Obituary for Ch.L" which he wrote around this time (*Poems 1913–1956*, p. 418):

> Speak of the weather
> Be thankful he's dead
> Who before he had spoken
> Took back what he said.

At any rate this put paid for the moment to all further plans, since the play could hardly be staged by Brecht's own company the Berliner Ensemble till they had a suitable actor and a revised German text. In 1953 however Brecht set his collaborators (Hauptmann, Besson, Berlau) to work translating and expanding the "American" version so as to include certain elements of that of 1938, notably the plague scenes and the great introductory speech about the "new time" in scene 1. He then went over the results himself, also adding German versions of the ballad, the poems and the inter-scene verses. In 1955 this was given its première in Cologne in West Germany, after which he at last—in the final year of his life—began preparing to stage the play with the Berliner Ensemble.

In ten years a lot had changed. The text had grown longer by half, the production envisaged (with Neher as designer) was more lavish, there was no actor of Laughton's calibre available. Brecht himself was to direct it, but he could only conduct rehearsals from mid-December up to the end of March 1956 when he became too ill to go on. As Galileo he cast his old Communist friend Ernst Busch, who had been in *The Mother*, *Kuhle Wampe* and *The Threepenny Opera* film before 1933, had sung Brecht-Eisler songs to the troops in Spain, been interned by the French, then handed over to the Gestapo and wounded in the bombing of Berlin. Since returning to the German stage Busch had tended to specialise in cunning or lovable rogues: Mephisto and Iago for the Deutsches Theater, Azdak and the Cook (in *Mother Courage*) for Brecht. A much less intellectual actor than Laughton, he found it even more difficult to alienate the audience's sympathies at the end of the play; and when Erich Engel took over the production after Brecht's death he was allowed to present the handing-over of the *Discorsi* as a piece of justified foxiness which made his recantation ultimately forgiveable. Brecht himself had underlined two points in connection with this production: the first, his view that the recantation was an absolute crime (see p. 127), the second, that Galileo's line in scene 9 "My object is not to establish that I was right but to find out if I am" is the most important sentence in the play. Others have stressed that the new version followed the manufacture and testing of the hydrogen bomb, so that the social responsibility of the scientist became a particularly topical theme. It is difficult however to see this play as a member of an East European audience without feeling that it is above all about scientific enquiry and the human reason. For the parallels are too clear: the Catholic Church is the Communist Party, Aristotle is Marxism-Leninism with its incontrovertible scriptures, the late "reactionary" pope is Joseph Stalin, the Inquisition the KGB. Obviously Brecht did not write it to mean this, and if he had seen how the local context prompted this interpretation he might have been less keen for the production to go on. But as things turned out it has proved to be among the most successful of all his plays in the Communist world.

———

In our view *Galileo* is Brecht's greatest play, and it is worth tracing its long and involved history in order to understand why. Not just one, but three crucial moments of our recent history helped to give it its multiple relevance to our time: Hitler's triumphs in 1938, the dropping of the first nuclear bomb in 1945, the death of Stalin in 1953. Each found Brecht writing or rewriting his play. And on each occasion the conditions of work were different: thus it was first written in his measured, stylish yet utterly down-to-earth German, then re-thought in English for Anglo-Saxon tongues and ears, then put back into German so as to combine the strengths of both. At none of these three stages was its form in any way mannered or gimmicky: sprawl as it might, particularly in the two German versions, it was outwardly a straightforward chronicle of seventeenth-century intellectual history, sticking surprisingly closely to the known facts. This was not "opportunist" as Brecht at one moment termed it, even if it did represent a reaction against the conventionally realistic small-scale forms which he had used in 1937. Undoubtedly however his new approach did make for accessibility, and as a result almost any competent and unpretentious production of the play will grab the audience's attention and get the meaning across.

What is that meaning? In fact there are several that can be read into the play, nor is this surprising when you think that Brecht's active concern with it covered nearly twenty years. So the problem for the modern director is to sift out those that matter from those that don't. First of all, this is not only a hymn to reason, but one that centres specifically on the need to be sceptical, to doubt. The theme is one that recurs more briefly in others of Brecht's writings of the later 1930s—for instance the poems "The Doubter" and "In Praise of Doubt" and the "On Doubt" section of the as yet untranslated *Me-Ti*—and it very clearly conflicts with the kind of "positive" thinking called for by both Nazis and the more rigid-minded of the Communists, which must not be critical ("negative") but optimistic. This notion of Brecht's that doubt and even self-doubt can be highly productive—that "disbelief can move mountains," as he later put it in the *Short Organum*—is deeply engrained in the play; and although it ties in with his doctrine of "alienation" or the need to take nothing for granted it also surely represents a reaction against the orthodox Socialist Realist view. How far it can be attributed to the historical Galileo is another matter. As Eric Bentley and, more recently, Paul Feierabend have pointed out, Galileo's reliance on the evidence of his senses was largely limited to the observations which he made with the telescope; elsewhere he was more speculative and less rational than Brecht suggests. What is true however is the conflict between authority and free scientific enquiry, both on the institutional level and within Galileo's own character (for he was indeed a believing Catholic). If anything, the former's position is presented too reasonably, both Barberini and the Inquisitor having in fact behaved much worse than Brecht let them do.

Brecht all along was writing about attitudes which he could understand and even sympathise with; it is a play that contains very little element of caricature. This does not turn his Galileo into the self-portrait it is sometimes alleged to be, particularly by those who wish to present Brecht as a "survivor"—as if surviving was not a very reputable thing for him to have done. Nor does it bear out the late Isaac Deutscher's interpretation of the first version as an apologia for those who, like Brecht himself, supported Stalin whilst disliking many aspects of his regime. Not that such autobiographical considerations—which can of course be clamped on to almost any play—are much help to the director, who has first and foremost to take the work at its face value. What matters here is the overlaying of the original message, about the need at all costs to establish and communicate the truth in defiance of authority, by Brecht's growing recognition of the losses that this may involve: for instance, the creation of such a cleft between the intellectual and the average man that the former eventually comes to overlook the social consequences of his research. The intertwining of these two contradictory morals has presented problems to actor and director alike, and of course it devalues the original happy ending. None the less it represents a considerable enrichment both of the Galileo figure and of the story; while taking away nothing from the vividness with which the scientific attitude is depicted, it cuts down the improbabilities and brings the whole thing closer to the uneasy compromises of real life. The problem in production, then, is how to compress the play into a length appropriate to its audience without losing essential elements of so carefully thought-out a mixture. As a reading text it has a balance which needs also to be achieved under the very different conditions of the stage.

By turning it back, finally, into something of a meditation on the notion of a "new time," Brecht reemphasised another general theme of particular significance to himself. Between 1929 and 1933 (and even, less pardonably, for two or three years afterwards) the German Communists thought that the Revolution was round the corner, and men like Brecht were stimulated much as he describes in the Foreword on p. 113. At the end of the 1930s, however, when he wrote the poem "To Those Born Later" (*Poems 1913–1956*, pp. 318–320), their goal

> Lay far in the distance
> It was clearly visible, though I myself
> Was hardly likely to reach it.

"Terrible is the disappointment," says the Foreword, when the new time fails to arrive and the old times prove stronger than anyone thought. For what had actually arrived was the "dark times" of the first line of "To Those Born Later," and with this the whole concept of "old" and "new" got confused. "So the Old strode in disguised as the New," says the prose poem "Parade of the Old New" which he wrote at the time of the first version as one of five "Visions" foreshadowing the coming war. The temptation was to look nostalgically backwards, as the end of the Foreword suggests:

> Is that why I occupy myself with that epoch of the flowering of the arts and sciences three hundred years ago? I hope not.

And in this hope he was determined to hold on to his old belief in the New, writing for instance to Karin Michaelis in March 1942, when the war was still going Hitler's way, that

> the time we live in is an excellent time for fighters. Was there ever a time when Reason had such a chance?

What is significant in the final version is not just that it reinstates and even extends Galileo's opening "aria" of 1938 on the new age—that Elizabethan-Jacobean age which always fascinated Brecht, not least because of Germany's failure to benefit from it. The really crucial remark, rather, comes in the final summing up of the same idea, which differs subtly from one version to another. "Reason," says Galileo in the first version, "is not coming to an end but beginning.

And I still believe that this is a new age. It may look like a
bloodstained old harridan, but if so that must be the way new
ages look."

In the American version, which omits the reference to Reason,
Andrea asks Galileo outright if he doesn't now think that his
"new age" was an illusion, and is again given the same answer.
In the third version, far more tellingly, he gets the almost indifferent response *"Doch"*—"On the contrary," almost implying
"despite all"—followed by a quick change of subject. And it is
this one word, with all its overtones from the history of Brecht's
own time—at once so new and so dark—that wryly wraps up
the whole optimistic tragedy, pinning the beginning and the end
together with a single jab.

                                                      THE EDITORS

Life of Galileo

Collaborator: M. STEFFIN
Translator: JOHN WILLETT

Characters

GALILEO GALILEI

ANDREA SARTI

MRS SARTI, *Galileo's housekeeper, Andrea's mother*

LUDOVICO MARSILI, *a rich young man*

THE PROCURATOR OF PADUA UNIVERSITY, *Mr Priuli*

SAGREDO, *Galileo's friend*

VIRGINIA, *Galileo's daughter*

FEDERZONI, *a lens-grinder, Galileo's assistant*

THE DOGE

SENATORS

COSIMO DE MEDICI, *Grand Duke of Florence*

THE COURT CHAMBERLAIN

THE THEOLOGIAN

THE PHILOSOPHER

THE MATHEMATICIAN

THE OLDER COURT LADY

THE YOUNGER COURT LADY

GRAND-DUCAL FOOTMAN

TWO NUNS

TWO SOLDIERS

THE OLD WOMAN

A FAT PRELATE

TWO SCHOLARS

TWO MONKS

TWO ASTRONOMERS

A VERY THIN MONK

THE VERY OLD CARDINAL

FATHER CHRISTOPHER CLAVIUS, *astronomer*

THE LITTLE MONK
THE CARDINAL INQUISITOR
CARDINAL BARBERINI, *subsequently Pope Urban* VIII
CARDINAL BELLARMIN
TWO CLERICAL SECRETARIES
TWO YOUNG LADIES
FILIPPO MUCIUS, *a scholar*
MR GAFFONE, *Rector of the University of Pisa*
THE BALLAD-SINGER
HIS WIFE
VANNI, *an ironfounder*
AN OFFICIAL
A HIGH OFFICIAL
AN INDIVIDUAL
A MONK
A PEASANT
A FRONTIER GUARD
A CLERK
Men, women, children

I

GALILEO GALILEI, A TEACHER OF MATHEMATICS AT PADUA, SETS OUT TO PROVE COPERNICUS'S NEW COSMOGONY

In the year sixteen hundred and nine
Science's light began to shine.
At Padua city in a modest house
Galileo Galilei set out to prove
The sun is still, the earth is on the move.

Galileo's rather wretched study in Padua. It is morning. A boy, Andrea, the housekeeper's son, brings in a glass of milk and a roll.

GALILEO *washing down to the waist, puffing and cheerful*: Put that milk on the table, and don't you shut any of those books.

ANDREA: Mother says we must pay the milkman. Or he'll start making a circle round our house, Mr Galilei.

GALILEO: Describing a circle, you mean, Andrea.

ANDREA: Whichever you like. If we don't pay the bill he'll start describing a circle round us, Mr Galilei.

GALILEO: Whereas when Mr Cambione the bailiff comes straight for us what sort of distance between two points is he going to pick?

ANDREA *grinning*: The shortest.

GALILEO: Right. I've got something for you. Look behind the star charts.

Andrea rummages behind the star charts and brings out a big wooden model of the Ptolemaic system.

ANDREA: What is it?

GALILEO: That's an armillary sphere. It's a contraption to

show how the planets move around the earth, according to our forefathers.

ANDREA: How?

GALILEO: Let's examine it. Start at the beginning. Description?

ANDREA: In the middle there's a small stone.

GALILEO: That's the earth.

ANDREA: Round it there are rings, one inside another.

GALILEO: How many?

ANDREA: Eight.

GALILEO: That's the crystal spheres.

ANDREA: Stuck to the rings are little balls.

GALILEO: The stars.

ANDREA: Then there are bands with words painted on them.

GALILEO: What sort of words?

ANDREA: Names of stars.

GALILEO: Such as . . .

ANDREA: The lowest ball is the moon, it says. Above that's the sun.

GALILEO: Now start the sun moving.

ANDREA *moves the rings*: That's great. But we're so shut in.

GALILEO *drying himself*: Yes, I felt that first time I saw one of those. We're not the only ones to feel it. *He tosses the towel to Andrea, for him to dry his back with.* Walls and spheres and immobility! For two thousand years people have believed that the sun and all the stars of heaven rotate around mankind. Pope, cardinals, princes, professors, captains, merchants, fishwives and schoolkids thought they were sitting motionless inside this crystal sphere. But now we are breaking out of it, Andrea, at full speed. Because the old days are over and this is a new time. For the last hundred years mankind has seemed to be expecting something.

Our cities are cramped, and so are men's minds. Superstition and the plague. But now the word is 'that's how things are, but they won't stay like that'. Because everything is in motion, my friend.

I like to think that it began with the ships. As far as men could remember they had always hugged the coast, then suddenly they abandoned the coast line and ventured out across the seas. On our old continent a rumour sprang up: there might be new ones. And since our ships began sailing to them the laughing continents have got the message: the great ocean they feared, is a little puddle. And a vast desire has sprung up to know the reasons for everything: why a stone falls when you let it go and why it rises when you toss it up. Each day something fresh is discovered. Men of a hundred, even, are getting the young people to bawl the latest example into their ear. There have been a lot of discoveries, but there is still plenty to be found out. So future generations should have enough to do.

As a young man in Siena I watched a group of building workers argue for five minutes, then abandon a thousand-year-old method of shifting granite blocks in favour of a new and more efficient arrangement of the ropes. Then and there I knew, the old days are over and this is a new time. Soon humanity is going to understand its abode, the heavenly body on which it dwells. What is written in the old books is no longer good enough. For where faith has been enthroned for a thousand years doubt now sits. Everyone says: right, that's what it says in the books, but let's have a look for ourselves. That most solemn truths are being familiarly nudged; what was never doubted before is doubted now.

This has created a draught which is blowing up the gold-embroidered skirts of the prelates and princes, revealing the fat and skinny legs underneath, legs like our own. The heavens, it turns out, are empty. Cheerful laughter is our response. But the waters of the earth drive the new spinning machines, while in the shipyards, the ropewalks and sail-lofts five hundred hands are moving together in a new system.

It is my prophecy that our own lifetime will see astronomy being discussed in the marketplaces. Even the fishwives' sons will hasten off to school. For these novelty-seeking people in our cities will be delighted with a new astronomy that sets the earth moving too. The old idea was always that the stars were fixed to a crystal vault to stop them falling down. Today we have found the courage to let them soar through space without support; and they are travelling at full speed just like our ships, at full speed and without support.

And the earth is rolling cheerfully around the sun, and the fishwives, merchants, princes, cardinals and even the Pope are rolling with it.

The universe has lost its centre overnight, and woken up to find it has countless centres. So that each one can now be seen as the centre, or none at all. Suddenly there is a lot of room.

Our ships sail far overseas, our planets move far out into space, in chess too the rooks have begun sweeping far across the board.

What does the poet say? O early morning of beginnings . . .

ANDREA:

O early morning of beginnings
O breath of wind that
Cometh from new shores!

And you'd better drink up your milk, because people are sure to start arriving soon.

GALILEO: Have you understood what I told you yesterday?

ANDREA: What? All that about Copper Knickers and turning?

GALILEO: Yes.

ANDREA: No. What d'you want me to understand that for? It's very difficult, and I'm not even eleven till October.

GALILEO: I particularly want you to understand it. Getting people to understand it is the reason why I go on working and buying expensive books instead of paying the milkman.

ANDREA: But I can see with my own eyes that the sun goes down in a different place from where it rises. So how can it stay still? Of course it can't.

GALILEO: You can see, indeed! What can you see? Nothing at all. You just gawp. Gawping isn't seeing. *He puts the iron washstand in the middle of the room.* Right: this is the sun. Sit down. *Andrea sits on one of the chairs, Galileo stands behind him.* Where's the sun, right or left of you?

ANDREA: Left.

GALILEO: And how does it get to be on your right?

ANDREA: By you carrying it to my right, of course.

GALILEO: Isn't there any other way? *He picks him up along with the chair and makes an about-turn.* Now where's the sun?

ANDREA: On my right.

GALILEO: Did it move?

ANDREA: Not really.

GALILEO: So what did move?

ANDREA: Me.

GALILEO *bellows*: Wrong! You idiot! The chair!

ANDREA: But me with it!

GALILEO: Of course. The chair's the earth. You're sitting on it.

MRS SARTI *has entered in order to make the bed. She has been watching*: Just what are you up to with my boy, Mr Galilei?

GALILEO: Teaching him to see, Mrs Sarti.

MRS SARTI: What, by lugging him round the room?

ANDREA: Lay off, mother. You don't understand.

MRS SARTI: Oh, don't I? And you do: is that it? There's a young gentleman wants some lessons. Very well dressed, got a letter of introduction too. *Hands it over.* You'll have Andrea believing two and two makes five any minute now, Mr Galilei. As if he didn't already muddle up everything you tell him. Only last night he was arguing that the earth goes round the sun. He's got it into his head that some gentleman called Copper Knickers worked that one out.

ANDREA: Didn't Copper Knickers work it out, Mr Galilei? You tell her.

MRS SARTI: You surely can't tell him such stories? Making him trot it all out at school so the priests come and see me because he keeps on coming out with blasphemies. You should be ashamed of yourself, Mr Galilei.

GALILEO *eating his breakfast*: In consequence of our researches, Mrs Sarti, and as a result of intensive argument, Andrea and I have made discoveries which we can no longer hold back from the world. A new time has begun, a time it's a pleasure to live in.

MRS SARTI: Well. Let's hope your new time will allow us to pay the milkman, Mr Galilei. *Indicating the letter of introduction.* Just do me a favour and don't send this man away. I'm thinking of the milk bill.

GALILEO *laughing*: Let me at least finish my milk! *To Andrea*: So you did understand something yesterday?

ANDREA: I only told her to wake her up a bit. But it isn't true. All you did with me and that chair was turn it sideways, not like this. *He makes a looping motion with his arm.* Or I'd have fallen off, and that's a fact. Why didn't you turn the chair over? Because it would have proved I'd fall off if you turned it that way. So there.

GALILEO: Look, I proved to you . . .

ANDREA: But last night I realised that if the earth turned that way I'd be hanging head downwards every night, and that's a fact.

GALILEO *takes an apple from the table*: Right, now this is the earth.

ANDREA: Don't keep on taking that sort of example, Mr Galilei. They always work.

GALILEO *putting back the apple*: Very well.

ANDREA: Examples always work if you're clever. Only I can't lug my mother round in a chair like you did me. So you see it's a rotten example really. And suppose your apple is the earth like you say? Nothing follows.

GALILEO *laughing*: You just don't want to know.

ANDREA: Pick it up again. Why don't I hang head downwards at night, then?

GALILEO: Right: here's the earth and here's you standing on it. *He takes a splinter from a piece of firewood and sticks it into the apple.* Now the earth's turning around.

ANDREA: And now I'm hanging head downwards.

GALILEO: What d'you mean? Look at it carefully. Where's your head?

ANDREA *pointing*: There. Underneath.

GALILEO: Really? *He turns it back*: Isn't it in precisely the same position? Aren't your feet still underneath? You don't stand like this when I turn it, do you? *He takes out the splinter and puts it in upside down.*

ANDREA: No. Then why don't I notice it's turning?

GALILEO: Because you're turning with it. You and the air above you and everything else on this ball.

ANDREA: Then why does it look as if the sun's moving?

GALILEO *turns the apple and the splinter round again*: Right:

you're seeing the earth below you; that doesn't change, it's always underneath you and so far as you're concerned it doesn't move. But then look what's above you. At present the lamp's over your head, but once I've turned the apple what's over it now; what's above?

ANDREA *turns his head similarly*: The stove.

GALILEO: And where's the lamp?

ANDREA: Underneath.

GALILEO: Ha.

ANDREA: That's great: that'll give her something to think about. *Enter Ludovico Marsili, a rich young man.*

GALILEO: This place is getting like a pigeon loft.

LUDOVICO: Good morning, sir. My name is Ludovico Marsili.

GALILEO *reading his letter of introduction*: So you've been in Holland?

LUDOVICO: Where they were all speaking about you, Mr Galilei.

GALILEO: Your family owns estates in the Campagna?

LUDOVICO: Mother wanted me to have a look-see, find out what's cooking in the world and all that.

GALILEO: And in Holland they told you that in Italy, for instance, I was cooking?

LUDOVICO: And since Mother also wanted me to have a look-see in the sciences . . .

GALILEO: Private tuition: ten scudi a month.

LUDOVICO: Very well, sir.

GALILEO: What are your main interests?

LUDOVICO: Horses.

GALILEO: Ha.

LUDOVICO: I've not got the brains for science, Mr Galilei.

GALILEO: Ha. In that case we'll make it fifteen scudi a month.

LUDOVICO: Very well, Mr Galilei.

GALILEO: I'll have to take you first thing in the morning. That'll be your loss, Andrea. You'll have to drop out of course. You don't pay, see?

ANDREA: I'm off. Can I have the apple?

GALILEO: Yes.

Exit Andrea.

LUDOVICO: You'll have to be patient with me. You see, everything in the sciences goes against a fellow's good sound commonsense. I mean, look at that queer tube thing they're selling in Amsterdam. I gave it a good looking-over. A green leather casing and a couple of lenses, one this way—*he indicates a concave lens*—and the other that way—*he indicates a convex lens*. One of them's supposed to magnify and the other reduces. Anyone in his right mind would expect them to cancel out. They don't. The thing makes everything appear five times the size. That's science for you.

GALILEO: What appears five times the size?

LUDOVICO: Church spires, pigeons, anything that's a long way off.

GALILEO: Did you yourself see church spires magnified in this way?

LUDOVICO: Yes sir.

GALILEO: And this tube has two lenses? *He makes a sketch on a piece of paper*. Did it look like that? *Ludovico nods*. How old's this invention?

LUDOVICO: Not more than a couple of days, I'd say, when I left Holland; at least that's how long it had been on the market.

GALILEO *almost friendly*: And why does it have to be physics? Why not horsebreeding?

Enter Mrs Sarti unobserved by Galileo.

LUDOVICO: Mother thinks you can't do without a bit of science. Nobody can drink a glass of wine without science these days, you know.

GALILEO: Why didn't you pick a dead language or theology? That's easier. *Sees Mrs Sarti*. Right, come along on Tuesday morning. *Ludovico leaves*.

GALILEO: Don't give me that look. I accepted him.

MRS SARTI: Because I caught your eye in time. The procurator of the university is out there.

GALILEO: Show him in, he matters. There may be 500 scudi in this. I wouldn't have to bother with pupils.

Mrs Sarti shows in the procurator. Galileo has finished dressing, meanwhile jotting down figures on a piece of paper.

GALILEO: Good morning. Lend us half a scudo. *The procurator digs a coin out of his purse and Galileo gives it to Sarti.* Sarti, tell Andrea to go to the spectacle-maker's and get two lenses: there's the prescription.

Exit Mrs Sarti with the paper.

PROCURATOR: I have come in connection with your application for a rise in salary to 1000 scudi. I regret that I cannot recommend it to the university. As you know, courses in mathematics do not attract new students. Mathematics, so to speak, is an unproductive art. Not that our Republic doesn't esteem it most highly. It may not be so essential as philosophy or so useful as theology, but it nonetheless offers infinite pleasures to its adepts.

GALILEO *busy with his papers*: My dear fellow, I can't manage on 500 scudi.

PROCURATOR: But, Mr Galilei, your week consists of two two-hour lectures. Given your outstanding reputation you can certainly get plenty of pupils who can afford private lessons. Haven't you got private pupils?

GALILEO: Too many, sir. I teach and I teach, and when am I supposed to learn? God help us, I'm not half as sharp as those gentlemen in the philosophy department. I'm stupid. I understand absolutely nothing. So I'm compelled to fill the gaps in my knowledge. And when am I supposed to do that? When am I to get on with my research? Sir, my branch of knowledge is still avid to know. The greatest problems still find us with nothing but hypotheses to go on. Yet we keep asking ourselves for proofs. How am I to provide them if I can only maintain my home by having to take any thickhead who can afford the money and din it into him that parallel lines meet at infinity?

PROCURATOR: Don't forget that even if the Republic pays less well than certain princes it does guarantee freedom of research. In Padua we even admit Protestants to our lectures. And give them doctors' degrees too. In Mr Cremonini's case we not only failed to hand him over to the Inquisition when he was proved, proved, Mr Galilei—to have made irreligious remarks, but actually granted him a rise in salary. As far as

Holland Venice is known as the republic where the Inquisition has no say. That should mean something to you, being an astronomer, that's to say operating in a field where for some time now the doctrines of the church have hardly been treated with proper respect.

GALILEO: You people handed Mr Giordano Bruno over to Rome. Because he was propagating the ideas of Copernicus.

PROCURATOR: Not because he was propagating the ideas of Mr Copernicus, which anyway are wrong, but because he was not a Venetian citizen and had no regular position here. So you needn't drag in the man they burned. Incidentally, however free we are, I wouldn't go around openly citing a name like his, which is subject to the express anathema of the church: not even here, not even here.

GALILEO: Your protection of freedom of thought is pretty good business, isn't it? By showing how everywhere else the Inquisition prevails and burns people, you get good teachers cheap for this place. You make up for your attitude to the Inquisition by paying lower salaries than anyone.

PROCURATOR: That's most unfair. What use would it be to you to have limitless spare time for research if any ignorant monk in the Inquisition could just put a ban on your thoughts? Every rose has its thorn, Mr Galilei, and every ruler has his monks.

GALILEO: So what's the good of free research without free time to research in? What happens to its results? Perhaps you'd kindly show this paper about falling bodies to the gentlemen at the Signoria—*he indicates a bundle of manuscript*—and ask them if it isn't worth a few extra scudi.

PROCURATOR: It's worth infinitely more than that, Mr Galilei.

GALILEO: Sir, not infinitely more, a mere 500 scudi more.

PROCURATOR: What is worth scudi is what brings scudi in. If you want money you'll have to produce something else. When you're selling knowledge you can't ask more than the buyer is likely to make from it. Philosophy, for instance, as taught by Mr Colombe in Florence, nets the prince at least 10,000 scudi a year. I know your laws on falling bodies have made a stir. They've applauded you in Prague and Paris. But the people who applaud don't pay Padua University what you cost it. You made an unfortunate choice of subject, Mr Galilei.

GALILEO: I see. Freedom of trade, freedom of research. Free trading in research, is that it?

PROCURATOR: Really, Mr Galilei, what a way of looking at it! Allow me to tell you that I don't quite understand your flippant remarks. Our Republic's thriving foreign trade hardly strikes me as a matter to be sneered at. And speaking from many years of experience as procurator of this university I would be even more disinclined to speak of scientific research in what I would term with respect, so frivolous a manner. *While Galileo glances longingly at his work table*: Consider the conditions that surround us. The slavery under whose whips the sciences in certain places are groaning. Whips cut from old leather bindings. Nobody there needs to know how a stone falls, merely what Aristotle wrote about it. Eyes are only for reading with. Why investigate falling bodies, when it's the laws governing grovelling bodies that count? Contrast the infinite joy with which our Republic welcomes your ideas, however daring they may be. Here you have a chance to research, to work. Nobody supervises you, nobody suppresses you. Our merchants know the value of better linen in their struggle with their competitors in Florence; they listen interestedly to your cry for better physics, and physics in turn owes much to their cry for better looms. Our most prominent citizens take an interest in your researches, call on you, get you to demonstrate your findings: men whose time is precious. Don't underrate trade, Mr Galilei. Nobody here would stand for the slightest interference with your work or let outsiders make difficulties for you. This is a place where you can work, Mr Galilei, you have to admit it.

GALILEO *in despair*: Yes.

PROCURATOR: As for the material aspects: why can't you give us another nice piece of work like those famous proportional compasses of yours, the ones that allow complete mathematical dunces to trace lines, reckon compound interest on capital, reproduce a land survey on varying scales and determine the weight of cannon balls?

GALILEO: Kids' stuff.

PROCURATOR: Here's something that fascinated and astonished our top people and brought in good money, and you call it kids' stuff. I'm told even General Stefano Gritti can work out square roots with your instrument.

GALILEO: A real miracle. —All the same, Priuli, you've given me something to think about. Priuli, I think I might be able to let you have something of the kind you want. *He picks up the paper with the sketch.*

PROCURATOR: Could you? That would be the answer. *Gets up:* Mr Galilei, we realise that you are a great man. A great but dissatisfied man, if I may say so.

GALILEO: Yes, I am dissatisfied, and that's what you'd be paying me for if you had any brains. Because I'm dissatisfied with myself. But instead of doing that you force me to be dissatisfied with you. I admit I enjoy doing my stuff for you gentlemen of Venice in your famous arsenal and in the shipyards and cannon foundries. But you never give me the time to follow up the hunches which come to me there and which are important for my branch of science. That way you muzzle the threshing ox. I am 46 years old and have achieved nothing that satisfies me.

PROCURATOR: I mustn't interrupt you any longer.

GALILEO: Thank you.

Exit the Procurator.

Galileo is left alone for a moment or two and begins to work. Then Andrea hurries in.

GALILEO *working*: Why didn't you eat the apple?

ANDREA: I need it to convince her that it turns.

GALILEO: Listen to me, Andrea: don't talk to other people about our ideas.

ANDREA: Why not?

GALILEO: The big shots won't allow it.

ANDREA: But it's the truth.

GALILEO: But they're forbidding it. —And there's something more. We physicists may think we have the answer, but that doesn't mean we can prove it. Even the ideas of a great man like Copernicus still need proving. They are only hypotheses. Give me those lenses.

ANDREA: Your half scudo wasn't enough. I had to leave my coat. As security.

GALILEO: How will you manage without a coat this winter? *Pause. Galileo arranges the lenses on the sheet with the sketch on it.*

ANDREA: What's a hypothesis?

GALILEO: It's when you assume that something's likely, but haven't any facts. Look at Felicia down there outside the basket-maker's shop breastfeeding her child: it remains a hypothesis that she's giving it milk and not getting milk from it, till one actually goes and sees and proves it. Faced with the stars we are like dull-eyed worms that can hardly see at all. Those old constructions people have believed in for the last thousand years are hopelessly rickety: vast buildings most of whose wood is in the buttresses propping them up. Lots of laws that explain very little, whereas our new hypothesis has very few laws that explain a lot.

ANDREA: But you proved it all to me.

GALILEO: No, only that that's how it could be. I'm not saying it isn't a beautiful hypothesis; what's more there's nothing against it.

ANDREA: I'd like to be a physicist too, Mr Galilei.

GALILEO: That's understandable, given the million and one questions in our field still waiting to be cleared up. *He has gone to the window and looked through the lenses. Mildly interested*: Have a look through that, Andrea.

ANDREA: Holy Mary, it's all quite close. The bells in the campanile very close indeed. I can even read the copper letters: GRACIA DEI.

GALILEO: That'll get us 500 scudi.

2

GALILEO PRESENTS THE VENETIAN REPUBLIC
WITH A NEW INVENTION

No one's virtue is complete:
Great Galileo liked to eat.
You will not resent, we hope
The truth about his telescope.

The great arsenal of Venice, alongside the harbour.

*Senators, headed by the Doge. To one side, Galileo's friend
Sagredo and the fifteen-year-old Virginia Galilei with a velvet
cushion on which rests a two-foot-long telescope in a crimson
leather case. On a dais, Galileo. Behind him the telescope's
stand, supervised by Federzoni the lens-grinder.*

GALILEO: Your Excellency; august Signoria! In my capacity as
mathematics teacher at your university in Padua and director
of your great arsenal here in Venice I have always seen it as
my job not merely to fulfil my exalted task as a teacher but
also to provide useful inventions that would be of exceptional advantage to the Venetian Republic. Today it is with
deep joy and all due deference that I find myself able to
demonstrate and hand over to you a completely new instrument, namely my spyglass or telescope, fabricated in your
world-famous Great Arsenal on the loftiest Christian and scientific principles, the product of seventeen years of patient research by your humble servant. *Galileo leaves the dais and
stands alongside Sagredo. Applause. Galileo bows.*
GALILEO *softly to Sagredo*: Waste of time.
SAGREDO *softly*: You'll be able to pay the butcher, old boy.

GALILEO: Yes, they'll make money on this. *He bows again.*

PROCURATOR *steps on to the dais*: Your Excellency, august Signoria! Once again a glorious page in the great book of the arts is inscribed in a Venetian hand. *Polite applause*: Today a world-famous scholar is offering you, and you alone, a highly marketable tube, for you to manufacture and sell as and how you wish. *Louder applause.* What is more, has it struck you that in wartime this instrument will allow us to distinguish the number and types of the enemy's ships at least two hours before he does ours, with the result that we shall know how strong he is and be able to choose whether to pursue, join battle or run away? *Very loud applause.* And now, your Excellency, august Signoria, Mr Galileo invites you to accept this instrument which he has invented, this testimonial to his intuition, at the hand of his enchanting daughter. *Music. Virginia steps forward, bows and hands the telescope to the Procurator, who passes it to Federzoni. Federzoni puts it on the stand and focusses it. Doge and Senators mount the dais and look through the tube.*

GALILEO *softly*: I'm not sure how long I'll be able to stick this circus. These people think they're getting a lucrative plaything, but it's a lot more than that. Last night I turned it on the moon.

SAGREDO: What did you see?

GALILEO: The moon doesn't generate its own light.

SAGREDO: What?

SENATORS: I can make out the fortifications of Santa Rosita, Mr Galilei. —They're having their dinner on that boat. Fried fish. Makes me feel peckish.

GALILEO: I'm telling you astronomy has stagnated for the last thousand years because they had no telescope.

SENATOR: Mr Galilei!

SAGREDO: They want you.

SENATOR: That contraption lets you see too much. I'll have to tell my women they can't take baths on the roof any longer.

GALILEO: Know what the Milky Way consists of?

SAGREDO: No.

GALILEO: I do.

SENATOR: One should be able to ask 10 scudi for a thing like that, Mr Galilei. *Galileo bows.*

VIRGINIA *leading Ludovico up to her father*: Ludovico wants to congratulate you, Father.

LUDOVICO *embarrassed*: I congratulate you, sir.

GALILEO: I've improved it.

LUDOVICO: Yes, sir. I see you've made the casing red. In Holland it was green.

GALILEO *turning to Sagredo*: I've even begun to wonder if I couldn't use it to prove a certain theory.

SAGREDO: Watch your step.

PROCURATOR: Your 500 scudi are in the bag, Galileo.

GALILEO *disregarding him*: Of course I'm sceptical about jumping to conclusions.

The Doge, a fat unassuming man, has come up to Galileo and is trying to address him with a kind of dignified awkwardness.

PROCURATOR: Mr Galilei, His Excellency the Doge.

The Doge shakes Galileo's hand.

GALILEO: Of course, the 500! Are you satisfied, your Excellency?

DOGE: I'm afraid our republic always has to have some pretext before the city fathers can do anything for our scholars.

PROCURATOR: But what other incentive can there be, Mr Galilei?

DOGE *smiling*: We need that pretext.

The Doge and the Procurator lead Galileo towards the Senators, who gather round him. Virginia and Ludovico slowly go away.

VIRGINIA: Did I do all right?

LUDOVICO: Seemed all right to me.

VIRGINIA: What's the matter?

LUDOVICO: Nothing, really. I suppose a green casing would have been just as good.

VIRGINIA: It strikes me they're all very pleased with Father.

LUDOVICO: And it strikes me I'm starting to learn a thing or two about science.

3

10 JANUARY 1610. USING THE TELESCOPE, GALILEO
DISCOVERS CELESTIAL PHENOMENA THAT CONFIRM
THE COPERNICAN SYSTEM. WARNED BY HIS FRIEND
OF THE POSSIBLE CONSEQUENCES OF HIS RESEARCH,
GALILEO PROCLAIMS HIS BELIEF IN HUMAN REASON

> January ten, sixteen ten:
> Galileo Galilei abolishes heaven.

Galileo's study in Padua. Night. Galileo and Sagredo at the telescope, wrapped in heavy overcoats.

SAGREDO *looking through the telescope, half to himself*: The crescent's edge is quite irregular, jagged and rough. In the dark area, close to the luminous edge, there are bright spots. They come up one after the other. The light starts from the spots and flows outwards over bigger and bigger surfaces, where it merges into the larger luminous part.

GALILEO: What's your explanation of these bright spots?

SAGREDO: It's not possible.

GALILEO: It is. They're mountains.

SAGREDO: On a star?

GALILEO: Huge mountains. Whose peaks are gilded by the rising sun while the surrounding slopes are still covered by night. What you're seeing is the light spreading down into the valleys from the topmost peaks.

SAGREDO: But this goes against two thousand years of astronomy.

GALILEO: It does. What you are seeing has been seen by no mortal except myself. You are the second.

SAGREDO: But the moon can't be an earth complete with mountains and valleys, any more than the earth can be a star.

GALILEO: The moon can be an earth complete with mountains and valleys, and the earth can be a star. An ordinary celestial body, one of thousands. Take another look. Does the dark part of the moon look completely dark to you?

SAGREDO: No. Now that I look at it, I can see a feeble ashygrey light all over it.

GALILEO: What sort of light might that be?

SAGREDO: ?

GALILEO: It comes from the earth.

SAGREDO: You're talking through your hat. How can the earth give off light, with all its mountains and forests and waters; it's a cold body.

GALILEO: The same way the moon gives off light. Both of them are lit by the sun, and so they give off light. What the moon is to us, we are to the moon. It sees us sometimes as a crescent, sometimes as a half-moon, sometimes full and sometimes not at all.

SAGREDO: In other words, there's no difference between the moon and earth.

GALILEO: Apparently not.

SAGREDO: Ten years ago in Rome they burnt a man at the stake for that. His name was Giordano Bruno, and that is what he said.

GALILEO: Exactly. And that's what we can see. Keep your eye glued to the telescope, Sagredo, my friend. What you're seeing is the fact that there is no difference between heaven and earth. Today is 10 January 1610. Today mankind can write in its diary: Got rid of Heaven.

SAGREDO: That's frightful.

GALILEO: There is another thing I discovered. Perhaps it's more appalling still.

MRS SARTI *quietly*: Mr Procurator.
The Procurator rushes in.

PROCURATOR: I'm sorry to come so late. Do you mind if I speak to you alone?

GALILEO: Mr Sagredo can listen to anything I can, Mr Priuli.

PROCURATOR: But you may not exactly be pleased if the gentleman hears what has happened. Unhappily it is something quite unbelievable.

GALILEO: Mr Sagredo is quite used to encountering unbelievable when I am around, let me tell you.

PROCURATOR: No doubt, no doubt. *Pointing at the telescope*: Yes, that's the famous contraption. You might just as well throw it away. It's useless, utterly useless.

SAGREDO, *who has been walking around impatiently*: Why's that?

PROCURATOR: Are you aware that this invention of yours which you said was the fruit of seventeen years of research can be bought on any street corner in Italy for a few scudi? Made in Holland, what's more. There is a Dutch merchant-man unloading 500 telescopes down at the harbour at this very moment.

GALILEO: Really?

PROCURATOR: I find your equanimity hard to understand, sir.

SAGREDO: What are you worrying about? Thanks to this instrument, let me tell you, Mr Galilei has just made some revolutionary discoveries about the universe.

GALILEO *laughing*: Have a look, Priuli.

PROCURATOR: And let me tell you it's quite enough for me to have made my particular discovery, after getting this unspeakable man's salary doubled, what's more. It's a pure stroke of luck that the gentlemen of the signoria, in their confidence that they had secured the republic a monopoly of this instrument, didn't look through it and instantly see an ordinary streetseller at the nearest corner, magnified to the power of seven and hawking an identical tube for twice nothing. *Galileo laughs resoundingly.*

SAGREDO: My dear Mr Priuli. I may not be competent to judge this instrument's value for commerce but its value for philosophy is so boundless that . . .

PROCURATOR: For philosophy indeed. What's a mathematician like Mr Galilei got to do with philosophy? Mr Galilei, you did once invent a very decent water pump for the city and your irrigation system works well. The weavers too report favourably on your machine. So how was I to expect something like this?

GALILEO: Not so fast, Priuli. Sea passages are still long, hazardous and expensive. We need a clock in the sky we can rely on. A guide for navigation, right? Well, I have reason to believe that the telescope will allow us to make clear sightings of certain stars that execute extremely regular movements. New star charts might save our shipping several million scudi, Priuli.

PROCURATOR: Don't bother. I've listened too long already. In return for my help you've made me the laughing-stock of the city. I'll go down to history as the procurator who fell for a worthless telescope. It's all very well for you to laugh. You've got your 500 scudi. But I'm an honourable man, and I tell you this world turns my stomach.

He leaves, slamming the door.

GALILEO: He's really quite likeable when he's angry. Did you hear that? A world where one can't do business turns his stomach.

SAGREDO: Did you know about these Dutch instruments?

GALILEO: Of course, by hearsay. But the one I made these skinflints in the Signoria was twice as good. How am I supposed to work with the bailiffs in the house? And Virginia will soon have to have a dowry: she's not bright. Then I like buying books about other things besides physics, and I like a decent meal. Good meals are when I get most of my ideas. A degraded age! They were paying me less than the carter who drives their wine barrels. Four cords of firewood for two courses on mathematics. Now I've managed to squeeze 500 scudi out of them, but I've still got debts, including some dating from twenty years back. Give me five years off to research, and I'd have proved it all. I'm going to show you another thing.

SAGREDO *is reluctant to go to the telescope*: I feel something not all that remote from fear, Galileo.

GALILEO: I'm about to show you one of the shining milk-white clouds in the Milky Way. Tell me what it's made up of.

SAGREDO: They're stars, an infinite number.

GALILEO: In Orion alone there are 500 fixed stars. Those are the countless other worlds, the remote stars the man they burned talked about. He never saw them, he just expected them to be there.

SAGREDO: But even supposing our earth is a star, that's still a long way from Copernicus's view that it goes round the sun. There's not a star in the sky that has another star going round it. But the moon does go round the earth.

GALILEO: Sagredo, I wonder. I've been wondering since yesterday. Here we have Jupiter. *He focuses on it.* Round it we have four smaller neighbouring stars that are invisible except through the tube. I saw them on Monday but without bothering to note their position. Yesterday I looked again. I could swear the position of all four had changed. I noted them down. They've changed again. What's this? I saw four. *Agitated*: Have a look.

SAGREDO: I can see three.

GALILEO: Where's the fourth? There are the tables. We must work out what movements they might have performed. *Excited, they sit down to work. The stage darkens, but Jupiter and its accompanying stars can be seen on the cyclorama. As it grows light once more they are still sitting there in their winter coats.*

GALILEO: That's the proof. The fourth one can only have gone behind Jupiter, where it can't be seen. So here you've a star with another one going round it.

SAGREDO: What about the crystal sphere Jupiter is attached to?

GALILEO: Yes, where has it got to? How can Jupiter be attached if other stars circle round it? It's not some kind of prop in the sky, some base in the universe. It's another sun.

SAGREDO: Calm down. You're thinking too quickly.

GALILEO: What d'you mean, quickly? Wake up, man! You're seeing something nobody has ever seen before. They were right.

SAGREDO: Who, Copernicus and his lot?

GALILEO: And the other fellow. The whole world was against them, and they were right. Andrea must see this! *In great excitement he hurries to the door and shouts*: Mrs Sarti! Mrs Sarti!

SAGREDO: Don't get worked up, Galileo!

GALILEO: Get worked up, Sagredo! Mrs Sarti!

SAGREDO *turns the telescope away*: Stop bellowing like an idiot.

GALILEO: Stop standing there like a stuffed dummy when the truth has been found.

SAGREDO: I'm not standing like a stuffed dummy; I'm trembling with fear that it may be the truth.

GALILEO: Uh?

SAGREDO: Have you completely lost your head? Don't you realise what you'll be getting into if what you see there is true? And if you go round telling all and sundry that the earth is a planet and not the centre of the universe?

GALILEO: Right, and that the entire universe full of stars isn't turning around our tiny little earth, anyone could guess.

SAGREDO: In other words that it's just a lot of stars. Then where's God?

GALILEO: What d'you mean?

SAGREDO: God! Where is God?

GALILEO *angrily*: Not there anyway. Any more than he'd be here on earth, suppose there were creatures out there wanting to come and look for him.

SAGREDO: So where is God?

GALILEO: I'm not a theologian. I'm a mathematician.

SAGREDO: First and foremost you're a human being. And I'm asking: where is God in your cosmography?

GALILEO: Within ourselves or nowhere.

SAGREDO *shouting*: Like the man they burned said?

GALILEO: Like the man they burned said.

SAGREDO: That's what they burned him for. Less than ten years back.

GALILEO: Because he couldn't prove it. Because it was just a hypothesis. Mrs Sarti!

SAGREDO: Galileo, ever since I've known you you've known how to cover yourself. For seventeen years here in Padua and three more in Pisa you have been patiently teaching the Ptolemaic system proclaimed by the Church and confirmed by the writings the Church is based on. Like Copernicus you thought it was wrong but you taught it just the same.

GALILEO: Because I couldn't prove anything.

SAGREDO *incredulously*: And do you imagine that makes any difference!

GALILEO: A tremendous difference. Look, Sagredo, I believe in Humanity, which means to say I believe in human reason. If it weren't for that belief each morning I wouldn't have the power to get out of bed.

SAGREDO: Then let me tell you something. I don't. Forty years spent among human beings has again and again brought it home to me that they are not open to reason. Show them a comet with a red tail, scare them out of their wits, and they'll rush out of their houses and break their legs. But try making one rational statement to them, and back it up with seven proofs, and they'll just laugh at you.

GALILEO: That's quite untrue, and it's a slander. I don't see how you can love science if that's what you believe. Nobody who isn't dead can fail to be convinced by proof.

SAGREDO: How can you imagine their pathetic shrewdness has anything to do with reason?

GALILEO: I'm not talking about their shrewdness. I know they call a donkey a horse when they want to sell it and a horse a donkey when they want to buy. That's the kind of shrewdness you mean. But the horny-handed old woman who gives her mule an extra bundle of hay on the eve of a journey, the sea captain who allows for storms and doldrums when laying in stores, the child who puts on his cap once they have convinced him that it may rain: these are the people I pin my hopes to, because they all accept proof. Yes, I believe in reason's gentle tyranny over people. Sooner or later they have to give in to it. Nobody can go on indefinitely watching me—*he drops a pebble on the ground*—drop a pebble, then say it doesn't fall. No human being is capable of that. The lure of a proof is too great. Nearly everyone succumbs to it; sooner or later we all do. Thinking is one of the chief pleasures of the human race.

MRS SARTI *enters*: Do you want something, Mr Galilei?

GALILEO *who is back at his telescope making notes; in a very friendly voice*: Yes, I want Andrea.

MRS SARTI: Andrea? He's asleep in bed.

GALILEO: Can't you wake him up?

MRS SARTI: Why d'you want him?

GALILEO: I want to show him something he'll appreciate. He's to see something nobody but us two has seen since the earth was made.

MRS SARTI: Something more through your tube?

GALILEO: Something through my tube, Mrs Sarti.

MRS SARTI: And I'm to wake him up in the middle of the night for that? Are you out of your mind? He's got to have his sleep. I wouldn't think of waking him.

GALILEO: Definitely not?

MRS SARTI: Definitely not.

GALILEO: In that case, Mrs Sarti, perhaps you can help me. You see, a question has arisen where we can't agree, probably because both of us have read too many books. It's a question about the heavens, something to do with the stars. This is it: are we to take it that the greater goes round the smaller, or does the smaller go round the greater?

MRS SARTI *cautiously*: I never know where I am with you, Mr Galilei. Is that a serious question, or are you pulling my leg again?

GALILEO: A serious question.

MRS SARTI: Then I'll give you a quick answer. Do I serve your dinner or do you serve mine?

GALILEO: You serve mine. Yesterday it was burnt.

MRS SARTI: And why was it burnt? Because I had to fetch you your shoes in the middle of my cooking. Didn't I fetch you your shoes?

GALILEO: I suppose so.

MRS SARTI: You see, you're the one who has studied and is able to pay.

Mrs Sarti, amused, goes off.

GALILEO: Don't tell me people like that can't grasp the truth. They grab at it.

The bell has begun sounding for early morning Mass. Enter Virginia in a cloak, carrying a shielded light.

VIRGINIA: Good morning, Father.

GALILEO: Why are you up at this hour?

VIRGINIA: Mrs Sarti and I are going to early mass. Ludovico's coming too. What sort of night was it, Father?

GALILEO: Clear.

VIRGINIA: Can I have a look?

GALILEO: What for? *Virginia does not know what to say.* It's not a toy.

VIRGINIA: No, Father.

GALILEO: Anyhow the tube is a flop, so everybody will soon be telling you. You can get it for 3 scudi all over the place and the Dutch invented it ages ago.

VIRGINIA: Hasn't it helped you see anything fresh in the sky?

GALILEO: Nothing in your line. Just a few dim little spots to the left of a large planet; I'll have to do something to draw attention to them. *Talking past his daughter to Sagredo*: I might christen them 'the Medicean Stars' after the Grand Duke of Florence. *Again to Virginia*: You'll be interested to hear, Virginia, that we'll probably be moving to Florence. I've written to them to ask if the Grand Duke can use me as his court mathematician.

VIRGINIA *radiant*: At Court?

SAGREDO: Galileo!

GALILEO: My dear fellow, I'll need time off. I need proofs. And I want the fleshpots. And here's a job where I won't have to take private pupils and din the Ptolemaic system into them, but shall have the time, time, time, time, time—to work out my proofs; because what I've got so far isn't enough. It's nothing, just wretched odds and ends. I can't take on the whole world with that. There's not a single shred of proof to show that any heavenly body whatever goes round the sun. But I am going to produce the proofs, proofs for everyone, from Mrs Sarti right up to the Pope. The only thing that worries me is whether the court will have me.

VIRGINIA: Of course they'll have you, Father, with your new stars and all that.

GALILEO: Run along to your mass.

Exit Virginia.

GALILEO: I'm not used to writing to important people. *He hands Sagredo a letter.* Do you think this is well expressed?

SAGREDO *reads out the end of the letter*: 'My most ardent desire is to be closer to you, the rising sun that will illuminate this age.' The grand duke of Florence is aged nine.

GALILEO: That's it. I see; you think my letter is too submissive. I'm wondering if it is submissive enough—not too formal, lacking in authentic servility. A reticent letter would be all right for someone whose distinction it is to have proved Aristotle correct, but not for me. A man like me can only get a halfway decent job by crawling on his belly. And you know what I think of people whose brains aren't capable of filling their stomachs.

Mrs Sarti and Virginia pass the men on their way to mass.

SAGREDO: Don't go to Florence, Galileo.

GALILEO: Why not?

SAGREDO: Because it's run by monks.

GALILEO: The Florentine Court includes eminent scholars.

SAGREDO: Flunkeys.

GALILEO: I'll take them by the scruff of the neck and I'll drag them to the telescope. Even monks are human beings, Sagredo. Even they are subject to the seduction of proof. Copernicus, don't forget, wanted them to believe his figures; but I only want them to believe their eyes. If the truth is too feeble to stick up for itself then it must go over to the attack. I'm going to take them by the scruff of the neck and force them to look through this telescope.

SAGREDO: Galileo, I see you embarking on a frightful road. It is a disastrous night when mankind sees the truth. And a delusive hour when it believes in human reason. What kind of person is said to go into things with his eyes open? One who is going to his doom. How could the people in power give free rein to somebody who knows the truth, even if it concerns the remotest stars? Do you imagine the Pope will hear the truth when you tell him he's wrong, and not just hear that he's wrong? Do you imagine he will merely note in his diary: January 10th 1610—got rid of heaven? How can you propose to leave the Republic with the truth in your pocket, risking the traps set by monks and princes and brandishing your tube. You may be a sceptic in science, but you're childishly credulous as soon as anything seems likely to help you to pursue it. You don't believe in Aristotle, but you do believe in the Grand Duke of Florence. Just now, when I was watching you at the telescope and you were watching those new stars, it seemed to me I was watching you stand on blazing faggots; and when you said you believed in proof I smelt burnt flesh. I am fond of science, my friend, but I am fonder of you. Don't go to Florence, Galileo.

GALILEO: If they'll have me I shall go.

On a curtain appears the last page of his letter:

In giving the noble name of the house of Medici to the new stars which I have discovered I realise that whereas the old gods and heroes were immortalised by being raised to the realm of the stars in this case the noble name of Medici will ensure that these stars are remembered forever. For my own part I commend myself to you as one of your loyalest and most humble servants who considers it the height of privilege to have been born as your subject.

There is nothing for which I long more ardently than to be closer to you, the rising sun which will illuminate this epoch.

GALILEO GALILEI.

4

GALILEO HAS EXCHANGED THE VENETIAN REPUBLIC
FOR THE COURT OF FLORENCE. HIS DISCOVERIES
WITH THE TELESCOPE ARE NOT BELIEVED
BY THE COURT SCHOLARS

The old says: What I've always done I'll always do.
The new says: If you're useless you must go.

Galileo's house in Florence. Mrs Sarti is preparing Galileo's study for the reception of guests. Her son Andrea is sitting tidying the star charts.

MRS SARTI: There has been nothing but bowing and scraping ever since we arrived safe and sound in this marvellous Florence. The whole city files past the tube, with me mopping the floor after them. If there was anything to all these discoveries the clergy would be the first to know. I spent four years in service with Monsignor Filippo without ever managing to get all his library dusted. Leather bound books up to the ceiling—and no slim volumes of poetry either. And that good Monsignor had a whole cluster of sores on his bottom from sitting and poring over all that learning; d'you imagine a man like that doesn't know the answers? And today's grand visit will be such a disaster that I'll never be able to meet the milkman's eye tomorrow. I knew what I was about when I advised him to give the gentlemen a good supper first, a proper joint of lamb, before they inspect his tube. But no: *she imitates Galileo:* 'I've got something else for them.'
There is knocking downstairs.
MRS SARTI *looks through the spyhole in the window*: My

goodness, the Grand Duke's arrived. And Galileo is still at the University.

She hurries down the stairs and admits the Grand Duke of Tuscany, Cosimo de Medici, together with his chamberlain and two court ladies.

COSIMO: I want to see that tube.

CHAMBERLAIN: Perhaps your Highness will possess himself until Mr Galilei and the other university gentlemen have arrived. *To Mrs Sarti*: Mr Galileo was going to ask our astronomers to test his newly discovered so-called Medicean stars.

COSIMO: They don't believe in the tube, not for one moment. So where is it?

MRS SARTI: Upstairs in the study.

The boy nods, points up the staircase and runs up it at a nod from Mrs Sarti.

CHAMBERLAIN *a very old man*: Your Highness! *To Mrs Sarti*: Have we *got* to go up there? I wouldn't have come at all if his tutor had not been indisposed.

MRS SARTI: The young gentleman will be all right. My own boy is up there.

COSIMO *entering above*: Good evening!

The two boys bow ceremoniously to each other. Pause. Then Andrea turns back to his work.

ANDREA *very like his master*: This place is getting like a pigeon loft.

COSIMO: Plenty of visitors?

ANDREA: Stump around here staring, and don't know the first thing.

COSIMO: I get it. That the . . . ? *Pointing to the telescope.*

ANDREA: Yes, that's it. Hands off, though.

COSIMO: And what's that? *He points to the wooden model of the Ptolemaic system.*

ANDREA: That's Ptolemy's thing.

COSIMO: Showing how the sun goes round, is that it?

ANDREA: So they say.

COSIMO *sitting down on a chair, takes the model on his lap*: My tutor's got a cold. I got off early. It's all right here.

ANDREA *shambles around restlessly and irresolutely shooting doubtful looks at the unknown boy, then finds that he cannot hold out any longer, and brings out a second model from behind the maps, one representing the Copernican system*: But really it's like this.

COSIMO: What's like this?

ANDREA *pointing at Cosimo's model*: That's how people think it is and—*pointing at his own*—this is how it is really. The earth turns round the sun, get it?

COSIMO: D'you really mean that?

ANDREA: Sure, it's been proved.

COSIMO: Indeed? I'd like to know why I'm never allowed to see the old man now. Yesterday he came to supper again.

ANDREA: They don't believe it, do they?

COSIMO: Of course they do.

ANDREA *suddenly pointing at the model on Cosimo's lap*: Give it back: you can't even understand that one.

COSIMO: Why should you have two?

ANDREA: Just you hand it over. It's not a toy for kids.

COSIMO: No reason why I shouldn't give it to you, but you need to learn some manners, you know.

ANDREA: You're an idiot, and to hell with manners, just give it over or you'll start something.

COSIMO: Hands off, I tell you.

They start brawling and are soon tangled up on the floor.

ANDREA: I'll teach you to handle a model properly! Say 'pax'.

COSIMO: It's broken. You're twisting my hand.

ANDREA: We'll see who's right. Say it turns or I'll bash you.

COSIMO: Shan't. Stop it, Ginger. I'll teach you manners.

ANDREA: Ginger: who are you calling Ginger?

They go on brawling in silence. Enter Galileo and a group of university professors downstairs. Federzoni follows.

CHAMBERLAIN: Gentlemen, his highness's tutor Mr Suri has a slight indisposition and was therefore unable to accompany his highness.

THEOLOGIAN: I hope it's nothing serious.

CHAMBERLAIN: Not in the least.

GALILEO *disappointed*: Isn't his highness here?

CHAMBERLAIN: His highness is upstairs. I would ask you gentlemen not to prolong matters. The court is so very eager to
know what our distinguished university thinks about Mr
Galileo's remarkable instrument and these amazing new
stars.
They go upstairs.
*The boys are now lying quiet, having heard the noise down-
stairs.*
COSIMO: Here they are. Let me get up.
They stand up quickly.
THE GENTLEMEN *on their way upstairs*: No, there's nothing
whatever to worry about. —Those cases in the old city: our
faculty of medicine says there's no question of it being
plague. Any miasmas would freeze at this temperature. —
The worst possible thing in such a situation is to panic. —It's
just the usual incidence of colds for this time of year. —Every
suspicion has been eliminated. —Nothing whatever to worry
about.
Greetings upstairs.
GALILEO: Your highness, I am glad to be able to introduce the
gentlemen of your university to these new discoveries in your
presence.
Cosimo bows formally in all directions, including Andrea's.
THEOLOGIAN *noticing the broken Ptolemaic model on the
floor*: Something seems to have got broken here.
*Cosimo quickly stoops down and politely hands Andrea the
model. Meantime Galileo unobtrusively shifts the other
model to one side.*
GALILEO *at the telescope*: As your highness no doubt realises,
we astronomers have been running into great difficulties in
our calculations for some while. We have been using a very
ancient system which is apparently consistent with our philosophy but not, alas, with the facts. Under this ancient,
Ptolemaic system the motions of the stars are presumed to be
extremely complex. The planet Venus, for instance, is supposed to have an orbit like this. *On a board he draws the
epicyclical orbit of Venus according to the Ptolemaic hypothesis.* But even if we accept the awkwardness of such motions

we are still unable to predict the position of the stars accu-
rately. We do not find them where in principle they ought to
be. What is more, some stars perform motions which the
Ptolemaic system just cannot explain. Such motions, it seems
to me, are performed by certain small stars which I have recently discovered around the planet Jupiter. Would you gentlemen care to start by observing these satellites of Jupiter,
the Medicean stars?

ANDREA *indicating the stool by the telescope*: Kindly sit here.

PHILOSOPHER: Thank you, my boy. I fear things are not quite
so simple. Mr Galileo, before turning to your famous tube, I
wonder if we might have the pleasure of a disputation? Its
subject to be: Can such planets exist?

MATHEMATICIAN: A formal dispute.

GALILEO: I was thinking you could just look through the telescope and convince yourselves?

ANDREA: This way, please.

MATHEMATICIAN: Of course, of course. I take it you are familiar with the opinion of the ancients that there can be no stars
which turn round centres other than the earth, nor any which
lack support in the sky?

GALILEO: I am.

PHILOSOPHER: Moreover, quite apart from the very possibility
of such stars, which our mathematicians—*he turns towards
the mathematician*—would appear to doubt, I would like in
all humility to pose the philosophical question: are such stars
necessary? Aristotelis divini universum . . .

GALILEO: Shouldn't we go on using the vernacular? My colleague Mr Federzoni doesn't understand Latin.

PHILOSOPHER: Does it matter if he understands us or not?

GALILEO: Yes.

PHILOSOPHER: I am so sorry. I thought he was your lens-
grinder.

ANDREA: Mr Federzoni is a lens-grinder and a scholar.

PHILOSOPHER: Thank you, my boy. Well, if Mr Federzoni
insists . . .

GALILEO: I insist.

PHILOSOPHER: The argument will be less brilliant, but it's

your house. The universe of the divine Aristotle, with the mystical music of its spheres and its crystal vaults, the orbits of its heavenly bodies, the slanting angle of the sun's course, the secrets of the moon tables, the starry richness catalogued in the southern hemisphere and the transparent structure of the celestial globe add up to an edifice of such exquisite proportions that we should think twice before disrupting its harmony.

GALILEO: How about your highness now taking a look at his impossible and unnecessary stars through this telescope?

MATHEMATICIAN: One might be tempted to answer that, if your tube shows something which cannot be there, it cannot be an entirely reliable tube, wouldn't you say?

GALILEO: What d'you mean by that?

MATHEMATICIAN: It would be rather more appropriate, Mr Galileo, if you were to name your reasons for assuming that there could be free-floating stars moving about in the highest sphere of the unalterable heavens.

PHILOSOPHER: Your reasons, Mr Galileo, your reasons.

GALILEO: My reasons! When a single glance at the stars themselves and my own notes makes the phenomenon evident? Sir, your disputation is becoming absurd.

MATHEMATICIAN: If one could be sure of not over-exciting you one might say that what is in your tube and what is in the skies is not necessarily the same thing.

PHILOSOPHER: That couldn't be more courteously put.

FEDERZONI: They think we painted the Medicean stars on the lens.

GALILEO: Are you saying I'm a fraud?

PHILOSOPHER: How could we? In his highness's presence too.

MATHEMATICIAN: Your instrument—I don't know whether to call it your brainchild or your adopted brainchild—is most ingeniously made, no doubt of that.

PHILOSOPHER: And we are utterly convinced, Mr Galilei, that neither you nor anyone else would bestow the illustrious name of our ruling family on stars whose existence was not above all doubt. *All bow deeply to the grand duke.*

COSIMO *turns to the ladies of the court*: Is something the matter with my stars?

THE OLDER COURT LADY: There is nothing the matter with your highness's stars. It's just that the gentlemen are wondering if they are really and truly there.
Pause.

THE YOUNGER COURT LADY: I'm told you can actually see the wheels on the Plough.

FEDERZONI: Yes, and all kinds of things on the Bull.

GALILEO: Well, are you gentlemen going to look through it or not?

PHILOSOPHER: Of course, of course.

MATHEMATICIAN: Of course.
Pause. Suddenly Andrea turns and walks stiffly out across the whole length of the room. His mother stops him.

MRS SARTI: What's the matter with you?

ANDREA: They're stupid. *He tears himself away and runs off.*

PHILOSOPHER: A lamentable boy.

CHAMBERLAIN: Your highness: gentlemen: may I remind you that the state ball is due to start in three quarters of an hour.

MATHEMATICIAN: Let's not beat about the bush. Sooner or later Mr Galilei will have to reconcile himself to the facts. Those Jupiter satellites of his would penetrate the crystal spheres. It is as simple as that.

FEDERZONI: You'll be surprised: the crystal spheres don't exist.

PHILOSOPHER: Any textbook will tell you that they do, my good man.

FEDERZONI: Right, then let's have new textbooks.

PHILOSOPHER: Your highness, my distinguished colleague and I are supported by none less than the divine Aristotle himself.

GALILEO *almost obsequiously*: Gentlemen, to believe in the authority of Aristotle is one thing, tangible facts are another. You are saying that according to Aristotle there are crystal spheres up there, so certain motions just cannot take place because the stars would penetrate them. But suppose those motions could be established? Mightn't that suggest to you that those crystal spheres don't exist? Gentlemen, in all humility I ask you to go by the evidence of your eyes.

MATHEMATICIAN: My dear Galileo, I may strike you as very

old-fashioned, but I'm in the habit of reading Aristotle now and again, and there, I can assure you, I trust the evidence of my eyes.

GALILEO: I am used to seeing the gentlemen of the various faculties shutting their eyes to every fact and pretending that nothing has happened. I produce my observations and everyone laughs: I offer my telescope so they can see for themselves, and everyone quotes Aristotle.

FEDERZONI: The fellow had no telescope.

MATHEMATICIAN: That's just it.

PHILOSOPHER *grandly*: If Aristotle is going to be dragged in the mud—that's to say an authority recognized not only by every classical scientist but also by the chief fathers of the church—then any prolonging of this discussion is in my view a waste of time. I have no use for discussions which are not objective. Basta.

GALILEO: Truth is born of the times, not of authority. Our ignorance is limitless: let us lop one cubic millimeter off it. Why try to be clever now that we at last have a chance of being just a little less stupid? I have had the unimaginable luck to get my hands on a new instrument that lets us observe one tiny corner of the universe a little, but not all that much, more exactly. Make use of it.

PHILOSOPHER: Your highness, ladies and gentlemen, I just wonder where all this is leading?

GALILEO: I should say our duty as scientists is not to ask where truth is leading.

PHILOSOPHER *agitatedly*: Mr Galilei, truth might lead us anywhere!

GALILEO: Your highness. At night nowadays telescopes are being pointed at the sky all over Italy. Jupiter's moons may not bring down the price of milk. But they have never been seen before, and yet all the same they exist. From this the man in the street concludes that a lot else might exist if only he opened his eyes. It is your duty to confirm this. What has made Italy prick up its ears is not the movements of a few distant stars but the news that hitherto unquestioned dogmas have begun to totter—and we all know that there are too

many of those. Gentlemen, don't let us fight for questionable
truths.

FEDERZONI: You people are teachers: you should be stimulat-
ing the questions.

PHILOSOPHER: I would rather your man didn't tell us how to
conduct a scholarly disputation.

GALILEO: Your highness! My work in the Great Arsenal in
Venice brought me into daily contact with draughtsmen,
builders and instrument mechanics. Such people showed me
a lot of new approaches. They don't read much, but rely on
the evidence of their five senses, without all that much fear as
to where such evidence is going to lead them . . .

PHILOSOPHER: Oho!

GALILEO: Very much like our mariners who a hundred years
ago abandoned our coasts without knowing what other
coasts they would encounter, if any. It looks as if the only
way today to find that supreme curiosity which was the real
glory of classical Greece is to go down to the docks.

PHILOSOPHER: After what we've heard so far I'm not surprised that Mr Galilei finds admirers at the docks.

CHAMBERLAIN: Your highness, I am dismayed to note that this
exceptionally instructive conversation has become a trifle
prolonged. His highness must have some repose before the
court ball.

*At a sign, the grand duke bows to Galileo. The court quickly
gets ready to leave.*

MRS SARTI *blocks the grand duke's way and offers him a plate
of biscuits*: A biscuit, your highness? *The older court lady
leads the grand duke out.*

GALILEO *hurrying after them*: But all you gentlemen need do is
look through the telescope!

CHAMBERLAIN: His highness will not fail to submit your ideas
to our greatest living astronomer: Father Christopher Clavius, chief astronomer at the papal college in Rome.

5

(A)

*Early morning. Galileo at the telescope, bent over his notes.
Enter Virginia with a travelling bag.*

GALILEO: Virginia! Has something happened?

VIRGINIA: The convent's shut; they sent us straight home.
Arcetri has had five cases of plague.

GALILEO *calls*: Sarti!

VIRGINIA: Market Street was barricaded off last night. Two
people have died in the old town, they say, and there are
three more dying in hospital.

GALILEO: As usual they hushed it all up till it was too late.

MRS SARTI *entering*: What are you doing here?

VIRGINIA: The plague.

MRS SARTI: God alive! I'll pack. *Sits down.*

GALILEO: Pack nothing. Take Virginia and Andrea. I'll get my
notes.

*He hurries to his table and hurriedly gathers up papers. Mrs
Sarti puts Andrea's coat on him as he runs up, then collects
some food and bed linen. Enter a grand-ducal footman.*

FOOTMAN: In view of the spread of the disease his highness has
left the city for Bologna. However, he insisted that Mr Galilei
too should be offered a chance to get to safety. The carriage
will be outside your door in two minutes.

MRS SARTI *to Virginia and Andrea*: Go outside at once. Here,
take this.

ANDREA: What for? If you don't tell me why I shan't go.

MRS SARTI: It's the plague, my boy.

VIRGINIA: We'll wait for Father.

MRS SARTI: Mr Galilei, are you ready?

GALILEO *wrapping the telescope in the tablecloth*: Put Virginia and Andrea in the carriage. I won't be a moment.

VIRGINIA: No, we're not going without you. Once you start packing up your books you'll never finish.

MRS SARTI: The coach is there.

GALILEO: Have some sense, Virginia, if you don't take your seats the coachman will drive off. Plague is no joking matter.

VIRGINIA *protesting, as Mrs Sarti and Andrea escort her out*: Help him with his books, or he won't come.

MRS SARTI *from the main door*: Mr Galilei, the coachman says he can't wait.

GALILEO: Mrs Sarti, I don't think I should go. It's all such a mess, you see: three months' worth of notes which I might as well throw away if I can't spend another night or two on them. Anyway this plague is all over the place.

MRS SARTI: Mr Galilei! You must come now! You're crazy.

GALILEO: You'll have to go off with Virginia and Andrea. I'll follow.

MRS SARTI: Another hour, and nobody will be able to get away. You must come. *Listens.* He's driving off. I'll have to stop him.
Exit.
Galileo walks up and down. Mrs Sarti re-enters, very pale, without her bundle.

GALILEO: What are you still here for? You'll miss the children's carriage.

MRS SARTI: They've gone. Virginia had to be held in. The children will get looked after in Bologna. But who's going to see you get your meals?

GALILEO: You're crazy. Staying in this city in order to cook! *Picking up his notes*: Don't think I'm a complete fool, Mrs Sarti. I can't abandon these observations. I have powerful enemies and I must collect proofs for certain hypotheses.

MRS SARTI: You don't have to justify yourself. But it's not exactly sensible.

(B)

Outside Galileo's house in Florence. Galileo steps out and looks down the street. Two nuns pass by.

GALILEO *addresses them*: Could you tell me, sisters, where I can buy some milk? The milk woman didn't come this morning, and my housekeeper has left.
ONE NUN: The only shops open are in the lower town.
THE OTHER NUN: Did you come from here? *Galileo nods.* This is the street!
The two nuns cross themselves, mumble a Hail Mary and hurry away. A man goes by.
GALILEO *addresses him*: Aren't you the baker that delivers our bread to us? *The man nods.* Have you seen my housekeeper? She must have left last night. She hasn't been around all day. *The man shakes his head. A window is opened across the way and a woman looks out.*
WOMAN *yelling*: Hurry! They've got the plague opposite! *The man runs off horrified.*
GALILEO: Have you heard anything about my housekeeper?
WOMAN: Your housekeeper collapsed in the street up there. She must have realised. That's why she went. So inconsiderate! *She slams the window shut.*
Children come down the street. They see Galileo and run away screaming. Galileo turns round; two soldiers hurry up, encased in armour.
SOLDIERS: Get right back indoors!
They push Galileo back into his house with their long pikes. They bolt the door behind him.
GALILEO *at the window*: Can you tell me what happened to the woman?
SOLDIERS: They throw them on the heap.

WOMAN *reappears at the window*: That whole street back there is infected. Why can't you close it off?
The soldiers rope the street off.

WOMAN: But that way nobody can get into our house. This part doesn't have to be closed off. This part's all right. Stop it! Stop! Can't you listen? My husband's still in town, he won't be able to get through to us. You animals! *She can be heard inside weeping and screaming. The soldiers leave. At another window an old woman appears.*

GALILEO: That must be a fire back there.

THE OLD WOMAN: They've stopped putting them out where there's any risk of infection. All they can think about is the plague.

GALILEO: Just like them. It's their whole system of government. Chopping us off like the diseased branch of some barren figtree.

THE OLD WOMAN: That's not fair. It's just that they're powerless.

GALILEO: Are you the only one in your house?

THE OLD WOMAN: Yes. My son sent me a note. Thank God he got a message last night to say somebody back there had died, so he didn't come home. There were eleven cases in our district during the night.

GALILEO: I blame myself for not making my housekeeper leave in time. I had some urgent work, but she had no call to stay.

THE OLD WOMAN: We can't leave either. Who's to take us in? No need for you to blame yourself. I saw her. She left early this morning, around seven o'clock. She must have been ill; when she saw me coming out to fetch in the bread she deliberately kept away from me. She didn't want them to close off your house. But they're bound to find out.
A rattling sound is heard.

GALILEO: What's that?

THE OLD WOMAN: They're trying to make noises to drive away the clouds with the plague seeds in them.
Galileo roars with laughter.

THE OLD WOMAN: Fancy being able to laugh now.
A man comes down the street and finds it roped off.

GALILEO: Hey, you! This street's closed off and I've nothing to eat. Hey! Hey!

The man has quickly hurried away.

THE OLD WOMAN: They may bring something. If not I can leave a jug of milk outside your door tonight, if you're not scared.

GALILEO: Hey! Hey! Can't anybody hear us?

All of a sudden Andrea is standing by the rope. He looks desperate.

GALILEO: Andrea! How did you get here?

ANDREA: I was here first thing. I knocked but you didn't open your door. They told me you . . .

GALILEO: Didn't you go off in the carriage?

ANDREA: Yes. But I managed to jump out. Virginia went on. Can't I come in?

THE OLD WOMAN: No, you can't. You'll have to go to the Ursulines. Your mother may be there.

ANDREA: I've been. But they wouldn't let me see her. She's too ill.

GALILEO: Did you walk the whole way back? It's three days since you left, you know.

ANDREA: It took all that time. Don't be cross with me. They arrested me once.

GALILEO *helplessly*: Don't cry. You know, I've found out lots of things since you went. Shall I tell you? *Andrea nods between his sobs.* Listen carefully or you won't understand. You remember me showing you the planet Venus? Don't bother about that noise, it's nothing. Can you remember? You know what I saw? It's like the moon! I've seen it as a half-circle and I've seen it as a sickle. What d'you say to that? I can demonstrate the whole thing to you with a lamp and a small ball. That proves it's yet another planet with no light of its own. And it turns round the sun in a simple circle; isn't that marvellous?

ANDREA *sobbing*: Yes, and that's a fact.

GALILEO *quietly*: I never asked her to stay.

Andrea says nothing

GALILEO: But of course if I hadn't stayed myself it wouldn't have happened.

ANDREA: They'll have to believe you now, won't they?

GALILEO: I've got all the proofs I need now. Once this is over, I tell you, I shall go to Rome and show them.

Down the street come two masked men with long poles and buckets. They use these to pass bread through the window to Galileo and the old woman.

THE OLD WOMAN: And there's a woman across there with three children. Leave something for her too.

GALILEO: But I've got nothing to drink. There's no water left in the house. *The two shrug their shoulders.* Will you be coming back tomorrow?

ONE MAN *in a muffled voice, since he has a rag over his mouth*: Who knows what'll happen tomorrow?

GALILEO: If you do come, could you bring me a small book I need for my work?

THE MAN *gives a stifled laugh*: As if a book could make any difference. You'll be lucky if you get bread.

GALILEO: But this boy is my pupil, and he'll be there and can give it you for me. It's the chart giving the periodicity of Mercury, Andrea: I've mislaid it. Can you get me one from the school?

The men have gone on.

ANDREA: Of course. I'll get it, Mr Galilei. *Exit. Galileo likewise goes in. The old woman comes out of the house opposite and puts a jug outside Galileo's door.*

6

1616. THE VATICAN RESEARCH INSTITUTE,
THE COLLEGIUM ROMANUM,
CONFIRMS GALILEO'S FINDINGS

> Things take indeed a wondrous turn
> When learned men do stoop to learn.
> Clavius, we are pleased to say
> Upheld Galileo Galilei.

Hall of the Collegium Romanum in Rome. It is night-time. High ecclesiastics, monks and scholars in groups. On his own, to one side, Galileo. The atmosphere is extremely hilarious. Before the beginning of the scene a great wave of laughter is heard.

A FAT PRELATE *clasps his belly with laughing*: Stupidity! Stupidity! I'd like to hear a proposition that people won't believe.

A SCHOLAR: For instance: that you have an incurable aversion to meals, Monsignor.

A FAT PRELATE: They'd believe it; they'd believe it. Things have to make sense to be disbelieved. That Satan exists: that's something they doubt. But that the earth spins round like a marble in the gutter; that's believed all right. O sancta simplicatas!

A MONK *play-acting*: I'm getting giddy. The earth's spinning round too fast. Permit me to hold on to you, professor. *He pretends to lurch and clutches one of the scholars.*

THE SCHOLAR *following suit*: Yes, the old girl has been on the bottle again.

He clutches another.

THE MONK: Stop, stop! We're skidding off. Stop, I said!

A SECOND SCHOLAR: Venus is all askew. I can only see one half of her backside. Help!

A group of laughing monks forms, acting as if they were doing their best not to be swept off a ship's deck in a storm.

A SECOND MONK: As long as we aren't flung on to the moon! It's said to have terribly sharp peaks, my brethren.

THE FIRST SCHOLAR: Dig your heels in and resist.

THE FIRST MONK: And don't look down. I'm losing my balance.

THE FAT PRELATE *intentionally loudly, aiming at Galileo*: Oh, that's impossible. Nobody is unbalanced in the Collegium Romanum.

Much laughter. Two of the Collegium astronomers enter from a door. There is a silence.

A MONK: Are you still going over it? That's scandalous.

THE FIRST ASTRONOMER *angrily*: Not us.

THE SECOND ASTRONOMER: What's this meant to lead to? I don't understand Clavius's attitude ... One can't treat everything as gospel that has been put forward in the past fifty years. In 1572 a new star appeared in the eighth and highest sphere, the sphere of the fixed stars, which seemed larger and more brilliant than all the stars round it, and within eighteen months it had gone out and been annihilated. Does that mean we must question the eternity and immutability of the heavens?

PHILOSOPHER: Give them half a chance and they'll smash up our whole starry sky.

THE FIRST ASTRONOMER: Yes, what are we coming to? Five years later Tycho Brahe in Denmark established the course of a comet. It started above the moon and broke through one crystal sphere after another, the solid supports on which all the moving of the heavenly bodies depend. It encountered no obstacles, there was no deflection of its light. Does that mean we must doubt the existence of the spheres?

THE PHILOSOPHER: It's out of the question. As Italy's and the Church's greatest astronomer, how can Christopher Clavius stoop to examine such a proposition?

THE FAT PRELATE: Outrageous.

THE FIRST ASTRONOMER: He is examining it, though. He's sitting in there staring through that diabolical tube.

THE SECOND ASTRONOMER: Principiis obsta! It all started when we began reckoning so many things—the length of the solar year, the dates of solar and lunar eclipses, the position of the heavenly bodies—according to the tables established by Copernicus, who was a heretic.

A MONK: Which is better, I ask you: to have an eclipse of the moon happen three days later than the calendar says, or never to have eternal salvation at all?

A VERY THIN MONK *comes forward with an open bible, fanatically thrusting his finger at a certain passage*: What do the Scriptures say? "Sun, stand thou still on Gibeon and thou, moon, in the valley of Ajalon." How can the sun stand still if it never moves at all as suggested by this heretic? Are the Scriptures lying?

THE FIRST ASTRONOMER: No, and that's why we walked out.

THE SECOND ASTRONOMER: There *are* phenomena that present difficulties for us astronomers, but does mankind have to understand everything? *Both go out.*

THE VERY THIN MONK: They degrade humanity's dwelling place to a wandering star. Men, animals, plants and the kingdoms of the earth get packed on a cart and driven in a circle round an empty sky. Heaven and earth are no longer distinct, according to them. Heaven because it is made of earth, and earth because it is just one more heavenly body. There is no more difference between top and bottom, between eternal and ephemeral. That we are short-lived we know. Now they tell us that heaven is short-lived too. There are sun, moon and stars, and we live on the earth, it used to be said, and so the Book has it; but now these people are saying the earth is another star. Wait till they say man and animal are not distinct either, man himself is an animal, there's nothing but animals!

THE FIRST SCHOLAR *to Galileo*: Mr Galilei, you've let something fall.

GALILEO *who had meanwhile taken his stone from his pocket, played with it and finally allowed it to drop on the floor, bending to pick it up*: Rise, monsignor; I let it rise.

THE FAT PRELATE *turning round*: An arrogant fellow.

Enter a very old cardinal supported by a monk. They respectfully make way for him.

THE VERY OLD CARDINAL: Are they still in there? Can't they settle such a trivial matter more quickly? Clavius must surely know his astronomy. I am told that this Mr Galilei moves mankind away from the centre of the universe and dumps it somewhere on the edge. Clearly this makes him an enemy of the human race. We must treat him as such. Mankind is the crown of creation, as every child knows, God's highest and dearest creature. How could He take something so miraculous, the fruit of so much effort, and lodge it on a remote, minor, constantly elusive star? Would he send His Son to such a place? How can there be people so perverse as to pin their faith to these slaves of the multiplication table! Which of God's creatures would stand for anything like that?

THE FAT PRELATE *murmurs*: The gentleman is present.

THE VERY OLD CARDINAL *to Galileo*: It's you, is it? You know, my eyesight is not what it was, but I can still see one thing: that you bear a remarkable likeness to what's-his-name, you know, that man we burned.

THE MONK: Your Eminence should avoid excitement. The doctor . . .

THE VERY OLD CARDINAL *shakes him off. To Galileo*: You want to debase the earth even though you live on it and derive everything from it. You are fouling your own nest. But I for one am not going to stand for that. *He pushes the monk away and begins proudly striding to and fro.* I am not just any old creature on any insignificant star briefly circling in no particular place. I am walking, with a firm step, on a fixed earth, it is motionless, it is the centre of the universe, I am at the centre and the eye of the Creator falls upon me and me alone. Round about me, attached to eight crystal spheres, revolve the fixed stars and the mighty sun which has been created to light my surroundings. And myself too, that God may see me. In this way everything comes visibly and incontrovertibly to depend on me, mankind, God's great effort, the creature on whom it all centres, made in God's own image, indestructible and . . . *He collapses.*

THE MONK: Your Eminence has overstrained himself.
At this moment the door at the back opens and the great Clavius enters at the head of his astronomers. Swiftly and in silence he crosses the hall without looking to one side or the other and addresses a monk as he is on the way out.

CLAVIUS: He's right. *He leaves, followed by the astronomers. The door at the back remains open. Deadly silence. The very old Cardinal recovers consciousness.*

THE VERY OLD CARDINAL: What's that? Have they reached a conclusion?
Nobody dares tell him.

THE MONK: Your Eminence must be taken home. *The old man is assisted out. All leave the hall, worried. A little monk from Clavius's committee of experts pauses beside Galileo.*

THE LITTLE MONK *confidentially*: Mr Galilei, before he left Father Clavius said: Now it's up to the theologians to see how they can straighten out the movements of the heavens once more. You've won. *Exit*

GALILEO *tries to hold him back*: It has won. Not me: reason has won.
The little monk has already left. Galileo too starts to go. In the doorway he encounters a tall cleric, the Cardinal Inquisitor, who is accompanied by an astronomer. Galileo bows. Before going out he whispers a question to the guard at the door.

GUARD *whispers back*: His Eminence the Cardinal Inquisitor. *The astronomer leads the Cardinal Inquisitor up to the telescope.*

7

BUT THE INQUISITION PUTS COPERNICUS'S
TEACHINGS ON THE INDEX (MARCH 5TH, 1616)

> When Galileo was in Rome
> A cardinal asked him to his home.
> He wined and dined him as his guest
> And only made one small request.

Cardinal Bellarmin's house in Rome. A ball is in progress. In the vestibule, where two clerical secretaries are playing chess and making notes about the guests, Galileo is received with applause by a small group of masked ladies and gentlemen. He arrives accompanied by his daughter Virginia and her fiancé Ludovico Marsili.

VIRGINIA: I'm not dancing with anybody else, Ludovico.

LUDOVICO: Your shoulder-strap's undone.

GALILEO:
> Fret not, daughter, if perchance
> You attract a wanton glance.
> The eyes that catch a trembling lace
> Will guess the heartbeat's quickened pace.
> Lovely woman still may be
> Careless with felicity.

VIRGINIA: Feel my heart.

GALILEO *puts his hand on her heart*: It's thumping.

VIRGINIA: I'd like to look beautiful.

GALILEO: You'd better, or they'll go back to wondering whether it turns or not.

LUDOVICO: Of course it doesn't turn. *Galileo laughs.* Rome is talking only of you. But after tonight, sir, they will be talking about your daughter.

GALILEO: It's supposed to be easy to look beautiful in the Roman spring. Even I shall start looking like an overweight Adonis. *To the secretaries*: I am to wait here for his Eminence the Cardinal. *To the couple*: Go off and enjoy yourselves. *Before they leave for the ball offstage Virginia again comes running back*.

VIRGINIA: Father, the hairdresser in the Via del Trionfo took me first, and he made four other ladies wait. He knew your name right away. *Exit*.

GALILEO *to the secretaries as they play chess*: How can you go on playing old-style chess? Cramped, cramped. Nowadays the play is to let the chief pieces roam across the whole board. The rooks like this—*he demonstrates*—and the bishops like that and the Queen like this and that. That way you have enough space and can plan ahead.

FIRST SECRETARY: It wouldn't go with our small salaries, you know. We can only do moves like this. *He makes a small move*.

GALILEO: You've got it wrong, my friend, quite wrong. If you live grandly enough you can afford to sweep the board. One has to move with the times, gentlemen. Not just hugging the coasts; sooner or later one has to venture out. *The very old cardinal from the previous scene crosses the stage, led by his monk. He notices Galileo, walks past him, turns round hesitantly and greets him. Galileo sits down. From the ballroom boys' voices are heard singing Lorenzo di Medici's famous poem on transience,*

> I who have seen the summer's roses die
> And all their petals pale and shrivelled lie
> Upon the chilly ground, I know the truth:
> How evanescent is the flower of youth.

GALILEO: Rome—A large party?

THE FIRST SECRETARY: The first carnival since the plague

years. All Italy's great families are represented here tonight. The Orsinis, the Villanis, the Nuccolis, the Soldanieris, the Canes, the Lecchis, the d'Estes, the Colombinis . . .

SECOND SECRETARY *interrupting*: Their Eminences Cardinals Bellarmin and Barberini.

Enter Cardinal Bellarmin and Cardinal Barberini. They are holding sticks with the masks of a lamb and a dove over their faces.

BARBERINI *pointing at Galileo*: 'The sun also ariseth, and the sun goeth down, and hasteth to his place where he arose.' So says Solomon, and what does Galileo say?

GALILEO: When I was so high—*he indicates with his hand*—your Eminence, I stood on a ship and called out 'The shore is moving away.' Today I realise that the shore was standing still and the ship moving away.

BARBERINI: Ingenious, ingenious—what our eyes see, Bellarmin, in other words the rotation of the starry heavens, is not necessarily true—witness the ship and the shore. But what is true—i.e. the rotation of the earth—cannot be perceived. Ingenious. But his moons of Jupiter are a tough nut for our astronomers to crack. Unfortunately I once studied some astronomy, Bellarmin. It sticks to you like the itch.

BELLARMIN: We must move with the times, Barberini. If new star charts based on a new hypothesis help our mariners to navigate, then they should make use of them. We only disapprove of such doctrines as run counter to the Scriptures.

He waves toward the ballroom in greeting.

GALILEO: The Scriptures . . . 'He that withholdeth corn, the people shall curse him.' Proverbs of Solomon.

BARBERINI: 'A prudent man concealeth knowledge.' Proverbs of Solomon.

GALILEO: 'Where no oxen are the crib is clean: but much increase is by the strength of ox.'

BARBERINI: 'He that ruleth his spirit is better than he that taketh a city.'

GALILEO: 'But a broken spirit drieth the bones.' *Pause.* 'Doth not wisdom cry?'

BARBERINI: 'Can one go upon hot coals, and his feet not be

burned?'—Welcome to Rome, Galileo my friend. You know its origins? Two little boys, so runs the legend, were given milk and shelter by a she-wolf. Since that time all her children have had to pay for their milk. The she-wolf makes up for it by providing every kind of pleasure, earthly and heavenly, ranging from conversations with my friend Bellarmin to three or four ladies of international repute; let me point them out to you . . .

He takes Galileo upstage to show him the ballroom. Galileo follows reluctantly.

BARBERINI: No? He would rather have a serious discussion. Right. Are you sure, Galileo my friend, that you astronomers aren't merely out to make astronomy simpler for yourselves? *He leads him forward once more.* You think in circles and ellipses and constant velocities, simple motions such as are adapted to your brains. Suppose it had pleased God to make his stars move like this? *With his finger he traces an extremely complicated course at an uneven speed.* What would that do to your calculations?

GALILEO: Your Eminence, if God had constructed the world like that—*he imitates Barberini's course*—then he would have gone on to construct our brains like that, so that they would regard such motions as the simplest. I believe in men's reason.

BARBERINI: I think men's reason is not up to the job. *Silence.* He's too polite to go on and say he thinks mine is not up to the job.

Laughs and walks back to the balustrade.

BELLARMIN: Men's reason, my friend, does not take us very far. All around us we see nothing but crookedness, crime and weakness. Where is truth?

GALILEO *angrily*: I believe in men's reason.

BARBERINI *to the secretaries*: You needn't take this down; it's a scientific discussion among friends.

BELLARMIN: Think for an instant how much thought and effort it cost the Fathers of the Church and their countless successors to put some sense into this appalling world of ours. Think of the brutality of the landowners in the Campagna who have their half-naked peasants flogged to work, and of the stupidity of those poor people who kiss their feet in return.

GALILEO: Horrifying. As I was driving here I saw . . .

BELLARMIN: We have shifted the responsibility for such occurrences as we cannot understand—life is made up of them—to a higher Being, and argued that all of them contribute to the fulfilment of certain intentions, that the whole thing is taking place according to a great plan. Admittedly this hasn't satisfied everybody, but now you come along and accuse this higher Being of not being quite clear how the stars move, whereas you yourself are. Is that sensible?

GALILEO *starts to make a statement*: I am a faithful son of the Church . . .

BARBERINI: He's a terrible man. He cheerfully sets out to convict God of the most elementary errors in astronomy. I suppose God hadn't got far enough in his studies before he wrote the bible; is that it? My *dear* fellow . . .

BELLARMIN: Wouldn't you also think it possible that the Creator had a better idea of what he was making than those he has created?

GALILEO: But surely, gentlemen, mankind may not only get the motions of the stars wrong but the Bible too?

BELLARMIN: But isn't interpreting the Bible the business of Holy Church and her theologians, wouldn't you say? *Galileo is silent.*

BELLARMIN: You have no answer to that, have you? *He makes a sign to the secretaries*: Mr Galilei, tonight the Holy Office decided that the doctrine of Copernicus, according to which the sun is motionless and at the centre of the cosmos, while the earth moves and is not at the centre of the cosmos, is foolish, absurd, heretical and contrary to our faith. I have been charged to warn you that you must abandon this view.

GALILEO: What does this mean?

From the ballroom boys can be heard singing a further verse of the madrigal:

> I said: This lovely springtime cannot last
> So pluck your roses before May is past.

Barberini gestures Galileo not to speak till the song is finished. They listen.

GALILEO: And the facts? I understand that the Collegium Romanum had approved my observations.

BELLARMIN: And expressed their complete satisfaction, in terms very flattering to you.

GALILEO: But the moons of Jupiter, the phases of Venus . . .

BELLARMIN: The Holy Congregation took its decision without going into such details.

GALILEO: In other words, all further scientific research . . .

BELLARMIN: Is explicitly guaranteed, Mr Galilei. In line with the Church's view that it is impossible for us to know, but legitimate for us to explore. *He again greets a guest in the ballroom.* You are also at liberty to treat the doctrine in question mathematically, in the form of a hypothesis. Science is the rightful and much-loved daughter of the Church, Mr Galilei. None of us seriously believes that you want to shake men's faith in the Church.

GALILEO *angrily*: What destroys faith is invoking it.

BARBERINI: Really? *He slaps him on the shoulder with a roar of laughter. Then he gives him a keen look and says in a not unfriendly manner*: Don't tip the baby out with the bathwater, Galileo my friend. We shan't. We need you more than you need us.

BELLARMIN: I cannot wait to introduce Italy's greatest mathematician to the Commissioner of the Holy Office, who has the highest possible esteem for you.

BARBERINI *taking Galileo's other arm*: At which he turns himself back into a lamb. You too, my dear fellow, ought really to have come disguised as a good orthodox thinker. It's my own mask that permits me certain freedoms today. Dressed like this I might be heard to murmur: If God didn't exist we should have to invent him. Right, let's put on our masks once more. Poor old Galileo hasn't got one. *They put Galileo between them and escort him into the ballroom.*

FIRST SECRETARY: Did you get that last sentence?

SECOND SECRETARY: Just doing it. *They write rapidly.* Have

you got that bit where he said he believes in men's reason? *Enter the Cardinal Inquisitor.*

THE INQUISITOR: Did the conversation take place?

FIRST SECRETARY *mechanically*: To start with Mr Galilei arrived with his daughter. She has become engaged today to Mr . . . *The Inquisitor gestures him not to go on.* Mr Galilei then told us about the new way of playing chess in which, contrary to all the rules, the pieces are moved right across the board.

THE INQUISITOR *with a similar gesture*: The transcript. *A secretary hands him the transcripts and the cardinal sits down and skims through it. Two young ladies in masks cross the stage; they curtsey to the cardinal.*

ONE YOUNG LADY: Who's that?

THE OTHER: The Cardinal Inquisitor.

They giggle and go off. Enter Virginia, looking around for something.

THE INQUISITOR *from his corner*: Well, my daughter?

VIRGINIA *gives a slight start, not having seen him*: Oh, your Eminence . . .

Without looking up, the Inquisitor holds out his right hand to her.

She approaches and kisses his ring.

THE INQUISITOR: A splendid night. Permit me to congratulate you on your engagement. Your future husband comes from a distinguished family. Are you staying long in Rome?

VIRGINIA: Not this time, your Eminence. A wedding takes so much preparing.

THE INQUISITOR: Ah, then you'll be returning to Florence like your father. I am glad of that. I expect that your father needs you. Mathematics is not the warmest of companions in the home, is it? Having a creature of flesh and blood around makes all the difference. It's easy to get lost in the world of the stars, with its immense distances, if one is a great man.

VIRGINIA *breathlessly*: You are very kind, your Eminence. I really understand practically nothing about such things.

THE INQUISITOR: Indeed? *He laughs.* In the fisherman's house no one eats fish, eh? It will tickle your father to hear that al-most all your knowledge about the world of the stars comes ultimately from me, my child. *Leafing through the transcript*: It says here that our innovators, whose acknowledged leader is your father—a great man, one of the greatest—consider our present ideas about the significance of the dear old earth to be a little exaggerated. Well, from Ptolemy's time—and he was a wise man of antiquity—up to the present day we used to reckon that the whole of creation—in other words the en-tire crystal ball at whose centre the earth lies—measured about twenty thousand diametres of the earth across. Nice and roomy, but not large enough for innovators. Apparently they feel that it is unimaginably far-flung and that the earth's distance from the sun—quite a respectable distance, we al-ways found it—is so minute compared with its distance from the fixed stars on the outermost sphere that our calculations can simply ignore it. So who can say that the innovators themselves aren't living on a very grand scale?

Virginia laughs. So does the Inquisitor.

THE INQUISITOR: True enough, there are a few gentlemen of the Holy Office who have started objecting, as it were, to such a view of the world, compared with which our picture so far has been a little miniature such as one might hang round the neck of certain young ladies. What worries them is that a prelate or even a cardinal might get lost in such vast distances and the Almighty might lose sight of the Pope him-self. Yes, it's very amusing, but I am glad to know that you will remain close to your great father whom we all esteem so highly, my dear child. By the way, do I know your Father Confessor . . . ?

VIRGINIA: Father Christopherus of Saint Ursula.

THE INQUISITOR: Ah yes, I am glad that you will be going with your father. He will need you; perhaps you cannot imag-ine this, but the time will come. You are still so young and so very much flesh and blood, and greatness is occasionally a difficult burden for those on whom God has bestowed it; it can be. No mortal is so great that he cannot be contained in a prayer. But I am keeping you, my dear child, and I'll be making your fiancé jealous and maybe your father too by telling you something about the stars which is possibly out of date. Run off and dance; only mind you remember me to Father Christopherus.

Virginia makes a deep bow and goes.

8

A CONVERSATION

Galileo, feeling grim,
A young monk came to visit him.
The monk was born of common folk.
It was of science that they spoke.

In the Florentine Ambassador's palace in Rome Galileo is listening to the little monk who whispered the papal astronomer's remark to him after the meeting of the Collegium Romanum.

GALILEO: Go on, go on. The habit you're wearing gives you the right to say whatever you want.

THE LITTLE MONK: I studied mathematics, Mr Galilei.

GALILEO: That might come in handy if it led you to admit that two and two sometimes makes four.

THE LITTLE MONK: Mr Galilei, I have been unable to sleep for three days. I couldn't see how to reconcile the decree I had read with the moons of Jupiter which I had observed. Today I decided to say an early mass and come to you.

GALILEO: In order to tell me Jupiter has no moons?

THE LITTLE MONK: No. I have managed to see the wisdom of the decree. It has drawn my attention to the potential dangers for humanity in wholly unrestricted research, and I have decided to give astronomy up. But I also wanted to explain to you the motives which can make even an astronomer renounce pursuing that doctrine any further.

GALILEO: I can assure you that such motives are familiar to me.

THE LITTLE MONK: I understand your bitterness. You have in mind certain exceptional powers of enforcement at the Church's disposal.

GALILEO: Just call them instruments of torture.

THE LITTLE MONK: But I am referring to other motives. Let me speak about myself. My parents were peasants in the Campagna, and I grew up there. They are simple people. They know all about olive trees, but not much else. As I study the phases of Venus I can visualise my parents sitting round the fire with my sister, eating their curded cheese. I see the beams above them, blackened by hundreds of years of smoke, and I see every detail of their old worn hands and the little spoons they are holding. They are badly off, but even their misfortunes imply a certain order. There are so many cycles, ranging from washing the floor, through the seasons of the olive crop to the paying of taxes. There is a regularity about the disasters that befall them. My father's back does not get bent all at once, but more and more each spring he spends in the olive groves; just as the successive childbirths that have made my mother increasingly sexless have followed well-defined intervals. They draw the strength they need to carry their baskets sweating up the stony tracks, to bear children and even to eat, from the feeling of stability and necessity that comes of looking at the soil, at the annual greening of the trees and at the little church, and of listening to the bible passages read there every Sunday. They have been assured that God's eye is always on them—probingly, even anxiously—: that the whole drama of the world is constructed around them so that they, the performers, may prove themselves in their greater or lesser roles. What would my people say if I told them that they happen to be on a small knob of stone twisting endlessly through the void round a second-rate star, just one among myriads? What would be the value or necessity then of so much patience, such understanding of their own poverty? What would be the use of Holy Scripture, which has explained and justified it all—the sweat, the patience, the hunger, the submissiveness—and now turns out to be full of errors? No: I can see their eyes wavering, I can see them letting their spoons drop, I can see how betrayed and deceived they will feel. So nobody's eye is on us, they'll say. Have we got to look after ourselves, old, uneducated and worn-out as we are? The only part anybody has devised for us is this wretched, earthly one, to be played out on a tiny star wholly dependent on others, with nothing revolving round it. Our poverty has no meaning: hunger is no trial of strength, it's merely not having eaten: effort is no virtue, it's just bending and carrying. Can you see now why I read into the Holy Congregations decree a noble motherly compassion; a vast goodness of soul?

GALILEO: Goodness of soul! Aren't you really saying that there's nothing for them, the wine has all been drunk, their lips are parched, so they had better kiss the cassock? Why is there nothing for them? Why does order in this country mean the orderliness of a bare cupboard, and necessity nothing but the need to work oneself to death? When there are teeming vineyards and cornfields on every side? Your Campagna peasants are paying for the wars which the representative of gentle Jesus is waging in Germany and Spain. Why does he make the earth the centre of the universe? So that the See of St Peter can be the centre of the earth! That's what it is all about. You're right, it's not about the planets, it's about the peasants of the Campagna. And don't talk to me about the beauty given to phenomena by the patina of age! You know how the Margaritifera oyster produces its pearl? By a mortally dangerous disease which involves taking some unassimilable foreign body, like a grain of sand, and wrapping it in a slimy ball. The process all but kills it. To hell with the pearl, give me the healthy oyster. Virtues are not an offshoot of poverty, my dear fellow. If your people were happy and prosperous they could develop the virtues of happiness and prosperity. At present the virtues of exhaustion derive from exhausted fields, and I reject them. Sir, my new pumps will perform more miracles in that direction than all your ridiculous superhuman slaving.—'Be fruitful and multiply', since your fields are not fruitful and you are being decimated by wars. Am I supposed to tell your people lies?

THE LITTLE MONK *much agitated*: We have the highest of all motives for keeping our mouths shut—the peace of mind of the less fortunate.

GALILEO: Would you like me to show you a Cellini clock that Cardinal Bellarmin's coachman brought round this morning? My dear fellow, authority is rewarding me for not disturbing the peace of mind of people like your parents, by offering me the wine they press in the sweat of their countenance which we all know to have been made in God's image. If I were to agree to keep my mouth shut my motives would be thoroughly low ones: an easy life, freedom from persecution, and so on.

THE LITTLE MONK: Mr Galilei, I am a priest.

GALILEO: You're also a physicist. And you can see that Venus has phases. Here, look out there! *He points at the window.* Can you see the little Priapus on the fountain next the laurel bush? The god of gardens, birds and thieves, rich in two thousand years of bucolic indecency. Even he was less of a liar. All right, let's drop it. I too am a son of the Church. But do you know the eighth Satire of Horace? I've been rereading it again lately, it acts as a kind of counterweight. *He picks up a small book.* He makes his Priapus speak—a little statue which was then in the Esquiline gardens. Starting:

> Stump of a figtree, useless kind of wood
> Was I once; then the carpenter, not sure
> Whether to make a Priapus or a stool
> Opted for the god . . .

Can you imagine Horace being told not to mention stools and agreeing to put a table in the poem instead? Sir, it offends my sense of beauty if my cosmogony has a Venus without phases. We cannot invent mechanisms to pump water up from rivers if we are not to be allowed to study the greatest of all mechanisms right under our nose, that of the heavenly bodies. The sum of the angles in a triangle cannot be varied to suit the Vatican's convenience. I can't calculate the courses of flying bodies in such a way as also to explain witches taking trips on broomsticks.

THE LITTLE MONK: But don't you think that the truth will get through without us, so long as it's true?

GALILEO: No, no, no. The only truth that gets through will be what we force through: the victory of reason will be the victory of people who are prepared to reason, nothing else. Your picture of the Campagna peasants makes them look like the moss on their own huts. How can anyone imagine that the sum of the angles in a triangle conflicts with *their* needs? But unless they get moving and learn how to think, they will find even the finest irrigation systems won't help them. Oh, to hell with it: I see your people's divine patience, but where is their divine anger?

THE LITTLE MONK: They are tired.

GALILEO *tosses him a bundle of manuscripts*: Are you a physicist, my son? Here you have the reasons why the ocean moves, ebbing and flowing. But you're not supposed to read it, d'you hear? Oh, you've already started. You are a physicist, then? *The little monk is absorbed in the papers.*

GALILEO: An apple from the tree of knowledge! He's wolfing it down. He is damned forever, but he has got to wolf it down, the poor glutton. I sometimes think I'll have myself shut up in a dungeon ten fathoms below ground in complete darkness if only it will help me to find out what light is. And the worst thing is that what I know I have to tell people, like a lover, like a drunkard, like a traitor. It is an absolute vice and leads to disaster. How long can I go on shouting it into the void, that's the question.

THE LITTLE MONK *indicating a passage in the papers*: I don't understand this sentence.

GALILEO: I'll explain it you, I'll explain it to you.

AFTER KEEPING SILENT FOR EIGHT YEARS, GALILEO
IS ENCOURAGED BY THE ACCESSION OF A NEW POPE,
HIMSELF A SCIENTIST, TO RESUME HIS RESEARCHES
INTO THE FORBIDDEN AREA: THE SUNSPOTS

> Eight long years with tongue in cheek
> Of what he knew he did not speak.
> Then temptation grew too great
> And Galileo challenged fate.

Galileo's house in Florence. Galileo's pupils—Federzoni, the little monk and Andrea Sarti, a young man now—have gathered to see an experiment demonstrated. Galileo himself is standing reading a book. Virginia and Mrs Sarti are sewing her trousseau.

VIRGINIA: Sewing one's trousseau is fun. That one's for entertaining at the long table; Ludovico likes entertaining. It's got to be neat, though; his mother can spot every loose thread. She doesn't like Father's books. Nor does Father Christopherus.

MRS SARTI: He hasn't written a book for years.

VIRGINIA: I think he realises he was wrong. A very high church person in Rome told me a lot about astronomy. The distances are too great.

ANDREA *writing the day's programme on the board*: 'Thursday p.m. Floating bodies'—as before, ice, bucket of water, balance, iron needle, Aristotle.

He fetches these things.

The others are reading books.

Enter Filippo Mucius, a scholar in middle age. He appears somewhat distraught.

MUCIUS: Could you tell Mr Galilei that he has got to see me? He is condemning me unheard.

MRS SARTI: But he won't receive you.

MUCIUS: God will recompense you if you will only ask. I must speak to him.

VIRGINIA *goes to the stairs*: Father!

GALILEO: What is it?

VIRGINIA: Mr Mucius.

GALILEO *looking up sharply, goes to the head of the stairs, followed by his pupils*: What do you want?

MUCIUS: Mr Galilei, may I be allowed to explain those passages from my book which seem to contain a condemnation of Copernicus's theories about the rotation of the earth? I have . . .

GALILEO: What do you want to explain? You are fully in line with the Holy Congregation's decree of 1616. You cannot be faulted. You did of course study mathematics here, but that's no reason why we should need to hear you say that two and two makes four. You are quite within your rights in saying that this stone—*he takes a little stone from his pocket and throws it down to the hall*—has just flown up to the ceiling.

MUCIUS: Mr Galilei, there are worse things than the plague.

GALILEO: Listen to me: someone who doesn't know the truth is just thick-headed. But someone who does know it and calls it a lie is a crook. Get out of my house.

MUCIUS *tonelessly*: You're quite right.
He goes out.
Galileo goes back into his work room.

FEDERZONI: I am afraid so. He's not a great man and no one would take him seriously for one moment if he hadn't been your pupil. Now of course people are saying 'he's heard everything Galileo had to teach and he's forced to admit that it's all nonsense'.

MRS SARTI: I'm sorry for the poor gentleman.

VIRGINIA: Father was too good to him.

MRS SARTI: I really wanted to talk to you about your marriage,

Virginia. You're such a child still, and got no mother, and your father keeps putting those little bits of ice on water. Anyhow I wouldn't ask him anything to do with your marriage if I were you. He'd keep on for days saying the most dreadful things, preferably at meals and when the young people are there, because he hasn't got half a scudo's worth of shame in his make-up, and never had. But I'm not talking about that kind of thing, just about how the future will turn out. Not that I'm in a position to know anything myself. I'm not educated. But nobody goes blindly into a serious affair like this. I really think you ought to go to a proper astronomer at the university and get him to cast your horoscope so you know what you're in for. Why are you laughing?

VIRGINIA: Because I've been.

MRS SARTI *very inquisitive*: What did he say?

VIRGINIA: For three months I'll have to be careful, because the sun will be in Aries, but then I shall get a particularly favourable ascendant and the clouds will part. So long as I keep my eye on Jupiter I can travel as much as I like, because I'm an Aries.

MRS SARTI: And Ludovico?

VIRGINIA: He's a Leo. *After a little pause*: That's supposed to be sensual. *Pause*.

VIRGINIA: I know whose step that is. It's Mr Gaffone, the Rector.

Enter Mr Gaffone, Rector of the University.

GAFFONE: I'm just bringing a book which I think might interest your father. For heaven's sake please don't disturb him. I can't help it; I always feel that every moment stolen from that great man is a moment stolen from Italy. I'll lay it neatly and daintily in your hands and slip away, on tiptoe. *He goes. Virginia gives the book to Federzoni.*

GALILEO: What's it about?

FEDERZONI: I don't know. *Spelling out*: 'De maculis in sole'.

ANDREA: About sunspots. Yet another.

Federzoni irritably passes it on to him.

ANDREA: Listen to the dedication. 'To the greatest living authority on physics, Galileo Galilei.'

Galileo is once more deep in his book.

ANDREA: I've read the treatise on sunspots which Fabricius has written in Holland. He thinks they are clusters of stars passing between the earth and the sun.

THE LITTLE MONK: Doubtful, don't you think, Mr Galilei?
Galileo does not answer.

ANDREA: In Paris and in Prague they think they are vapours from the sun.

FEDERZONI: Hm.

ANDREA: Federzoni doubts it.

FEDERZONI: Leave me out of it, would you? I said 'Hm', that's all. I'm your lens-grinder, I grind lenses and you make observations of the sky through them and what you see isn't spots but 'maculis'. How am I to doubt anything? How often do I have to tell you I can't read the books, they're in Latin? *In his anger he gesticulates with the scales. One of the pans falls to the floor. Galileo goes over and picks it up without saying anything.*

THE LITTLE MONK: There's happiness in doubting: I wonder why.

ANDREA: Every sunny day for the past two weeks I've gone up to the attic, under the roof. The narrow chinks between the shingles let just a thin ray of light through. If you take a sheet of paper you can catch the sun's image upside down. I saw a spot as big as a fly, as smudged as a cloud. It was moving. Why aren't we investigating those spots, Mr Galilei?

GALILEO: Because we're working on floating bodies.

ANDREA: Mother's got great baskets full of letters. The whole of Europe wants to know what you think, you've such a reputation now, you can't just say nothing.

GALILEO: Rome allowed me to get a reputation because I said nothing.

FEDERZONI: But you can't afford to go on saying nothing now.

GALILEO: Nor can I afford to be roasted over a wood fire like a ham.

ANDREA: Does that mean you think the sunspots are part of this business?
Galileo does not answer.

ANDREA: All right, let's stick to our bits of ice, they can't hurt you.

GALILEO: Correct.—Our proposition, Andrea?

ANDREA: As for floating, we assume that it depends not on a body's form but on whether it is lighter or heavier than water.

GALILEO: What does Aristotle say?

THE LITTLE MONK: 'Discus latus platique . . .'

GALILEO: For God's sake translate it.

THE LITTLE MONK: 'A broad flat piece of ice will float on water whereas an iron needle will sink.'

GALILEO: Why does the ice not sink, in Aristotle's view?

THE LITTLE MONK: Because it is broad and flat and therefore cannot divide the water.

GALILEO: Right. *He takes a piece of ice and places it in the bucket.* Now I am pressing the ice hard against the bottom of the bucket. I release the pressure of my hands. What happens?

THE LITTLE MONK: It shoots up to the top again.

GALILEO: Correct. Apparently it can divide the water all right as it rises. Fulganzio!

THE LITTLE MONK: But why can it float in the first place? It's heavier than water, because it is concentrated water.

GALILEO: Suppose it were thinned-down water?

ANDREA: It has to be lighter than water, or it wouldn't float.

GALILEO: Aha.

ANDREA: Any more than an iron needle can float. Everything lighter than water floats and everything heavier sinks. QED.

GALILEO: Andrea, you must learn to think cautiously. Hand me the needle. A sheet of paper. Is iron heavier than water?

ANDREA: Yes.

Galileo lays the needle on a piece of paper and launches it on the water. A pause.

GALILEO: What happens?

FEDERZONI: The needle's floating. Holy Aristotle, they never checked up on him!

They laugh.

GALILEO: One of the main reasons why the sciences are so poor is that they imagine they are so rich. It isn't their job to throw open the door to infinite wisdom but to put a limit to infinite error. Make your notes.

VIRGINIA: What is it?

MRS SARTI: Whenever they laugh it gives me a turn. What are they laughing about, I ask myself.

VIRGINIA: Father says theologians have their bells to ring: physicists have their laughter.

MRS SARTI: Anyway I'm glad he isn't looking through his tube so often these days. That was even worse.

VIRGINIA: All he's doing now is put bits of ice in water: that can't do much harm.

MRS SARTI: I don't know.

Enter Ludovico Marsili in travelling clothes, followed by a servant carrying items of luggage. Virginia runs up and throws her arms round him.

VIRGINIA: Why didn't you write and say you were coming?

LUDOVICO: I happened to be in the area inspecting our vineyards at Buccioli, and couldn't resist the chance.

GALILEO *as though short-sighted*: Who is it?

VIRGINIA: Ludovico.

THE LITTLE MONK: Can't you see him?

GALILEO: Ah yes, Ludovico. *Goes towards him.* How are the horses?

LUDOVICO: Doing fine, sir.

GALILEO: Sarti, we're celebrating. Get us a jug of that Sicilian wine, the old sort.

Exit Mrs Sarti with Andrea.

LUDOVICO *to Virginia*: You look pale. Country life will suit you. My mother is expecting you in September.

VIRGINIA: Wait a moment, I'll show you my wedding dress. *Runs out.*

GALILEO: Sit down.

LUDOVICO: I'm told there are over a thousand students going to your lectures at the university, sir. What are you working at just now?

GALILEO: Routine stuff. Did you come through Rome?

LUDOVICO: Yes. —Before I forget: my mother congratulates you on your remarkable tact in connection with those sunspot orgies the Dutch have been going in for lately.

GALILEO *drily*: Very kind of her.

Mrs Sarti and Andrea bring wine and glasses. Everyone gathers round the table.

LUDOVICO: I can tell you what all the gossip will be about in Rome this February. Christopher Clavius said he's afraid the whole earth-round-the-sun act will start up again because of these sunspots.

ANDREA: No chance.

GALILEO: Any other news from the Holy City, aside from hopes of fresh lapses on my part?

LUDOVICO: I suppose you know that His Holiness is dying?

THE LITTLE MONK: Oh.

GALILEO: Who do they think will succeed him?

LUDOVICO: The favourite is Barberini.

GALILEO: Barberini.

ANDREA: Mr Galilei knows Barberini.

THE LITTLE MONK: Cardinal Barberini is a mathematician.

FEDERZONI: A mathematician at the Holy See! *Pause.*

GALILEO: Well: so now they need people like Barberini who have read a bit of mathematics! Things are beginning to move. Federzoni, we may yet see the day when we no longer have to look over our shoulder like criminals every time we say two and two equals four. *To Ludovico*: I like this wine, Ludovico. What do you think of it?

LUDOVICO: It's good.

GALILEO: I know the vineyard. The hillside is steep and stony, the grapes almost blue. I love this wine.

LUDOVICO: Yes, sir.

GALILEO: It has got little shadows in it. And it is almost sweet but just stops short of it. —Andrea, clear all that stuff away, the ice, needle and bucket. —I value the consolations of the flesh. I've no use for those chicken-hearts who see them as weaknesses. Pleasure takes some achieving, I'd say.

THE LITTLE MONK: What have you in mind?

FEDERZONI: We're starting up the earth-round-the-sun act again.

ANDREA *hums*:

> It's fixed, the Scriptures say. And so
> Orthodox science proves.
> The Holy Father grabs its ears, to show
> It's firmly held. And yet it moves.

Andrea, Federzoni and the little monk hurry to the work table and clear it.

ANDREA: We might find that the sun goes round too. How would that suit you, Marsili?

LUDOVICO: What's the excitement about?

MRS SARTI: You're not going to start up that devilish business again, surely, Mr Galilei?

GALILEO: Now I know why your mother sent you to me. Barberini in the ascendant! Knowledge will become a passion and research an ecstasy. Clavius is right, those sunspots interest me. Do you like my wine, Ludovico?

LUDOVICO: I told you I did, Sir.

GALILEO: You really like it?

LUDOVICO *stiffly*: I like it.

GALILEO: Would you go so far as to accept a man's wine or his daughter without asking him to give up his profession? What has my astronomy got to do with my daughter? The phases of Venus can't alter my daughter's backside.

MRS SARTI: Don't be so vulgar. I am going to fetch Virginia.

LUDOVICO *holding her back*: Marriages in families like ours are not based on purely sexual considerations.

GALILEO: Did they stop you from marrying my daughter for eight years because I had a term of probation to serve?

LUDOVICO: My wife will also have to take her place in our pew in the village church.

GALILEO: You think your peasants will go by the saintliness of their mistress in deciding whether to pay rent or not?

LUDOVICO: In a sense, yes.

GALILEO: Andrea, Fulganzio, get out the brass reflector and the screen! We will project the sun's image on it so as to protect our eyes; that's your method, Andrea.

Andrea and the little monk fetch reflector and screen.

LUDOVICO: You did sign a declaration in Rome, you know, Sir, saying you would have nothing more to do with this earth-round-the-sun business.

GALILEO: Oh that. In those days we had a reactionary pope.

MRS SARTI: Had! And his Holiness not even dead yet!

GALILEO: Almost. Put a grid of squares on the screen. We will do this methodically. And then we'll be able to answer their letters, won't we, Andrea?

MRS SARTI: 'Almost' indeed. The man'll weigh his pieces of ice fifty times over, but as soon as it's something that suits his book he believes it blindly.

The screen is set up.

LUDOVICO: If His Holiness does die, Mr Galilei, irrespective who the next pope is and how intense his devotion to the sciences, he will also have to take into account the devotion felt for him by the most respected families in the land.

THE LITTLE MONK: God made the physical world, Ludovico; God made the human brain; God will permit physics.

MRS SARTI: Galileo, I am going to say something to you. I have watched my son slipping into sin with all those 'experiments' and 'theories' and 'observations' and there was nothing I could do about it. You set yourself up against the authorities and they have already warned you once. The highest cardinals spoke to you like to a sick horse. That worked for a time, but then two months ago, just after the Feast of the Immaculate Conception, I caught you secretly starting your 'observations' again. In the attic. I didn't say much but I knew what to do. I ran and lit a candle to St Joseph. It's more than I can cope with. When I get you on your own you show vestiges of sense and tell me you know you've got to behave or else it'll be dangerous; but two days of experiments and you're just as bad as before. If I choose to forfeit eternal bliss by sticking with a heretic that's my business, but you have no right to trample all over your daughter's happiness with your great feet.

GALILEO *gruffly*: Bring the telescope.

LUDOVICO: Giuseppe, take our luggage back to the coach. *The servant goes out.*

MRS SARTI: She'll never get over this. You can tell her yourself. *Hurries off, still carrying the jug.*

LUDOVICO: I see you have made your preparations. Mr Galileo, my mother and I spend three quarters of each year on our estate in the Campagna, and we can assure you that our peasants are not disturbed by your papers on Jupiter and its moons. They are kept too busy in the fields. But they could be upset if they heard that frivolous attacks on the church's sacred doctrines were in future to go unpunished. Don't forget that the poor things are little better than animals and get everything muddled up. They truly are like beasts, you can hardly imagine it. If rumour says a pear has been seen on an apple tree they will drop their work and hurry off to gossip about it.

GALILEO *interested*: Really?

LUDOVICO: Beasts. If they come up to the house to make some minor complaint or other, my mother is forced to have a dog whipped before their eyes, as the only way to recall them to discipline and order and a proper respect. You, Mr Galileo, may see rich cornfields from your coach as you pass, you eat our olives and our cheese, without a thought, and you have no idea how much trouble it takes to produce them, how much supervision.

GALILEO: Young man, I do not eat my olives without a thought. *Roughly*: You're holding me up. *Calls through the door*: Got the screen?

ANDREA: Yes. Are you coming?

GALILEO: You whip other things than dogs for the sake of discipline, don't you, Marsili?

LUDOVICO: Mr Galileo. You have a marvellous brain. Pity.

THE LITTLE MONK *amazed*: He's threatening you.

GALILEO: Yes, I might stir up his peasants to think new thoughts. And his servants and his stewards.

FEDERZONI: How? None of them can read Latin.

GALILEO: I might write in the language of the people, for the many, rather than in Latin for the few. Our new thoughts call for people who work with their hands. Who else cares about knowing the causes of things? People who only see bread on their table don't want to know how it got baked; that lot would sooner thank God than thank the baker. But the people who make the bread will understand that nothing moves unless it has been made to move. Your sister pressing olives, Fulganzio, won't be astounded but will probably laugh when she hears that the sun isn't a golden coat of arms but a motor: that the earth moves because the sun sets it moving.

LUDOVICO: You will always be the slave of your passions. Make my excuses to Virginia; I think it will be better if I don't see her.

GALILEO: Her dowry will remain available to you, at any time.

LUDOVICO: Good day. *He goes.*

ANDREA: And our kindest regards to all the Marsilis.

FEDERZONI: Who command the earth to stand still so their castles shan't tumble down.

ANDREA: And the Cenzis and the Villanis!

FEDERZONI: The Cervillis!

ANDREA: The Lecchis!

FEDERZONI: The Pirleonis!

ANDREA: Who are prepared to kiss the pope's toe only if he uses it to kick the people with!

THE LITTLE MONK *likewise at the instruments*: The new pope is going to be an enlightened man.

GALILEO: So let us embark on the examination of those spots on the sun in which we are interested, at our own risk and without banking too much on the protection of a new pope.

ANDREA *interrupting*: But fully convinced that we shall dispel Mr Fabricius's star shadows along with the sun vapours of Paris and Prague, and establish the rotation of the sun.

GALILEO: Somewhat convinced that we shall establish the rotation of the sun. My object is not to establish that I was right but to find out if I am. Abandon hope, I say, all ye who enter on observation. They may be vapours, they may be spots, but before we assume that they are spots—which is what would suit us best—we should assume that they are fried fish. In fact we shall question everything all over again. And we shall

go forward not in seven-league boots but at a snail's pace. And what we discover today we shall wipe off the slate tomorrow and only write it up again once we have again discovered it. And whatever we wish to find we shall regard, once found, with particular mistrust. So we shall approach the observation of the sun with an irrevocable determination to establish that the earth does *not* move. Only when we have failed, have been utterly and hopelessly beaten and are licking our wounds in the profoundest depression, shall we start asking if we weren't right after all, and the earth does go round. *With a twinkle*: But once every other hypothesis has crumbled in our hands then there will be no mercy for those who failed to research, and who go on talking all the same. Take the cloth off the telescope and point it at the sun!
He adjusts the brass reflector

THE LITTLE MONK: I knew you had begun working on this. I knew when you failed to recognise Mr Marsili.
In silence they begin their observations. As the sun's flaming image appears on the screen Virginia comes running in in her wedding dress.

VIRGINIA: You sent him away, father.
She faints. Andrea and the little monk hurry to her side.

GALILEO: I've got to know.

I O

DURING THE NEXT DECADE GALILEO'S DOCTRINE
SPREADS AMONG THE COMMON PEOPLE. BALLAD
SINGERS AND PAMPHLETEERS EVERYWHERE TAKE UP
THE NEW IDEAS. IN THE CARNIVAL OF 1632 MANY
ITALIAN CITIES CHOOSE ASTRONOMY AS THE THEME
FOR THEIR GUILDS' CARNIVAL PROCESSIONS

*A half-starved couple of fairground people with a baby and a
five-year-old girl enter a market place where a partly masked
crowd is awaiting the carnival procession. The two of them are
carrying bundles, a drum and other utensils.*

THE BALLAD SINGER *drumming*: Honoured inhabitants, ladies
and gentlemen! To introduce the great carnival procession of
the guilds we are going to perform the latest song from Florence which is now being sung all over north Italy and has
been imported by us at vast expense. It is called: Ye horrible
doctrine and opinions of Messer Galileo Galilei, physicist to
the court, or A Foretaste of ye Future. *He sings*:

> When the Almighty made the universe
> He made the earth and then he made the sun.
> Then round the earth he bade the sun to turn—
> That's in the Bible, Genesis, Chapter One.
> And from that time all creatures here below
> Were in obedient circles meant to go.
>
> So the circles were all woven:
> Around the greater went the smaller
> Around the pace-setter the crawler

On earth as it is in heaven.
Around the pope the cardinals
Around the cardinals the bishops
Around the bishops the secretaries
Around the secretaries the aldermen
Around the aldermen the craftsmen
Around the craftsmen the servants
Around the servants the dogs, the chickens and the beggars.

That, good people, is the Great Order of things, ordo ordinum as the theologians call it, regula aeternis, the rule of rules; but what, dear people, happened?
Sings:

Up stood the learned Galilei
(Chucked away the Bible, whipped out his telescope, took a
   quick look at the universe.)
And told the sun 'Stop there.
From now the whole creatio dei
Will turn as I think fair:
The boss starts turning from today
His servants stand and stare'.

Now that's no joke, my friends, it is no matter small.
Each day our servants' insolence increases
But one thing's true, pleasures are few. I ask you all:
Who wouldn't like to say and do just as he pleases?

Honourable inhabitants, such doctrines are utterly impossible.
He sings:

The serf stays sitting on his arse.
This turning's turned his head.
The altar boy won't serve the mass
The apprentice lies in bed.

No, no, my friends, the Bible is no matter small
Once let them off the lead indeed all loyalty ceases

> For one thing's true, pleasures are few. I ask you all:
> Who wouldn't like to say and do just as he pleases?

Good people all, kindly take a glance at the future as foretold
by the learned Doctor Galileo Galilei:

> Two housewives standing buying fish
> Don't like the fish they're shown
> The fishwife takes a hunk of bread
> And eats them up alone.
> The mason clears the building site
> And hauls the builders' stone.
> And when the house is finished quite
> He keeps it as his own.
>
> Can such things be my friends? It is no matter small
> For independent spirit spreads like foul diseases.
> But one thing's true, pleasures are few. I ask you all:
> Who wouldn't like to say and do just as he pleases?
>
> The tenant gives his landlord hell
> Not caring in the least.
> His wife now feeds her children well
> On the milk she fed the priest.
>
> No, no, my friends, the Bible is no matter small
> Once let them off the lead indeed all loyalty ceases.
> But one thing's true, pleasures are few. I ask you all:
> Who wouldn't like to say and do just as he pleases?

THE SINGER'S WIFE:
> I lately went a bit too far
> And told my husband I'd see
> If I could get some other fixed star
> To do what he does for me.

BALLAD SINGER:
> No, no, no, no, no, no! Stop, Galileo, stop.
> Once take a mad dog's muzzle off it spreads diseases

People must keep their place, some down and some on top.
(Although it's nice for once to do just as one pleases).

BOTH:
Good people who have trouble here below
In serving cruel lords and gentle Jesus
Who bid you turn the other cheek just so
They're better placed to strike the second blow:
Obedience isn't going to cure your woe
So each of you wake up, and do just as he pleases!

THE BALLAD SINGER: Honoured inhabitants, you will now see
Galileo Galilei's amazing discovery: the earth circling round
the sun!

*He belabours the drum violently. The woman and child step
forward. The woman holds a crude image of the sun while
the child, with a pumpkin over its head to represent the
earth, circles round her. The singer points elatedly at the
child as if it were performing a dangerous leap as it takes
jerky steps to single beats on the drum. Then comes drumming from the rear.*

A DEEP VOICE *calls*: The procession!

*Enter two men in rags pulling a little cart. On an absurd
throne sits the 'Grand-Duke of Florence', a figure with a
cardboard crown dressed in sacking and looking through a
telescope. Above his throne a sign saying 'Looking for trouble'. Then four masked men march in carrying a big tarpau-
lin. They stop and toss a puppet representing a cardinal into
the air. A dwarf has taken up position to one side with a sign
saying 'The new age'. In the crowd a beggar gets up on his
crutches and dances, stamping the ground till he crashes to
earth. Enter an over-lifesize puppet, Galileo Galilei, bowing
to the audience. Before it goes a boy carrying a gigantic
bible, open, with crossed-out pages.*

THE BALLAD SINGER: Galileo Galilei, the bible-buster!

Huge laughter among the crowd.

11

The depths are hot, the heights are chill
The streets are loud, the court is still.

*Antechamber and staircase in the Medici palace in Florence.
Galileo and his daughter are waiting to be admitted by the
Grand Duke.*

VIRGINIA: This is taking a long time.

GALILEO: Yes.

VIRGINIA: There's that fellow again who followed us here. *She
points out an individual who walks past without looking at
them.*

GALILEO *whose eyes have suffered*: I don't know him.

VIRGINIA: I've seen him several times in the past few days,
though. He gives me the creeps.

GALILEO: Rubbish. We're in Florence, not among Corsican
bandits.

VIRGINIA: Here's Rector Gaffone.

GALILEO: He makes me want to run. That idiot will involve me
in another of his interminable talks.

*Down the stairs comes Mr Gaffone, rector of the university.
He is visibly alarmed on seeing Galileo and walks stiffly past
them barely nodding, his head awkwardly averted.*

GALILEO: What's got into the man? My eyes are bad again.
Did he even greet us?

VIRGINIA: Barely. What's in your book? Could it be thought
heretical maybe?

GALILEO: You're wasting too much time in church. You'll spoil what's left of your complexion with all this early rising and scurrying off to mass. You're praying for me, is that it?

VIRGINIA: Here's Mr Vanni the ironfounder you designed the furnace for. Don't forget to thank him for those quails. *A man has come down the stairs.*

VANNI: Were those good quails I sent you, Mr Galilei?

GALILEO: The quails were first-rate, Messer Vanni, many thanks again.

VANNI: Your name was mentioned upstairs. They're blaming you for those pamphlets against the Bible that have been selling all over the place lately.

GALILEO: I know nothing about pamphlets. The Bible and Homer are my preferred reading.

VANNI: Even if that weren't so I'd like to take this chance to say that we manufacturers are behind you. I'm not the sort of fellow that knows much about the stars, but to me you're the man who's battling for freedom to teach what's new. Take that mechanical cultivator from Germany you were describing to me. In the past year alone five books on agriculture have been published in London. We'd be glad enough to have a book on the Dutch canals. The same sort of people as are trying to block you are stopping the Bologna doctors from dissecting bodies for medical research.

GALILEO: Your voice can be heard, Vanni.

VANNI: I should hope so. Do you realise that they've now got money markets in Amsterdam and London? Commercial schools too. Regularly printed papers with news in them. In this place we haven't even the freedom to make money. They're against ironfoundries because they imagine putting too many workers in one place leads to immorality. I sink or swim with people like you, Mr Galilei. If anybody ever tries launching anything against you, please remember you've friends in every branch of business. You've got the north Italian cities behind you, sir.

GALILEO: As far as I know nobody's thinking of launching anything against me.

VANNI: No?

GALILEO: No.

VANNI: I think you'd be better off in Venice. Fewer clerics. You could take up the cudgels from there. I've a travelling coach and horses, Mr Galilei.

GALILEO: I don't see myself as a refugee. I like my comforts.

VANNI: Surely. But from what I heard upstairs I'd say there was a hurry. It's my impression they'd be glad to know you weren't in Florence just now.

GALILEO: Nonsense. The Grand Duke is my pupil, and what's more the pope himself would never stand for any kind of attempt to trap me.

VANNI: I'm not sure you're good at distinguishing your friends from your enemies, Mr Galilei.

GALILEO: I can distinguish power from impotence. *He goes off brusquely.*

VANNI: Right. I wish you luck. *Exit.*

GALILEO *returning to Virginia*: Every local Tom, Dick and Harry with an axe to grind wants me to be his spokesman, particularly in places where it's not exactly helpful to me. I've written a book about the mechanics of the universe, that's all. What people make of it or don't make of it isn't my business.

VIRGINIA *loudly*: If they only knew how you condemned all those incidents at last carnival-time!

GALILEO: Yes. Give a bear honey and if the brute's hungry you risk losing your arm.

VIRGINIA *quietly*: Did the Grand Duke actually send for you today?

GALILEO: No, but I had myself announced. He wants to have the book, he has paid for it. Ask that official and tell him we don't like being kept waiting.

VIRGINIA *followed by the same individual, goes and addresses an official*: Mr Mincio, has his Highness been told my father wishes to speak with him?

THE OFFICIAL: How am I to know?

VIRGINIA: I don't call that an answer.

THE OFFICIAL: Don't you?

VIRGINIA: You're supposed to be polite.

The official half turns his back on her and yawns as he looks at the individual.

VIRGINIA *returning*: He says the Grand Duke is still occupied.

GALILEO: I heard you say something about 'polite'. What was it?

VIRGINIA: I was thanking him for his polite answer, that's all. Can't you just leave the book here? You could use the time.

GALILEO: I'm beginning to wonder how much my time is worth. Perhaps I'll accept Sagredo's invitation to spend a few weeks in Padua after all. My health's not what it was.

VIRGINIA: You couldn't live without your books.

GALILEO: We could take a crate or two of that Sicilian wine in the coach with us.

VIRGINIA: You've always said it doesn't travel. And the court owes you three months' salary. They'll never forward it.

GALILEO: That's true.

The Cardinal Inquisitor comes down the stairs.

VIRGINIA: The Cardinal Inquisitor.

As he walks past he makes a deep bow to Galileo.

VIRGINIA: What's the Cardinal Inquisitor doing in Florence, Father?

GALILEO: I don't know. He behaved quite respectfully. I knew what I was doing when I came to Florence and kept quiet for all those years. They've paid me such tributes that now they're forced to accept me as I am.

THE OFFICIAL *calls out*: His Highness the Grand Duke! *Cosimo de Medici comes down the staircase. Galileo goes to meet him. Cosimo stops somewhat embarrassedly.*

GALILEO: I wanted to bring my Dialogues on Two World Systems to your . . .

COSIMO: Ah, yes. How are your eyes?

GALILEO: Not too good, your Highness. If your Highness permits, I have the book . . .

COSIMO: The state of your eyes worries me. It worries me, truly. It shows me that you've been a little too eager to use that admirable tube of yours, haven't you?

He walks on without accepting the book.

GALILEO: He didn't take the book, did he?

VIRGINIA: Father, I'm scared.

GALILEO *firmly, in a low voice*: Control your feelings. We're not going home after this, we're going to Volpi the glazier's. I've fixed with him to have a cart full of empty barrels standing permanently in the yard of the winehouse next door, ready to take me out of the city.

VIRGINIA: So you knew . . .

GALILEO: Don't look round.

They start to go.

A HIGH OFFICIAL *comes down the stairs*: Mr Galilei, I have been charged to tell you that the court of Florence is no longer in a position to oppose the Holy Inquisition's wish to interrogate you in Rome. The coach of the Holy Inquisition awaits you, Mr Galilei.

12

THE POPE

Room in the Vatican. Pope Urban VIII (formerly Cardinal Barberini) has received the Cardinal Inquisitor. In the course of the audience he is robed. Outside is heard the shuffling of many feet.

THE POPE *very loudly*: No! No! No!

THE INQUISITOR: So it is your Holiness's intention to go before this gathering of doctors from every faculty, representatives of every order and the entire clergy, all with their naive faith in the word of God as set down in the scriptures, who are now assembling here to have that trust confirmed by your Holiness, and tell them that those scriptures can no longer be regarded as true?

THE POPE: I am not going to have the multiplication table broken. No!

THE INQUISITOR: Ah, it's the multiplication table, not the spirit of insubordination and doubt: that's what these people will tell you. But it isn't the multiplication table. No, a terrible restlessness has descended on the world. It is the restlessness of their own brain which these people have transferred to the unmoving earth. They shout 'But look at the figures'. But where do their figures come from? Everybody knows they originate in doubt. These people doubt everything. Are we to base human society on doubt and no longer on faith? 'You are my lord, but I doubt if that's a good thing'. 'This is your house and your wife, but I doubt if they shouldn't be mine.' Against that we have your Holiness's love of art, to which we owe our fine collections, being subjected to such disgraceful interpretations as we see scrawled on the walls of

Roman houses: 'The Barberinis take what the Barbarians left.' And abroad? Your Holiness's Spanish policy has been misinterpreted by short-sighted critics, its antagonising of the Emperor regretted. For the last fifteen years Germany has been running with blood, and men have quoted the Bible as they hacked each other to pieces. And at this moment, just when Christianity is being shrivelled into little enclaves by plague, war and the Reformation, a rumour is going through Europe that you have made a secret pact with protestant Sweden in order to weaken the Catholic emperor. So what do these wretched mathematicians do but go and point their tubes at the sky and inform the whole world that your Holiness is hopelessly at sea in the one area nobody has yet denied you? There's every reason to be surprised at this sudden interest in an obscure subject like astronomy. Who really cares how these spheres rotate? But thanks to the example of this wretched Florentine all Italy, down to the last stable boy, is now gossiping about the phases of Venus, nor can they fail at the same time to think about a lot of other irksome things that schools and others hold to be incontrovertible. Given the weakness of their flesh and their liability to excesses of all kinds, what would the effect be if they were to believe in nothing but their own reason, which this maniac has set up as the sole tribunal? They would start by wondering if the sun stood still over Gibeon, then extend their filthy scepticism to the offertory box. Ever since they began voyaging across the seas—and I've nothing against that—they have placed their faith in a brass ball they call a compass, not in God. This fellow Galileo was writing about machines even when he was young. With machines they hope to work miracles. What sort? God anyhow is no longer necessary to them, but what kind of miracle is it to be? The abolition of top and bottom, for one. They're not needed any longer. Aristotle, whom they otherwise regard as a dead dog, has said—and they quote this—that once the shuttle weaves by itself and the plectrum plays the zither of its own accord, then masters would need no apprentice and lords no servants. And they think they are already there. This evil man knows what he is up to when he writes his astronomical works not in Latin but in the idiom of fishwives and wool merchants.

THE POPE: That's very bad taste; I shall tell him.

THE INQUISITOR: He agitates some of them and bribes others. The north Italian ports are insisting more and more that they must have Mr Galilei's star charts for their ships. We'll have to give in to them, material interests are at stake.

THE POPE: But those star charts are based on his heretical theories. They presuppose certain notions on the part of the heavenly bodies which are impossible if you reject his doctrine. You can't condemn the doctrine and accept the charts.

THE INQUISITOR: Why not? It's the only way.

THE POPE: This shuffling is getting on my nerves. I cannot help listening to it.

THE INQUISITOR: It may speak to you more persuasively than I can, your Holiness. Are all these people to leave here with doubt in their hearts.

THE POPE: After all the man is the greatest physicist of our time, the light of Italy, and not just any old crank. He has friends. There is Versailles. There's the Viennese Court. They'll call the Holy Church a cesspool of decomposing prejudices. Hands off him!

THE INQUISITOR: Practically speaking one wouldn't have to push it very far with him. He is a man of the flesh. He would give in immediately.

THE POPE: He enjoys himself in more ways than any man I have ever met. His thinking springs from sensuality. Give him an old wine or a new idea, and he cannot say no. But I won't have any condemnation of the physical facts, no war cries of 'Up the Church' 'Up Reason'. I let him write his book on condition that he finished it by saying that the last word lay with faith, not science. He met that condition.

THE INQUISITOR: But how? His book shows a stupid man, representing the view of Aristotle of course, arguing with a clever one who of course represents Mr Galilei's own; and which do you think, your Holiness, delivers the final remark?

THE POPE: What did you say? Well, which of them expresses our view?

THE INQUISITOR: Not the clever one.

THE POPE: Yes, that is an impertinence. All this stamping in the corridors is really unbearable. Is the whole world coming here?

THE INQUISITOR: Not the whole of it but its best part.

Pause. The Pope is now in his full robes.

THE POPE: At the very most he can be shown the instruments.

THE INQUISITOR: That will be enough your Holiness. Instruments are Mr Galilei's speciality.

13

BEFORE THE INQUISITION, ON JUNE 22ND, 1633, GALILEO RECANTS HIS DOCTRINE OF THE MOTION OF THE EARTH

> June twenty-second, sixteen thirty-three
> A momentous day for you and me.
> Of all the days that was the one
> An age of reason could have begun.

In the Florentine ambassador's palace in Rome. Galileo's pupils are waiting for news. Federzoni and the little monk are playing new-style chess with its sweeping moves. In one corner Virginia kneels saying the Ave Maria.

THE LITTLE MONK: The Pope wouldn't receive him. No more discussions about science.

FEDERZONI: That was his last hope. It's true what he told him years back in Rome when he was still Cardinal Barberini: We need you. Now they've got him.

ANDREA: They'll kill him. The Discorsi will never get finished.

FEDERZONI *gives him a covert look*: You think so?

ANDREA: Because he'll never recant.

Pause

THE LITTLE MONK: You keep getting quite irrelevant thoughts when you can't sleep. Last night for instance I kept on thinking, he ought never to have left the Venetian Republic.

ANDREA: He couldn't write his book there.

FEDERZONI: And in Florence he couldn't publish it.

Pause

THE LITTLE MONK: I also wondered if they'd let him keep his little stone he always carries in his pocket. His proving stone.

FEDERZONI: You don't wear pockets where they'll be taking him.

ANDREA *shouting*: They daren't do that! And even if they do he'll not recant. 'Someone who doesn't know the truth is just thick-headed. But someone who does know it and calls it a lie is a crook.'

FEDERZONI: I don't believe it either and I wouldn't want to go on living if he did it. But they do have the power.

ANDREA: Power can't achieve everything.

FEDERZONI: Perhaps not.

THE LITTLE MONK *softly*: This is his twenty-fourth day in prison. Yesterday was the chief hearing. And today they're sitting on it. *Aloud, as Andrea is listening*: That time I came to see him here two days after the decree we sat over there and he showed me the little Priapus by the sundial in the garden— you can see it from here—and he compared his own work with a poem by Horace which cannot be altered either. He talked about his sense of beauty, saying that was what forced him to look for the truth. And he quoted the motto 'Hieme et aestate, et prope et procul, usque dum vivam et ultra'. And he was referring to truth.

ANDREA *to the little monk*: Have you told him the way he stood in the Collegium Romanum when they were testing his tube? Tell him! *The little monk shakes his head*. He behaved just as usual. He had his hands on his hams, thrust out his tummy and said 'I would like a bit of reason, please, gentlemen.'

Laughing, he imitates Galileo.

Pause.

ANDREA *referring to Virginia*: She is praying that he'll recant.

FEDERZONI: Leave her alone. She's been all confused ever since they spoke to her. They brought her father confessor down from Florence.

The individual from the Grand-Ducal palace in Florence enters.

INDIVIDUAL: Mr Galilei will be here shortly. He may need a bed.

FEDERZONI: Have they released him?

INDIVIDUAL: It is expected that Mr Galilei will recant around five o'clock at a full sitting of the Inquisition. The great bell of St Mark's will be rung and the text of his recantation will be proclaimed in public.

ANDREA: I don't believe it.

INDIVIDUAL: In view of the crowds in the streets Mr Galilei will be brought to the garden gate here at the back of the palace.

Exit.

ANDREA *suddenly in a loud voice*: The moon is an earth and has no light of its own. Likewise Venus has no light of its own and is like the earth and travels round the sun. And four moons revolve round the planet Jupiter which is on a level with the fixed stars and is unattached to any crystal sphere. And the sun is the centre of the cosmos and motionless, and the earth is not the centre and not motionless. And he is the one who showed us this.

THE LITTLE MONK: And no force will help them to make what has been seen unseen.

Silence.

FEDERZONI *looks at the sundial in the garden.* Five o'clock. *Virginia prays louder.*

ANDREA: I can't wait any more. They're beheading the truth. *He puts his hands over his ears, as does the little monk. But the bell is not rung. After a pause filled only by Virginia's murmured prayers, Federzoni shakes his head negatively. The others let their hands drop.*

FEDERZONI *hoarsely*: Nothing. It's three minutes past the hour.

ANDREA: He's holding out.

THE LITTLE MONK: He's not recanting.

FEDERZONI: No. Oh, how marvellous for us! *The embrace. They are ecstatically happy.*

ANDREA: So force won't do the trick. There are some things it can't do. So stupidity has been defeated, it's not invulnerable. So man is not afraid of death.

FEDERZONI: This truly is the start of the age of knowledge. This is the hour of its birth. Imagine if he had recanted.

THE LITTLE MONK: I didn't say, but I was worried silly. O ye of little faith!

ANDREA: But I knew.

FEDERZONI: Like nightfall in the morning, it would have been.

ANDREA: As if the mountain had said 'I'm a lake'.

THE LITTLE MONK *kneels down weeping*: Lord, I thank thee.

ANDREA: But today everything is altered. Man, so tormented, is lifting his head and saying 'I can live'. Such a lot is won when even a single man gets to his feet and says No. *At this moment the bell of Saint Mark's begins to toll. All stand rigid.*

VIRGINIA *gets up*: The bell of Saint Mark's. He is not damned!
From the street outside we hear the crier reading Galileo's recantation:

CRIER'S VOICE: 'I, Galileo Galilei, teacher of mathematics and physics in Florence, abjure what I have taught, namely that the sun is the centre of the cosmos and motionless and the earth is not the centre and not motionless. I foreswear, detest and curse, with sincere heart and unfeigned faith, all these errors and heresies as also any error and any further opinion repugnant to Holy Church.'
It grows dark.
When the light returns the bell is still tolling, but then stops. Virginia has left. Galileo's pupils are still there.

FEDERZONI: You know, he never paid you for your work. You could never publish your own stuff or buy yourself new breeches. You stood for it because it was 'working for the sake of science'.

ANDREA *loudly*: Unhappy the land that has no heroes!
Galileo has entered, so completely changed by his trial as to be almost unrecognisable. He has heard Andrea's remark. For a few moments he stands at the gate waiting to be greeted. When he is not, and his pupils back away from him, he goes slowly and, on account of his bad eyes, uncertainly forward till he finds a stool and sits down.

ANDREA: I can't look at him. Get him away.

FEDERZONI: Calm down.

ANDREA *yells at Galileo*: Wine-pump! Snail-eater! Did you save your precious skin? *Sits down*: I feel ill.

GALILEO *quietly*: Give him a glass of water.

The little monk fetches Andrea a glass of water from outside. The others do nothing about Galileo, who sits on his stool and listens. Outside the crier's voice can again be heard in the distance.

ANDREA: I think I can walk with a bit of help.

They escort him to the door. At this juncture Galileo starts to speak.

GALILEO: No. Unhappy the land where heroes are needed. *A reading before the curtain:*

Is it not obvious that a horse falling from a height of three or four ells will break its legs, whereas a dog would not suffer any damage, nor would a cat from a height of eight or nine ells, nor a cricket from a tower nor an ant even if it were to fall from the moon? And just as smaller animals are comparatively stronger than larger ones, so small plants too stand up better: an oak tree two hundred ells high cannot sustain its branches in the same proportion as a small oak tree, nor can nature let a horse grow as large as twenty horses or produce a giant ten times the size of man unless it changes all the proportions of the limbs and especially of the bones, which would have to be strengthened far beyond the size demanded by mere proportion. —The common assumption that large and small machines are equally durable is apparently erroneus.

GALILEO. DISCORSI.

14

*A large room with table, leather chair and globe. Galileo, old
now and half blind, is carefully experimenting with a bent
wooden rail and a small ball of wood. In the antechamber sits a
monk on guard. There is a knock at the door. The monk opens
it and a peasant comes in carrying two plucked geese. Virginia
emerges from the kitchen. She is now about forty years old.*

THE PEASANT: They told me to deliver these.

VIRGINIA: Who? I didn't order any geese.

THE PEASANT: They told me to say it was someone passing
through. *Exit. Virginia looks at the geese in amazement. The
monk takes them from her and examines them dubiously.
Then he gives them back to her, satisfied, and she carries
them by their necks to Galileo in the large room.*

VIRGINIA: Somebody passing through has sent us a present.

GALILEO: What is it?

VIRGINIA: Can't you see?

GALILEO: No. *He walks over.* Geese. Any name on them?

VIRGINIA: No.

GALILEO *takes one of the geese from her*: Heavy. I could eat
some of that.

VIRGINIA: Don't tell me you're hungry again; you've just had
your supper. And what's wrong with your eyes this time? You
should have been able to see them from where you are.

GALILEO: You're in the shadow.

VIRGINIA: I'm not in the shadow. *She takes the geese out.*

GALILEO: Put thyme with them, and apples.

VIRGINIA *to the monk*: We'll have to get the eye doctor in. Father couldn't see the geese from his table.

THE MONK: Not till I've cleared it with Monsignor Carpula. Has he been writing again?

VIRGINIA: No. He dictated his book to me, as you know. You've had pages 131 and 132, and those were the last.

THE MONK: He's an old fox.

VIRGINIA: He's doing nothing contrary to instructions. His repentance is genuine. I'll keep an eye on him. Tell them in the kitchen they're to fry the liver with an apple and an onion. *She goes back into the large room.* And now let's consider our eyes and leave that ball alone and dictate just a bit more of our weekly letter to the archbishop.

GALILEO: I'm not well enough. Read me some Horace.

VIRGINIA: Only last week Monsignor Carpula was telling me—and we owe him so much, you know; another lot of vegetables only the other day—that the archbishop keeps asking him what you think of those questions and quotations he sends you.

She has sat down to take dictation.

GALILEO: Where had I got to?

VIRGINIA: Section four: with respect to Holy Church's policy concerning the unrest in the Arsenal in Venice I agree with the attitude adopted by Cardinal Spoletti towards the disaffected rope-makers . . .

GALILEO: Yes. *He dictates*: I agree with the attitude adopted by Cardinal Spoletti towards the disaffected rope-makers, namely that it is better to hand out soup to them in the name of Christian brotherly love than to pay them more for their hawsers and bell ropes. Especially as it seems wiser to encourage their faith rather than their acquisitiveness. The apostle Paul says 'Charity never faileth'. —How's that?

VIRGINIA: That's wonderful, father.

GALILEO: You don't think a suspicion of irony might be read into it?

VIRGINIA: No, the archbishop will be delighted. He is so practical.

GALILEO: I trust your judgement. What's next?

VIRGINIA: A most beautiful saying: 'When I am weak then I am strong'.

GALILEO: No comment.

VIRGINIA: Why not?

GALILEO: What's next?

VIRGINIA: 'And to know the love of Christ, which passeth knowledge'. Saint Paul's Epistle to the Ephesians, iii, 19.

GALILEO: I am particularly grateful to your Eminence for the splendid quotation from the Epistle to the Ephesians. Stimulated by it I looked in our incomparable *Imitation* and found the following. *He quotes by heart*: 'He to whom speaketh the eternal word is free from much questioning.' May I take this opportunity to refer to my own affairs? I am still blamed for once having written an astronomical work in the language of the market-place. It was not my intention thereby to propose or approve the writing of books on infinitely more important matters, such as theology, in the jargon of pasta merchants. The argument for holding services in Latin—that it is a universal language and allows every nationality to hear holy mass in exactly the same way—seems to me a shade unfortunate in that our ever-present cynics might say this prevents any nationality from understanding the text. That sacred matters should be made cheaply understandable is something I can gladly do without. The church's Latin, which protects its eternal verities from the curiosity of the ignorant, inspires confidence when spoken by the priestly sons of the lower classes in the accents of the appropriate local dialect.—No, strike that out.

VIRGINIA: All of it?

GALILEO: Everything after the pasta merchants.

There is a knock at the door. Virginia goes into the antechamber. The monk opens. It is Andrea Sarti. He is now a man in his middle years.

ANDREA: Good evening. I am leaving Italy to do research in Holland and they asked me to look him up on the way through so I can say how he is.

VIRGINIA: I don't know that he'll want to see you. You never came.

ANDREA: Ask him. *Galileo has recognised his voice. He sits motionless. Virginia goes in to him.*

GALILEO: Is that Andrea?

VIRGINIA: Yes. Shall I send him away?

GALILEO *after a moment*: Show him in.
  Virginia brings Andrea in.

VIRGINIA *to the monk*: He's harmless. Used to be his pupil. So now he's his enemy.

GALILEO: Leave us, Virginia.

VIRGINIA: I want to hear what he's got to say. *She sits down.*

ANDREA *coolly*: How are you?

GALILEO: Come closer. What are you doing now? Tell us about your work. I'm told you're on hydraulics.

ANDREA: Fabricius in Amsterdam has commissioned me to inquire about your health.
  Pause.

GALILEO: My health is good. They pay me every attention.

ANDREA: I am glad I can report that your health is good.

GALILEO: Fabricius will be glad to hear it. And you can tell him that I live in corresponding comfort. The depth of my repentance has earned me enough credit with my superiors to be permitted to conduct scientific studies on a modest scale under clerical supervision.

ANDREA: That's right. We too heard that the church is more than pleased with you. Your utter capitulation has been effective. We understand the authorities are happy to note that not a single paper expounding new theories has been published in Italy since you toed the line.

GALILEO *listening*: Unhappily there are still countries not under the wing of the church. I'm afraid the condemned doctrines are being pursued there.

ANDREA: There too your recantation caused a setback most gratifying to the church.

GALILEO: Really? *Pause.* Nothing from Descartes? No news from Paris?

ANDREA: On the contrary. When he heard about your recantation he shoved his treatise on the nature of light away in a drawer.

Long pause.

GALILEO: I feel concern for certain scientific friends whom I
led into error. Did they learn anything from my recantation?

ANDREA: The only way I can do research is by going to Holland. They won't permit the ox anything that Jove won't permit himself.

GALILEO: I see.

ANDREA: Federzoni is back to grinding lenses in some shop in
Milan.

GALILEO *laughs*: He doesn't know Latin.

ANDREA: Fulganzio, our little monk, has given up science and
gone back to the bosom of the church.

GALILEO: Yes. *Pause.*

GALILEO: My superiors hope to achieve a spiritual cure in my
case too. I am progressing better than anyone expected.

ANDREA: Indeed.

VIRGINIA: The Lord be praised.

GALILEO *roughly*: See to the geese, Virginia.

*Virginia goes out angrily. The monk speaks to her as she
passes.*

THE MONK: I don't like that man.

VIRGINIA: He's harmless. You heard them. *Walking away*:
There's some fresh goats-milk cheese arrived.

The monk follows her out.

ANDREA: I have to travel all night if I'm to cross the frontier
early tomorrow. May I go?

GALILEO: I don't know why you came, Sarti. Was it to unsettle
me? I've been living prudently and thinking prudently since
coming here. Even so I get relapses.

ANDREA: I have no wish to arouse you, Mr Galilei.

GALILEO: Barberini called it the itch. He wasn't entirely free of
it himself. I've been writing again.

ANDREA: Indeed.

GALILEO: I finished the 'Discorsi'.

ANDREA: What? The 'Discourses Concerning Two New Sciences: Mechanics and Local Motion'? Here?

GALILEO: Oh, they let me have pens and paper. My masters
aren't stupid. They realise that deeply engrained vices can't

be snapped off just like that. They shield me from any unde-
sirable consequences by locking the pages away as I write
them.

ANDREA: O God!

GALILEO: Did you say something?

ANDREA: They're making you plough water. They allow you
pens and paper to keep you quiet. How can you possibly
write when you know that's the purpose?

GALILEO: Oh, I'm a creature of habit.

ANDREA: The 'Discorsi' in the hands of the monks! With Amsterdam and London and Prague all slavering for it!

GALILEO: I can hear Fabricius grumbling away, insisting on his
pound of flesh, meanwhile sitting safe and sound himself in
Amsterdam.

ANDREA: Two new branches of science as good as lost!

GALILEO: It will no doubt relieve him and one or two others to
hear that I've been risking the last pathetic remnants of my
own comfort by making a transcript, more or less behind my
back, by squeezing the very last ounce of light out of each
reasonably clear night for the past six months.

ANDREA: You've got a transcript?

GALILEO: So far my vanity has stopped me destroying it.

ANDREA: Where is it?

GALILEO: 'If thine eye offend thee, pluck it out'. Whoever
wrote that knew more about comfort than me. I suppose it's
the height of folly to part with it. However, as I haven't managed to keep clear of scientific work you people might as well
have it. The transcript is inside that globe. Should you think
of taking it to Holland you would of course have to bear the
entire responsibility. In that case you would have bought it
from someone who had access to the original in the Holy Office.

Andrea has gone to the globe. He takes out the transcript.

ANDREA: The 'Discorsi'! *He leafs through the manuscript.
Reads*: 'It is my purpose to establish an entirely new science
in regard to a very old problem, namely, motion. By means
of experiments I have discovered some of its properties,
which are worth knowing.'

GALILEO: I had to do something with my time.

ANDREA: This will found a new physics.

GALILEO: Stuff it under your coat.

ANDREA: And we thought you had deserted! No voice against you was louder than mine!

GALILEO: Very proper. I taught you science and I denied the truth.

ANDREA: This alters everything. Everything.

GALILEO: Really?

ANDREA: You were hiding the truth. From the enemy. Even in matters of ethics you were centuries ahead of us.

GALILEO: Elaborate that, will you Andrea?

ANDREA: Like the man in the street we said 'He'll die, but he'll never recant.' You came back: 'I've recanted, but I'm going to live.'—'Your hands are stained', we said. You're saying: 'Better stained than empty'.

GALILEO: Better stained than empty. Sounds realistic. Sounds like me. New science, new ethics.

ANDREA: I of all people should have known. I was eleven when you sold another man's telescope to the Venetian Senate. And I saw you put that instrument to immortal use. Your friends shook their heads when you bowed to that boy in Florence: science gained an audience. Even then you used to laugh at heroes. 'People who suffer are boring' you said. 'Misfortune comes from miscalculation'. And 'When there are obstacles the shortest line between two points may be a crooked one.'

GALILEO: I remember.

ANDREA: So in '33 when you chose to recant a popular point in your doctrine I ought to have known that you were simply backing out of a hopeless political wrangle in order to get on with the real business of science.

GALILEO: Which is . . .

ANDREA: Studying the properties of motion, mother of those machines which alone are going to make the earth so good to live on that heaven can be cleared away.

GALILEO: Aha.

ANDREA: You gained the leisure to write a scientific work which could be written by nobody else. If you had ended up at the stake in a halo of flames the other side would have won.

GALILEO: They did win. And there is no scientific work that can only be written by one particular man.

ANDREA: Why did you recant, then?

GALILEO: I recanted because I was afraid of physical pain.

ANDREA: No!

GALILEO: They showed me the instruments.

ANDREA: So it wasn't planned?

GALILEO: It was not.

Pause.

ANDREA *loudly*: Science makes only one demand: contribution to science.

GALILEO: And I met it. Welcome to the gutter, brother in science and cousin in betrayal! Do you eat fish? I have fish. What stinks is not my fish but me. I sell out, you are a buyer. O irresistible glimpse of the book, the sacred commodity! The mouth waters and the curses drown. The great whore of Babylon, the murderous beast, the scarlet woman, opens her thighs and everything is altered. Blessed be our horse-trading, whitewashing, death-fearing community!

ANDREA: Fearing death is human. Human weaknesses don't matter to science.

GALILEO: Don't they?—My dear Sarti, even as I now am I think I can still give you a tip or two as to what matters to that science you have dedicated yourself to.

A short pause.

GALILEO *professorially, folding his hands over his stomach*:
In my spare time, of which I have plenty, I have gone over my case and considered how it is going to be judged by that world of science of which I no longer count myself a member. Even a wool merchant has not only to buy cheap and sell dear but also to ensure that the wool trade continues unimpeded. The pursuit of science seems to me to demand particular courage in this respect. It deals in knowledge procured through doubt. Creating knowledge for all about all, it aims to turn all of us into doubters. Now the bulk of the population is kept by its princes, landlords and priests in a pearly

haze of superstition and old saws which cloak what these people are up to. The poverty of the many is as old as the hills, and from pulpit and lecture platform we hear that it is as hard as the hills to get rid of. Our new art of doubting delighted the mass audience. They tore the telescope out of our hands and trained it on their tormentors, the princes, landlords and priests. These selfish and domineering men, having greedily exploited the fruits of science, found that the cold eye of science had been turned on a primaeval but contrived poverty that could clearly be swept away if they were swept away themselves. They showered us with threats and bribes, irresistible to feeble souls. But can we deny ourselves to the crowd and still remain scientists? The movements of the heavenly bodies have become more comprehensible, but the peoples are as far as ever from calculating the moves of their rulers. The battle for a measurable heaven has been won thanks to doubt; but thanks to credulity the Rome housewife's battle for milk will be lost time and time again. Science, Sarti, is involved in both these battles. A human race which shambles around in a pearly haze of superstition and old saws, too ignorant to develop its own powers, will never be able to develop those powers of nature which you people are revealing to it. To what end are you working? Presumably for the principle that science's sole aim must be to lighten the burden of human existence. If the scientists, brought to heel by self-interested rulers, limit themselves to piling up knowledge for knowledge's sake, then science can be crippled and your new machines will lead to nothing but new impositions. You may in due course discover all that there is to discover, and your progress will nonetheless be nothing but a progress away from mankind. The gap between you and it may one day become so wide that your cry of triumph at some new achievement will be echoed by a universal cry of horror. —As a scientist I had a unique opportunity. In my day astronomy emerged into the market place. Given this unique situation, if one man had put up a fight it might have had tremendous repercussions. Had I stood firm the scientists could have developed something like the doctors' Hippocratic oath, a vow to use their knowledge exclusively for mankind's benefit. As things are, the best that can be hoped for is a race of inventive dwarfs who can be hired for any purpose. What's more, Sarti, I have come to the conclusion that I was never in any real danger. For a few years I was as strong as the authorities. And I handed my knowledge to those in power for them to use, fail to use, misuse—whatever best suited their objectives. *Virginia has entered with a dish and come to a standstill.*

GALILEO: I betrayed my profession. A man who does what I did cannot be tolerated in the ranks of science.

VIRGINIA: You are accepted in the ranks of the faithful. *She moves on and puts the dish on the table.*

GALILEO: Correct. —Now I must eat. *Andrea holds out his hand. Galileo sees the hand but does not take it.*

GALILEO: You're a teacher yourself now. Can you afford to take a hand like mine? *He goes to the table.* Somebody passing through sent me some geese. I still enjoy eating.

ANDREA: So you no longer believe a new age has started?

GALILEO: On the contrary—Look out for yourself when you pass through Germany, with the truth under your coat.

ANDREA *unable to tear himself away*: About your opinion of the author we were talking about. I don't know how to answer. But I cannot think your devastating analysis will be the last word.

GALILEO: Thank you very much, sir. *He begins eating.*

VIRGINIA *escorting andrea out*: We don't like visitors from the past. They excite him. *Andrea leaves. Virginia comes back.*

GALILEO: Got any idea who might have sent the geese?

VIRGINIA: Not Andrea.

GALILEO: Perhaps not. What's the night like?

VIRGINIA *at the window*: Clear.

15

1637. GALILEO'S BOOK, THE 'DISCORSI', CROSSES THE ITALIAN FRONTIER

> The great book o'er the border went
> And, good folk, that was the end.
> But we hope you'll keep in mind
> He and I were left behind.
> May you now guard science's light
> Kindle it and use it right
> Lest it be a flame to fall
> Downward to consume us all.
> Yes, us all.

Little Italian frontier town in the early morning. Children are playing by the barrier. Andrea, standing beside a coachman, is waiting to have his papers checked by the frontier guards. He is sitting on a small box reading Galileo's manuscript. On the other side of the barrier stands the coach.

THE CHILDREN *sing*:

> Mary, Mary sat her down
> Had a little old pink gown
> Gown was shabby and bespattered.
> But when chilly winter came
> Gown went round her just the same.
> Bespattered don't mean tattered.

THE FRONTIER GUARD: Why are you leaving Italy?

ANDREA: I'm a scholar.

THE FRONTIER GUARD *to his clerk*: Put under 'reason for leaving': scholar.

I must examine your luggage.
He does so.

THE FIRST BOY *to Andrea*: Better not sit there. *He points to the hut outside which Andrea is sitting.* There's a witch lives inside.

THE SECOND BOY: Old Marina's no witch.

THE FIRST BOY: Want me to twist your wrist?

THE THIRD BOY: Course she's one. She flies through the air at night.

THE FIRST BOY: And why won't anyone in the town let her have a jug of milk even, if she's not a witch?

THE SECOND BOY: Who says she flies through the air? It can't be done. *To Andrea*: Can it?

THE FIRST BOY *referring to the second*: That's Giuseppe. He doesn't know a thing because he doesn't go to school because his trousers need patching.

THE FRONTIER GUARD: What's that book you've got?

ANDREA *without looking up*: It's by Aristotle, the great philosopher.

THE FRONTIER GUARD *suspiciously*: Who's he when he's at home?

ANDREA: He's been dead for years.

The boys mock Andrea's reading by walking round as if they were meanwhile reading books.

THE FRONTIER GUARD *to the clerk*: Have a look if there's anything about religion in it.

THE CLERK *turning the pages*: I can't see nothing.

THE FRONTIER GUARD: All this searching's a bit of a waste of time anyway. Nobody who wanted to hide something would put it under our noses like that. *To Andrea*: You're to sign that we've examined it all.

Andrea gets up reluctantly and accompanies the frontier guard into the house, still reading.

THE THIRD BOY *to the clerk, pointing at the box*: There's that too, see?

THE CLERK: Wasn't it there before?

THE THIRD BOY: The devil put it there. It's a box.

THE SECOND BOY: No, it belongs to that foreigner.

THE THIRD BOY: I wouldn't touch it. She put the evil eye on old Passi's horses. I looked through the hole in the roof made by the blizzard and heard them coughing.

THE CLERK *who was almost at the box, hesitates and turns back*: Devil's tricks, what? Well, we can't check everything. We'd never get done.

Andrea comes back with a jug of milk. He sits down on the box once more and goes on reading.

THE FRONTIER GUARD *following him with papers*: Shut the boxes. Is that everything?

THE CLERK: Yes.

THE SECOND BOY *to Andrea*: So you're a scholar. Tell us, can people fly through the air?

ANDREA: Wait a moment.

THE FRONTIER GUARD: You can go through.

The coachman has taken the luggage. Andrea picks up the box and is about to go.

THE FRONTIER GUARD: Halt! What's in that box?

ANDREA *taking up his book again*: Books.

THE FIRST BOY: It's the witch's.

THE FRONTIER GUARD: Nonsense. How could she bewitch a box?

THE THIRD BOY: She could if the devil helped.

THE FRONTIER GUARD *laughs*: That wouldn't work here.

To the clerk: Open it.

The box is opened.

THE FRONTIER GUARD *unenthusiastically*: How many are there?

ANDREA: Thirty-four.

THE FRONTIER GUARD *to the clerk*: How long will they take to go through?

THE CLERK *who has begun superficially rummaging through the box*: Nothing but printed stuff. It'll mean you miss your breakfast, and when am I going to get over to Passi's stables to collect the road tax due on the sale of his house if I'm to go through this lot?

THE FRONTIER GUARD: Right, we need that money. *He kicks at the books*: After all, what can there be in those?

To the coachman: Off with you!

Andrea crosses the frontier with the coachman carrying the box. Once across, he puts Galileo's manuscript in his travelling bag.

THE THIRD BOY *points at the jug which Andrea has left behind*: Look!

THE FIRST BOY: The box has gone too! Didn't I tell you it was the devil?

ANDREA *turning round*: No, it was me. You should learn to use your eyes. The milk's paid for, the jug too. The old woman can keep it. Oh, and I didn't answer your question, Giuseppe. People can't fly through the air on a stick. It'd have to have a machine on it, to say the least. But there's no machine like that so far. Maybe there never will be, as a human being's too heavy. But of course one never knows. There are a lot of things we don't know yet, Giuseppe. We're really just at the beginning.

NOTES AND VARIANTS

Texts by Brecht

FOREWORD

It is well known how beneficially people can be influenced by the conviction that they are poised on the threshold of a new age. At such a moment their environment appears to be still entirely unfinished, capable of the happiest improvements, full of dreamt-of and undreamt-of possibilities, like malleable raw material in their hands. They themselves feel as if they have awakened to a new day, rested, strong, resourceful. Old beliefs are dismissed as superstitions, what yesterday seemed a matter of course is today subject to fresh examination. We have been ruled, says mankind, but now we shall be the rulers.

Around the turn of this century no other line from a song so powerfully inspired the workers as the line: 'Now a new age is dawning'; old and young marched to it, the poorest, the down-and-outs and those who had already won something of civilisation for themselves—all felt young. Under a house painter the unprecedented seductive power of these selfsame words was also tried and proved; for he too promised a new age. Here the words revealed their emptiness and vagueness. Their strength lay in their very indefiniteness, which was now being exploited in demoralising the masses. The new age—that was something and is something that affects everything, leaves nothing unchanged, but is also still only unfolding its character gradually; something in which all imagination has scope to flower, and which is only restricted by too precise description. Glorious is the feeling of beginning, of pioneering; the fact of being a beginner inspires enthusiasm. Glorious is the feeling of happiness in those who oil a new machine before it is to display its strength, in those who fill in a blank space on an old map, in those who dig the foundation of a new house, their house.

This feeling comes to the researcher who makes a discovery that will change everything, to the orator who prepares a speech that will create an entirely new situation. Terrible is the disappointment when men

discover, or think they discover, that they have fallen victims to an illusion, that the old is stronger than the new, that the 'facts' are against
them and not for them, that their age—the new age—has not yet arrived. Then things are not merely as bad as before, but much worse because people have made immense sacrifices for their schemes and have
lost everything; they have ventured and are now defeated; the old is
taking its revenge on them. The researcher or the discoverer—an unknown but also unpersecuted man before he has published his
discovery—when once his discovery has been disproved or discredited
is a swindler and a charlatan, and all too well known; the victim of oppression and exploitation, when once his insurrection has been
crushed, is a rebel who is subject to special repression and punishment. Exertion is followed by exhaustion, possibly exaggerated hope
by possibly exaggerated hopelessness. Those who do not relapse into
indifference and apathy fall into worse; those who have not sacrificed
their energies for their ideals now turn those selfsame energies against
those very ideals. There is no more remorseless reactionary than a
frustrated innovator, no crueller enemy of the wild elephant than the
tame elephant.

And yet these disappointed men may still go on existing in a new
age, an age of great upheaval. Only, they know nothing of new ages.

In those days the conception of the new is itself falsified. The Old and
the Very Old, now re-entering the arena, proclaim themselves as new,
or else it is held to be new when the Old or the Very Old are put over
in a new way. But the really New, having been deposed today, is de-
clared old-fashioned, degraded to being a transitory phase whose day
is done. 'New' for example is the system of waging wars, whereas
'old,' so they say, is a system of economy, proposed but never put into
practice, which makes wars superfluous. In the new system, society is
being entrenched in classes; while old, so they say, is the desire to abol-
ish classes. The hopes of mankind do not so much become discouraged
in these times; rather, they become diverted. Men had hoped that one
day there would be bread to eat. Now they may hope that one day
there will be stones.

Amid the darkness gathering fast over a fevered world, a world surrounded by bloody deeds and no less bloody thoughts, by increasing
barbarism which seems to be leading irresistibly to perhaps the greatest and most terrible war of all time, it is difficult to adopt an attitude
appropriate to people on the threshold of a new and happier age. Does
not everything point to night's arrival and nothing to the dawning of a

new age? So shouldn't one, therefore, assume an attitude appropriate to people heading towards the night?

What is this talk of a 'new age'? Is not this expression itself obsolete? When it is shouted at us, it is bellowed from hoarse throats. Now indeed, it is mere barbarism which impersonates the new age. It says of itself that it hopes it will last a thousand years.

So should one hold fast to the old times? Should one discuss sunken Atlantis?

Am I already lying down for the night and thinking, when I think of the morning, of the one that has passed, in order to avoid thinking of the one to come? Is that why I occupy myself with that epoch of the flowering of the arts and sciences three hundred years ago? I hope not.

These images of the morning and the night are misleading. Happy times do not come in the same way as a morning follows a night's sleep.

[Dated 1939; not revised by Brecht. From Werner Hecht (ed.): *Materialien zu Brechts 'Leben des Galilei,'* Frankfurt, Suhrkamp, 1968, pp. 7ff.]

THE *LIFE OF GALILEO* IS NOT A TRAGEDY

So, from the point of view of the theatre, the question will arise whether the *Life of Galileo* is to be presented as a tragedy or as an optimistic play. Is the keynote to be found in Galileo's 'Salutation to the New Age' in scene 1 or in certain parts of scene 14? According to the prevailing rules of play construction, the end of a drama must carry the greater weight. But this play is not constructed according to these rules. The play shows the dawn of a new age and tries to correct some of the prejudices about the dawn of a new age.

[Dated 1939. From Werner Hecht (ed.), ibid., p. 13.]

PORTRAYAL OF THE CHURCH

For the theatre it is important to understand that this play must lose a great part of its effect if its performance is directed chiefly against the Roman Catholic Church.

Of the dramatis personae, many wear the church's garb. Actors who, because of that, try to portray these characters as odious would be doing wrong. But neither, on the other hand, has the church the right to have the human weaknesses of its members glossed over. It has all too often encouraged these weaknesses and suppressed their exposure. But in this play there is also no question of the church being admonished: 'Hands off science!' Modern science is a legitimate daughter of the church, a daughter who has emancipated herself and turned against the mother.

In the present play the church functions, even when it opposes free investigation, simply as authority.

Since science was a branch of theology, the church is the intellectual authority, the ultimate scientific court of appeal. The play shows the temporary victory of authority, not the victory of the priesthood. It corresponds to the historical truth in that the Galileo of the play never turns directly against the church. There is not a sentence uttered by Galileo in that sense. If there had been, such a thorough commission of investigation as the Inquisition would undoubtedly have brought it to light. And it equally corresponds to the historical truth that the greatest astronomer of the Papal Roman College, Christopher Clavius, confirmed Galileo's discoveries (scene 6). It is also true that clerics were among his pupils (scenes 8, 9, and 13).

To take satirical aim at the worldly interests of high dignitaries seems to me cheap (it would be in scene 7). But the casual way in which these high officials treat the physicist is only meant to show that, by reason of their past experiences, they think they can count on ready complaisance from Galileo. They are not mistaken.

When one looks at our bourgeois politicians, one cannot but extol the spiritual (and scientific) interests of those politicians of old.

The play, therefore, ignores the falsifications made to the protocol of 1616 by the Inquisition of 1633, falsifications established by recent historical studies under the direction of the German scholar Emil Wohlwill. Doubtless the judgment and sentence of 1633 were thereby made juridically possible. Anybody who understands the point of view outlined above will appreciate that the author was not concerned with this legal side of the trial.

There is no doubt that Urban VIII was personally incensed at Galileo and, in the most detestable manner, played a personal part in the proceedings against him. The play passes this over.

Anyone who understands the standpoint of the author will realise that this attitude implies no reverence for the church of the seventeenth, let alone of the twentieth century.

Casting the church as the embodiment of authority in this theatrical trial of the persecutors of the champions of free research certainly

does not help to get the church acquitted. But it would be highly dangerous, particularly nowadays, to treat a matter like Galileo's fight for
freedom of research as a religious one; for thereby attention would be
most unhappily deflected from present-day reactionary authorities of
a totally unecclesiastical kind.

[Dated 1939. From Werner Hecht (ed.), ibid., pp. 14f.]

THREE NOTES ON THE CHARACTER
OF GALILEO

1. [*The new type of physicist*]

[. . .] It's important that you shouldn't idealise Galileo: You know the
kind of thing—the stargazer, the pallid intellectualised idealist. I know
you wouldn't if left to yourself, but the pictures you'll see in the books
are already idealised. My Galileo is a powerful physicist with a tummy
on him, a face like Socrates, a vociferous, full-blooded man with a
sense of humour, the new type of physicist, earthly, a great teacher.
Favourite attitude: stomach thrust forward, both hands on the but-
tocks, head back, using one meaty hand all the time to gesticulate
with, but with precision; comfortable trousers for working in, shirt-
sleeves or (particularly at the end) a long whitish-yellow robe with
broad sleeves, tied with a cord round his stomach. You get the idea—
preferably an etching of this figure or some kind of steel engraving or
wood engraving to maintain its historical flavour: in other words, realistic. Or for that matter one could have pen drawings standing freely
on the page. Don't be scared of a bit of humour. History without humour is a ghastly thing . . .

N.B. As far as I know, Galileo's telescope was about two and a half
feet long and the thickness of a man's arm. You can stand it on an ordinary tripod. The model of the Ptolemaic system (in scene 1) is of
wood, some twenty inches in diameter. You could probably get a
rough idea from the keeper of the planetarium.

2. *The Sensual Element in Galileo*

Galileo of course is not a Falstaff: He insists on his physical pleasures
because of his materialist convictions. He wouldn't, for instance,
drink at his work; the point is that he works in a sensual way. He gets
pleasure from handling his instruments with elegance. A great part of

his sensuality is of an intellectual kind: for instance, the 'beauty' of an experiment, the little theatrical performance with which he gives shape to each of his lessons, the often abrupt way in which he will confront somebody with the truth, not to mention those passages in his speeches (in 1, 7, 13) where he picks good words and tests them like a spice. (This has nothing to do with that bel canto of the actor who may produce his arias as if he enjoyed them, but fails to show the enjoyment of the character he is playing.)

3. *About the Part of Galileo*

What gives this new historical character his quality of strangeness, novelty, strikingness, is the fact that he, Galileo, looks at the world of 1600 around him as if he himself were a stranger. He studies this world and finds it remarkable, outdated, in need of explanation. He studies:

in scene 1, Ludovico Marsili and Priuli
in scene 2, the way in which the senators look through the telescope
    (When am I going to be able to buy one of these things?)
in scene 3, Sagredo (the prince being a child of nine)
in scene 4, the court scholars
in scene 5, the monks
in scene 7, the young monk
in scene 8, Federzoni and Ludovico
in scene [11], (just for one second) Virginia
in scene [13], his pupils
in scene [14], Andrea and Virginia.

[From Werner Hecht (ed.), *ibid.*, pp. 27f. The first section comes from a letter from Brecht to the painter Hans Tombrock in March 1941, and refers to the first version of the play, which Tombrock illustrated for a proposed publication in the USSR which never materialised. The second and third are undated, but appear to refer to the second, American version.]

DRAFTS FOR A FOREWORD
TO *LIFE OF GALILEO*

The *Life of Galileo* was written in those last dark months of 1938, when many people felt fascism's advance to be irresistible and the final collapse of Western civilisation to have arrived. And indeed we were approaching the end of that great age to which the world owes the development of the natural sciences, together with such new arts as music and the theater. There was a more or less general expectation of a barbaric age 'outside history.' Only a minority saw the evolution of new forces and sensed the vitality of the new ideas. Even the significance of expressions like 'old' and 'new' had been obscured. The doctrines of the socialist classics had lost the appeal of novelty, and seemed to belong to a vanished day.

The bourgeois single out science from the scientist's consciousness, setting it up as an island of independence so as to be able in practice to interweave it with *their* politics, *their* economics, *their* ideology. The research scientist's object is 'pure' research; the product of that research is not so pure. The formula $E=mc^2$ is conceived of as eternal, not tied to anything. Hence other people can do the tying: suddenly the city of Hiroshima became very short-lived. The scientists are claiming the irresponsibility of machines.

Let us think back to the founding father of experimental science, Francis Bacon, whose phrase that one must obey nature in order to command her was not written in vain. His contemporaries obeyed his nature by bribing him with money, and so thoroughly commanded him when he was Lord Chief Justice that in the end Parliament had to lock him up. Macaulay, the puritan, drew a distinction between Bacon the scientist, whom he admired, and Bacon the politician, of whom he disapproved. Should we be doing the same thing with the German doctors of Nazi times?

Among other things, war promotes the sciences. What an opportunity! It creates discoverers as well as thieves. A higher responsibility (that of the higher ranks) replaces the lower (that for the lowly). Obedience is the midwife of arbitrariness. Disorder is perfectly in order. Those doctors who combatted yellow fever had to use themselves as guinea pigs; the fascist doctors had material supplied them. Justice played a part too; they had to freeze only 'criminals', in other words those who did not share their opinions. For their experiments in using 'animal warmth' as a means of thawing they were given prostitutes, women who had transgressed the rule of chastity. They had served sin; now they were being allowed to serve science. It incidentally emerged that hot water restores life better than a woman's body; in its small way it can do more for the fatherland. (Ethics must never be overlooked in war.) Progress all round. At the beginning of this century politicians of the lower classes were forced to treat the prisons as their universities. Now the prisons became universities for the warders (and doctors). Their experiments would of course have been perfectly in order—'from a scientific point of view', that is—even if the state had been forced to exceed the ethical bounds. None the less the bourgeois world still has a certain right to be outraged. Even if it is only a matter of degrees it is a matter of degrees. When Generals von Mackensen and Maltzer were being tried in Rome for shooting hostages, the English prosecutor, a certain Colonel Halse, admitted that 'reprisal killings' in war were not illegal so long as the victims were taken from the scene of the incident in question, some attempt was made to find the persons responsible for it, and there were not too many executions. The German generals however had gone too far. They took ten Italians for every German soldier killed (not twenty, though, as demanded by Hitler), and dispatched the whole lot too quickly, within some twenty-four hours. The Italian police, by an oversight, handed over several Italians too many, and by another oversight the Germans shot them too, out of a misplaced reliance on the Italians. But here again they had ransacked the prisons for hostages, taking criminals or suspects awaiting trial, and filling the gaps with Jews. So a certain humanity asserted itself, and not merely in the errors of arithmetic. All the same, bounds were exceeded in this case, and something had to be done to punish the excess.

It can none the less be shown that, in this period when the bourgeoisie has gone completely to pieces, those pieces are still made of the same stuff as the original polished article.

And so in the end the scientists get what they want: state resources, large-scale planning, authority over industry; their Golden Age has come. And their great production starts as the production of weapons of destruction; their planning leads to extreme anarchy, for they are arming the state against other states. As soon as he represents such a threat to the world, the people's traditional contempt for the unworldly professor turns into naked fear. And just when he has wholly cut himself off from the people as the complete specialist, he is appalled to see himself once again as one of the people, because the threat applies to him too; he has reason to fear for his own life, and the best reason of anybody to know just how much. His protests, of which we have heard quite a number, refer not only to the attacks on his science, which is to be hampered, sterilised, and perverted, but also to the threat which his knowledge represents to the world, and also to the threat to himself.

The Germans have just undergone one of those experiences that are so difficult to convert into usable conclusions. The leadership of the state had fallen to an ignorant person who associated himself with a gang of violent and 'uneducated' politicians to proclaim a vast war and utterly ruin the country. Shortly before the catastrophic end, and for some time after it, the blame was attributed to these people. They had conducted an almost total mobilisation of the intellectuals, providing every branch with trained manpower, and although they made a number of clumsy attempts to interfere, the catastrophe cannot be ascribed to clumsy interference alone. Not even the military and political strategy appears to have been all that wrong, while the courage of the army and of the civil population is beyond dispute. What won in the end was the enemy's superiority in men and technology, something that had been brought into play by a series of almost unpredictable events.

Many of those who see, or at any rate suspect, capitalism's short-comings are prepared to put up with them for the sake of the personal freedom which capitalism appears to guarantee. They believe in this freedom mainly because they scarcely ever make use of it. Under the scourge of Hitler they saw this freedom more or less abrogated; it was like a little nest-egg in the savings bank which could normally be drawn on at any time, though it was clearly more sensible not to touch it, but had now, as it were, been frozen—i.e., could not be drawn on, although it was still there. They regarded the Hitler period as abnormal; it was a matter of some warts on capitalism, or even of an anti-capitalist movement. The latter was something that one could only believe if one accepted the Nazis' own definition of capitalism, while as for the wart theory one was after all dealing with a system where warts flourished, and there was no question of the intellectuals being able to prevent them or make them go away. In either case freedom could only be restored by a catastrophe. And when the catastrophe came, not even that was able to restore freedom, not even that.

Among the various descriptions of the poverty prevailing in denazi-fied Germany was that of spiritual poverty. 'What they want, what they're waiting for, is a message,' people said. 'Didn't they have one?' I asked. 'Look at the poverty,' they said, 'and at the lack of leader-ship.' 'Didn't they have leadership enough?' I asked, pointing to the poverty. 'But they must have something to look forward to,' they said. 'Aren't they tired of looking forward to such things?' I asked. 'I understand they lived quite a while on looking forward either to getting rid of their leader or to having him lay the world at their feet for them to pillage.'

The hardest time to get along without knowledge is the time when knowledge is hardest to get. It is the condition of bottom-most poverty, where it seems possible to get along without knowledge. Nothing is calculable any longer, the measures went up in the fire, short-range objectives hide those in the distance, at that point chance decides.

[From Werner Hecht (ed.), *ibid.*, pp. 16 ff. These different items are given in the same order as there, though they appear to date from after the Second World War and not, as there suggested, mainly from 1938–1939.]

UNVARNISHED PICTURE OF A NEW AGE

Preamble to the American Version

When, during my first years in exile in Denmark, I wrote the play *Life of Galileo*, I was helped in the reconstruction of the Ptolemaic cosmology by assistants of Niels Bohr who were working on the problem of splitting the atom. My intention was, among others, to give an unvarnished picture of a new age—a strenuous undertaking since all those around me were convinced that our own era lacked every attribute of a new age. Nothing of this aspect had changed when, years later, I began together with Charles Laughton to prepare an American version of the play. The 'atomic' age made its debut at Hiroshima in the middle of our work. Overnight the biography of the founder of the new system of physics read differently. The infernal effect of the great bomb placed the conflict between Galileo and the authorities of his day in a new, sharper light. We had to make only a few alterations—not a single one to the structure of the play. Already in the original version the church was portrayed as a secular authority, its ideology as fundamentally interchangeable with many others. From the first, the keystone of the gigantic figure of Galileo was his conception of a science for the people. For hundreds of years and throughout the whole of Europe people had paid him the honour, in the Galileo legend, of not believing in his recantation, just as they had for long derided scientists as biased, unpractical and eunuch-like old fogeys. [. . .]

[Dated 1946. From Werner Hecht (ed.), *ibid.*, pp. 10ff. The rest of the note, here omitted, was incorporated in the Model Book (see pp. 238–239 below).]

PRAISE OR CONDEMNATION OF GALILEO?

It would be a great weakness in this work if those physicists were right who said to me—in a tone of approval—that Galileo's recantation of his teachings was, despite one or two 'waverings,' portrayed as being sensible, on the principle that this recantation enabled him to carry on with his scientific work and to hand it down to posterity. The fact is that Galileo enriched astronomy and physics by simultaneously robbing these sciences of a greater part of their social importance. By discrediting the Bible and the church, these sciences stood for a while at the barricades on behalf of all progress. It is true that a forward movement took place in the following centuries, and these sciences were involved in it, but it was a slow movement, not a revolution; the scandal, so to speak, degenerated into a dispute between experts. The church, and with it all the forces of reaction, was able to bring off an organised retreat and more or less reassert its power. As far as these particular sciences were concerned, they never again regained their high position in society, neither did they ever again come into such close contact with the people.

Galileo's crime can be regarded as the 'original sin' of modern natural sciences. From the new astronomy, which deeply interested a new class—the bourgeoisie—since it gave an impetus to the revolutionary social current of the time, he made a sharply defined special science which—admittedly through its very 'purity', i.e., its indifference to modes of production—was able to develop comparatively undisturbed.

The atom bomb is, both as a technical and as a social phenomenon, the classical end-product of his contribution to science and his failure to contribute to society.

Thus the 'hero' of this work is not Galileo but the people, as Walter Benjamin has said. This seems to me to be rather too briefly expressed. I hope this work shows how society extorts from its individuals what it needs from them. The urge to research, a social phenomenon no less delightful or compulsive than the urge to reproduce, steers Galileo into that most dangerous territory, drives him into agonising conflict with his violent desires for other pleasures. He raises his telescope to the stars and delivers himself to the rack. In the end he indulges his science like a vice, secretly, and probably with pangs of conscience. Confronted with such a situation, one can scarcely wish only to praise or only to condemn Galileo.

[Dated 1947. From Werner Hecht (ed.), *ibid.*, pp. 12f.]

PROLOGUE TO THE AMERICAN PRODUCTION

Respected public of the way called Broad-
Tonight we invite you to step on board
A world of curves and measurements, where you'll descry
The newborn physics in their infancy.
Here you will see the life of the great Galileo Galilei,
The law of falling bodies versus the GRATIAS DEI
Science's fight versus the rulers, which we stage
At the beginning of a brand-new age.
Here you'll see science in its blooming youth
Also its first compromises with the truth.
It too must eat, and quickly gets prostrated
Takes the wrong road, is violated—
Once Nature's master, now it is no more
Than just another cheap commercial whore.
The Good, so far, has not been turned to goods
But already there's something nasty in the woods
Which cuts it off from reaching the majority
So it won't relieve, but aggravate their poverty.
We think such sights are relevant today
The new age is so quick to pass away.
We hope you'll lend a charitable ear
To what we say, since otherwise we fear
If you won't learn from Galileo's experience
The Bomb might make a personal appearance.

[From Brecht's *Arbeitsjournal*, entry for 1 December 1945.]

EPILOGUE OF THE SCIENTISTS

And the lamp his work ignited
We have tried to keep alight
Stooping low, and yet high-minded
Unrestrained, yet laced up tight.
Making moon and stars obey us
Grovelling at our rulers' feet
We sell our brains for what they'll pay us
To satisfy our bodies' need.

So, despised by those above us
Ridiculed by those below
We have found out the laws that move us
Keep this planet on the go.
Knowledge grows too large for nitwits
Servitude expands as well
Truth becomes so many titbits
Liberators give us hell.
Riding in new railway coaches
To the new ships on the waves
Who is it that now approaches?
Only slave-owners and slaves.
Only slaves and slave-owners
Leave the trains
Taking the new aeroplanes
Through the heaven's age-old blueness.
Till the last device arrives
Astronomic
White, atomic
Obliterating all our lives.

[From Werner Hecht (ed.), *ibid.*, pp. 38f.]

NOTES ON INDIVIDUAL SCENES

[Scene 11]

Could Galileo have acted any differently?

This scene gives ample reasons for Galileo's hesitation about escaping from Florence and seeking asylum in the North Italian cities. None the less the audience can imagine him putting himself in the hands of Matti the ironfounder, and discover various tendencies in his character and situations which would support this.

The actor Laughton showed Galileo in a state of great inner agitation during his talk with the ironfounder. He played it as a moment of decision—the wrong one. (Connoisseurs of dialectics will find Galileo's possibilities further clarified in the ensuing scene 'The Pope', where the inquisitor insists that Galileo must be forced to recant his theory because the Italian maritime cities need his star charts, which derive from it and of which it would not be possible to deprive them.)

An objectivist approach is not permissible here.*

[Scene 14]

Galileo after his recantation

His crime has made a criminal of him. When he reflects on the *scale* of his crime he is pleased with himself. He defends himself against the outside world's impertinent expectations of its geniuses. What has Andrea done to oppose the Inquisition? Galileo applies his intellect to solving the problems of the clergy, which these blockheads have overlooked. His mind functions automatically, like a motor in neutral. His appetite for knowledge feels to him like the impetus that makes him twitch. Scholarly activity, for him, is a sin: mortally dangerous, but impossible to do without. He has a fanatical hatred for humanity. Andrea's readiness to revise his damning verdict as soon as he sees the book means that he has been corrupted. As to a lame and starving wolf, Galileo tosses him a crust, the logical scientific analysis of the Galileo phenomenon. Behind this lies his rejection of the moral demands of a humanity which does nothing to relieve the deadliness of that morality and those demands.

[...]

Once Galileo knows that his book has set out on its journey towards publication he changes his attitude again. He proposes that the book should be prefaced by an introduction sharply condemning the author's treachery. Andrea passionately refuses to pass on such a request, pointing out that everything is different now; that Galileo's recantation gave him the chance to finish this immensely significant work. What needs to be altered is the popular concept of heroism, ethical precepts and so on. The one thing that counts is one's contribution to science, and so forth.

At first Galileo listens in silence to Andrea's speech, which builds a golden bridge for his return to the esteem of his fellow scientists, then contemptuously and cuttingly contradicts him, accusing Andrea of squalidly recanting every principle of science. Starting with a denunciation of 'bad thinking' which seems designed as a brilliant demonstration of how the trained scientist ought to analyse a case like his own, he proves to Andrea that no achievement is valuable enough to make up for the damage caused by a betrayal of mankind.

---

*Objectivists who prove the necessity of a given sequence of facts are always in danger of slipping into the position of justifying those facts (Lenin).

Galileo's portrayal in scene 14

The fact that the author is known to all and sundry as an opponent of the church might lead a theatre to give the play's performance a primarily anticlerical slant. The church, however, is mainly being treated here as a secular establishment. Its specific ideology is being looked at in the light of its function as a prop to practical rule. The old cardinal (in scene 6) can be turned into a Tory or a Louisiana Democrat without much adjustment. Galileo's illusions concerning a 'scientist in the chair of St. Peter' have more than one parallel in contemporary history, and these are scarcely related to the church. In scene 13 Galileo is not returning 'to the bosom of the church'; as we know, he never left it. He is simply trying to make his peace with those in power. One can judge his demoralisation by his social attitude; he buys his comfort (even his scientific activity having degenerated to the status of a comfort) by means of hackwork, unashamedly prostituting his intellect. (His use of clerical quotations is thus sheer blasphemy.) On no account should the actor make use of his self-analysis to endear the hero to the audience by his self-reproaches. All it does is to show that his brain is unimpaired, never mind what area he directs it to. Andrea Sarti's final remark in no sense represents the playwright's own view of Galileo, merely his opinion of Andrea Sarti. The playwright was not out to have the last word.

Galileo is a measure of the standard of Italian intellectuals in the first third of the seventeenth century, when they were defeated by the feudal nobility. Northern countries like Holland and England developed productive forces further by means of what is called the Industrial Revolution. In a sense Galileo was responsible both for its technical creation and for its social betrayal.

[Crime and Cunning]

The first version of the play ended differently. Galileo had written the *Discorsi* in the utmost secrecy. He uses the visit of his favourite pupil Andrea to get him to smuggle the book across the frontier. His recantation had given him the chance to create a seminal work. He had been wise.

In the Californian version [. . .] Galileo interrupts his pupil's hymns of praise to prove to him that his recantation had been a crime, and was not to be compensated by this work, important as it might be.

In case anybody is interested, this is also the opinion of the playwright.

[Shortened from Werner Hecht (ed.), *ibid.*, pp. 32–37. These notes were written at various times, those on scene 14 mainly during Brecht's work on the Berliner Ensemble production. The reference to a new critical introduction to the *Discorsi* must relate to a proposed change which Brecht never made; it is not to be found in our text.]

BUILDING UP A PART: LAUGHTON'S GALILEO*

Preface

In describing Laughton's Galileo Galilei the playwright is setting out not so much to try and give a little more permanence to one of those fleeting works of art that actors create, as to pay tribute to the pains a great actor is prepared to take over a fleeting work of this sort. This is no longer at all common. It is not just that the under-rehearsing in our hopelessly commercialised theatre is to blame for lifeless and stereotyped portraits—give the average actor more time, and he would hardly do better. Nor is it simply that this century has very few outstanding individualists with rich characteristics and rounded contours—if that were all, care could be devoted to the portrayal of lesser figures. Above all it is that we seem to have lost any understanding and appreciation of what we may call a *theatrical conception*: what Garrick did when, as Hamlet, he met his father's ghost; Sorel when, as Phedre, she knew that she was going to die; Bassermann when, as Philip, he had finished listening to Posa. It is a question of inventiveness.

The spectator could isolate and detach such theatrical conceptions, but they combined to form a single rich texture. Odd insights into men's nature, glimpses of their particular way of living together, were brought about by the ingenious contrivance of the actors.

With works of art, even more than with philosophical systems, it is impossible to find out how they are made. Those who make them work hard to give the impression that everything just happens, as it were of its own accord, as though an image were forming in a clear mirror that is itself inert. Of course this is a deception, and apparently the idea is that if it comes off it will increase the spectator's pleasure. In fact it does not. What the spectator—anyway the experienced spectator—enjoys about art is the making of art, the active creative element. In art we view nature herself as if she were an artist.

*[The text referred to throughout this essay is that of the Brecht–Laughton translation, for which see p. 195ff.]

The ensuing account deals with this aspect, with the process of manufacture rather than with the result. It is less a matter of the artist's temperament than of the notions of reality which he has *and communicates*; less a matter of his vitality than of the observations which underlie his portraits and can be derived from them. This means neglecting much that seemed to us to be 'inimitable' in Laughton's achievement, and going on rather to what can be learned from it. For we cannot create talent; we can only set it tasks.

It is unnecessary here to examine how the artists of the past used to astonish their public. Asked why he acted, L. answered: 'Because people don't know what they are like, and I think I can show them.' His collaboration in the rewriting of the play showed that he had all sorts of ideas which were begging to be disseminated, about how people *really* live together, about the motive forces that need to be taken into account here. L.'s attitude seemed to the playwright to be that of a realistic artist of our time. For whereas in relatively stationary ('quiet') periods artists may find it possible to merge wholly with their public and to be a faithful 'embodiment' of the general conception, our profoundly unsettled time forces them to take special measures to penetrate to the truth. Our society will not admit of its own accord what makes it move. It can even be said to exist purely through the secrecy with which it surrounds itself. What attracted L. about *Life of Galileo* was not only one or two formal points but also the subject matter; he thought this might become what he called a contribution. And so great was his anxiety to show things as they really are that despite all his indifference (indeed timidity) in political matters he suggested and even demanded that not a few of the play's points should be made sharper, on the simple ground that such passages seemed 'somehow weak' to him, by which he meant that they did not do justice to things as they are.

We usually met in L.'s big house above the Pacific, as the dictionaries of synonyms were too bulky to lug about. He had continual and inexhaustibly patient recourse to these tomes, and used in addition to fish out the most varied literary texts in order to examine this or that gest, or some particular mode of speech: Aesop, the Bible, Molière, Shakespeare. In my house he gave readings of Shakespeare's works to which he would devote perhaps a fortnight's preparation. In this way he read *The Tempest* and *King Lear*, simply for me and one or two guests who happened to have dropped in. Afterward we would briefly discuss what seemed relevant, an 'aria' perhaps or an effective scene opening. These were exercises and he would pursue them in various directions, assimilating them in the rest of his work. If he had to give a reading on the radio he would get me to hammer out the syncopated rhythms of Whitman's poems (which he found somewhat strange) on a table with my fists, and once he hired a studio where we recorded half a dozen ways of telling the story of the creation, in which he was an African planter telling the Negroes how he had created the world, or an English butler ascribing it to His Lordship. We needed such broadly ramified studies, because he spoke no German whatever and we had to decide the gest of dialogue by my acting it all in bad English or even in German and his then acting it back in proper English in a variety of ways until I could say: That's it. The result he would write down sentence by sentence in longhand. Some sentences, indeed many, he carried around for days, changing them continually. This system of performance-and-repetition had one immense advantage in that psychological discussions were almost entirely avoided. Even the most fundamental gests, such as Galileo's way of observing, or his showmanship, or his craze for pleasure, were established in three dimensions by actual performance. Our first concern throughout was the smallest fragments, for sentences, even for exclamations—each treated separately, each needing to be given the simplest, freshly fitted form, giving so much away, hiding so much or leaving it more. More radical changes in the structure of entire scenes or of the work itself were meant to help the story to move and to bring out fairly general conclusions about people's attitudes to the great physicist. But this reluctance to tinker with the psychological aspect remained with L. all through our long period of collaboration, even when a rough draft of the play was ready and he was giving various readings in order to test reactions, and even during the rehearsals.

The awkward circumstance that one translator knew no German and the other scarcely any English compelled us, as can be seen, from the outset to use acting as our means of translation. We were forced to do what better-equipped translators should do too: to translate gests. For language is theatrical in so far as it primarily expresses the mutual attitude of the speakers. (For the 'arias', as has been described, we brought in the playwright's own gest, by observing the bel canto of Shakespeare or the writers of the Bible.)

In a most striking and occasionally brutal way L. showed his lack of interest in the 'book', to an extent the playwright could not always share. What we were making was just a text; the performance was all that counted. Impossible to lure him to translate passages which the playwright was willing to cut for the proposed performance but wanted to keep in the book. The theatrical occasion was what mattered, the text was only there to make it possible: it would be expended in the production, would be consumed in it like gunpowder in a firework. Although L.'s theatrical experience had been in a London which had become thoroughly indifferent to the theatre, the old Elizabethan London still lived in him, the London where theatre was such a passion that it could swallow immortal works of art greedily and barefacedly as so many 'texts'. These works which have survived the centuries were in fact like improvisations thrown off for an all-important moment. Printing them at all was a matter of little interest, and probably only took place so that the spectators—in other words, those who were present at the actual event, the performance—might have a souvenir of their enjoyment. And the theatre seems in those days to have been so potent that the cuts and interpolations made at rehearsal can have done little harm to the text.

We used to work in L.'s small library, in the mornings. But often L. would come and meet me in the garden, running barefoot in shirt and trousers over the damp grass, and would show me some changes in his flowerbeds, for his garden always occupied him, providing many problems and subtleties. The gaiety and the beautiful proportions of this world of flowers overlapped in a most pleasant way into our work. For quite a while our work embraced everything we could lay our hands on. If we discussed gardening it was only a digression from one of the scenes in *Galileo*; if we combed a New York museum for technical drawings by Leonardo to use as background pictures in the performance we would digress to Hokusai's graphic work. L., I could see, would make only marginal use of such material. The parcels of books or photocopies from books, which he persistently ordered, never turned him into a bookworm. He obstinately sought for the external: not for physics but for the physicists' behaviour. It was a matter of putting together a bit of theatre, something slight and superficial. As the material piled up, L. became set on the idea of getting a good draughtsman to produce entertaining sketches in the manner of Caspar Neher, to expose the anatomy of the action. 'Before you amuse others you have to amuse yourself,' he said.

For this no trouble was too great. As soon as L. heard of Caspar Neher's delicate stage sketches, which allow the actors to group themselves according to a great artist's compositions and to take up attitudes that are both precise and realistic, he asked an excellent draughtsman from the Walt Disney Studios to make similar sketches. They were a little malicious; L. used them, but with caution.

What pains he took over the costumes, not only his own, but those of all the actors! And how much time we spent on the casting of the many parts!

First we had to look through works on costume and old pictures in order to find costumes that were free of any element of fancy dress. We sighed with relief when we found a small sixteenth-century panel that showed long trousers. Then we had to distinguish the classes. There the elder Brueghel was of great service. Finally we had to work out the colour scheme. Each scene had to have its basic tone: the first, e.g., a delicate morning one of white, yellow, and grey. But the entire sequence of scenes had to have its development in terms of colour. In the first scene a deep and distinguished blue made its entrance with Ludovico Marsili, and this deep blue remained, set apart, in the second scene with the upper bourgeoisie in their blackish-green coats made of felt and leather. Galileo's social ascent could be followed by means of colour. The silver and pearl-grey of the fourth (court) scene led into a nocturne in brown and black (where Galileo is jeered by the monks of the Collegium Romanum), then on to the seventh, the cardinals' ball, with delicate and fantastic individual masks (ladies and gentlemen) moving about the cardinals' crimson figures. That was a burst of colour, but it still had to be fully unleashed, and this occurred in the tenth scene, the carnival. After the nobility and the cardinals the poor people too had their masquerade. Then came the descent into dull and sombre colours. The difficulty of such a plan of course lies in the fact that the costumes and their wearers wander through several scenes; they have always to fit in and contribute to the colour scheme of the new scene.

We filled the parts mainly with young actors. The speeches presented certain problems. The American stage shuns speeches except in (maybe because of) its frightful Shakespearean productions. Speeches just mean a break in the story; and, as commonly delivered, that is what they are. L. worked with the young actors in a masterly and conscientious manner, and the playwright was impressed by the freedom he allowed them, by the way in which he avoided anything Laughtonish and simply taught them the structure. To those actors who were too easily influenced by his own personality he read passages from Shakespeare, without rehearsing the actual text at all; to none did he read the text itself. The actors were incidentally asked on no account to prove their suitability for the part by putting something 'impressive' into it.

We jointly agreed on the following points:

1. The decorations should not be of a kind to suggest to the spectators that they are in a medieval Italian room or the Vatican. The audience should be conscious of being in a theatre.

2. The background should show more than the scene directly surrounding Galileo; in an imaginative and artistically pleasing way, it should show the historical setting, but still remain background. (This can be achieved when the decoration itself is not independently colourful, but helps the actors' costumes and enhances the roundedness of the figures by remaining two-dimensional even when it contains three-dimensional elements, etc.)

3. Furniture and props (including doors) should be realistic and above all be of social and historical interest. Costumes must be individualised and show signs of having been worn. Social differences were to be underlined since we find it difficult to distinguish them in ancient fashions. The colours of the various costumes should harmonise.

4. The characters' groupings must have the quality of historical paintings (but not to bring out the historical aspect as an aesthetic attraction; this is a directive which is equally valid for contemporary plays). The director can achieve this by inventing historical titles for the episodes. (In the first scene such titles might be *Galileo the physicist explains the new Copernican theory to his subsequent collaborator Andrea Sarti and predicts the great historical importance of astronomy—To make a living the great Galileo teaches rich pupils—Galileo who has requested support for his continued investigations is admonished by the university officials to invent profitable instruments—Galileo constructs his first telescope based on information from a traveller.*)

5. The action must be presented calmly and in a large sweep. Frequent changes of position involving irrelevant movements of the characters must be avoided. The director must not for a moment forget that many of the actions and speeches are hard to understand and that it is therefore necessary to express the underlying idea of an episode by the positioning. The audience must be assured that when someone walks, or gets up, or makes a gesture it has meaning and deserves attention. But groupings and movements must always remain realistic.

6. In casting the ecclesiastical dignitaries realism is of more than ordinary importance. No caricature of the church is intended, but the refined manner of speech and the 'breeding' of the seventeenth-century hierarchy must not mislead the director into picking spiritual types. In this play, the church mainly represents authority; as types the dignitaries should resemble our present-day bankers and senators.

7. The portrayal of Galileo should not aim at rousing the audience to sympathy or empathy; they should rather be encouraged to adopt a deliberate attitude of wonder and criticism. Galileo should be portrayed as a phenomenon of the order of Richard III; the audience's emotions will be engaged by the vitality of this strange figure.

8. The more profoundly the historical seriousness of a production is established, the more scope can be given to humour. The more sweeping the overall plan, the more intimately individual scenes can be played.

9. There is no reason why *Life of Galileo* cannot be performed without drastically changing the present-day style of production, as a historical 'war-horse', for instance, with a star part. Any conventional performance, however (which need not seem at all conventional to the actors, especially if it contained interesting inventions), would weaken the play's real strength considerably without making it any easier for the audience. The play's main effects will be missed unless the theatre changes its attitude. The stock reply, 'Won't work here,' is familiar to the author; he heard it at home too. Most directors treat such plays as a coachman would have treated an automobile when it was first invented. On the arrival of the machine, mistrusting the practical instructions accompanying it, this coachman would have harnessed horses in front—more horses, of course, than to a carriage, since the new car was heavier—and then, his attention being drawn to the engine, he would have said, 'Won't work here.'*

The performance took place in a small theatre in Beverly Hills, and L.'s chief worry was the prevailing heat. He asked that trucks full of ice be parked against the theatre walls and fans be set in motion 'so that the audience can think'.

---

*[Brecht added Note 9 at a later date for inclusion in his Notes to the Play.]

Notes on individual scenes

I

The Scholar, a Human Being

The first thing L. did when he set to work was to rid the figure of
Galileo of the pallid, spiritual, stargazing aura of the text books.
Above all, the scholar must be made into a man. The very term
'scholar' [Gelehrter] sounds somewhat ridiculous when used by simple
people; there is an implication of having been prepared and fitted, of
something passive. In Bavaria people used to speak of the Nuremberg
Funnel by which simpletons were more or less forcibly fed undue
quantities of knowledge, a kind of enema for the brain. When someone had 'crammed himself with learning', that too was considered
unnatural. The educated—again one of those hopelessly passive
words—talked of the revenge of the 'uneducated', of their innate hatred for the mind; and it is true that their contempt was often mixed
with hatred; in villages and working-class districts, the mind was
considered something alien, even hostile. The same contempt, however, could also be found among the 'better classes'. A scholar was an
impotent, bloodless, quaint figure, conceited and barely fit to live.
He was an easy prey for romantic treatment. L.'s Galileo never
strayed far from the engineer at the great arsenal in Venice. His eyes
were there to see with, not to flash, his hands to work with, not to
gesticulate. Everything worth seeing or feeling L. derived from
Galileo's profession, his pursuit of physics and his teaching, the
teaching, that is, of something very concrete with its concomitant
real difficulties. And he portrayed the external side not just for the
sake of the inner man—that is to say, research and everything con-
nected with it, not just for the sake of the resulting psychological
reactions—these reactions, rather, were never separated from the
everyday business and conflicts, they never became 'universally human', even though they never lost their universal appeal. In the case
of the Richard III of Shakespeare's theatre, the spectator can easily
change himself along with the actor, since the king's politics and
warfare play only a very vague role; there is hardly more of it than a
dreaming man would understand. But with Galileo it is a continual
handicap to the spectator that he knows much less about science than
does Galileo. It is a piquant fact that in representing the history of
Galileo, both playwright and actor had to undo the notion which
Galileo's betrayal had helped to create, the notion that schoolteachers

and scientists are by nature absent-minded, hybrid, castrated. (Only in our own day when, in the shape of ruling-class hirelings remote from the people, they delivered the latest product of Galileo's laws of motion, did popular contempt change to fear.) As for Galileo himself, for many centuries, all over Europe, the people honoured him for his belief in a popularly based science by refusing to believe in his recantation.

Subdivisions and Line

We divided the first scene into several parts:

We had the advantage that the beginning of the story was also a beginning for Galileo, that is, his encounter with the telescope, and since the significance of this encounter is hidden from him for the time being, our solution was to derive the joy of beginning from the early morning: having him wash with cold water—L., with bare torso, lifted a copper pitcher with a quick sweeping motion to let the jet of water fall into the basin—find his open books on the high desk, have his first sip of milk, and give his first lesson, as it happens, to a young boy. As the scene unfolds, Galileo keeps coming back to his reading at the high desk, annoyed at being interrupted by the returning student with his shallow preference for new-fangled inventions such as this spyglass, and by the procurator of the university who denies him a grant; finally reaching the last obstacle that keeps him from his work, the testing of the lenses which, however, would not have been possible without the two prior interruptions, and makes an entirely new field of work accessible.

Interest in Interest and Thinking as Expression of Physical Contentment

Two elements in the action with the child may be mentioned:

Washing himself in the background, Galileo observes the boy's interest in the astrolabe as little Andrea circles around the strange instrument. L. emphasised what was novel in G. at that time by letting him look at the world around him as if he were a stranger and as if it needed explanation. His chuckling observation made fossils out of the monks at the Collegium Romanum. In that scene he also showed amusement at their primitive method of proof.

Some people objected to L.'s delivering his speech about the new astronomy in the first scene with a bare torso, claiming that it would confuse the audience if it were to hear such intellectual utterances from a half-naked man. But it was just this mixture of the physical and the intellectual that attracted L. 'Galileo's physical contentment' at having his back rubbed by the boy is transformed into intellectual production. Again, in the ninth scene, L. brought out the fact that Galileo recovers his taste for wine on hearing of the reactionary pope's expected demise. His sensual walking, the play of his hands in his pockets while he is planning new researches, came close to being offensive. Whenever Galileo is creative, L. displayed a mixture of aggressiveness and defenceless softness and vulnerability.

Rotation of the Earth and Rotation of the Brain

L. arranges the little demonstration of the earth's rotation to be quick and offhand, leaving his high desk where he has begun to read and returning to it. He avoids anything emphatic, seems to pay no attention to the child's intellectual capacity, and at the end leaves him sitting there alone with his thoughts.

This casual manner, in keeping with his limited time, simultaneously admits the boy to the community of scholars. Thus L. demonstrated how for Galileo learning and teaching are one and the same—which makes his subsequent betrayal all the more horrible.

Balanced Acting

During this demonstration of the earth's rotation Galileo is surprised by Andrea's mother. Questioned about the nonsensical notions he is teaching the child he answers: 'Apparently we are on the threshold of a new era, Mrs. Sarti.' The way in which L. caressingly emptied his glass of milk while he said it was enchanting.

Response to a Good Answer

A small detail: the housekeeper has gone to let the new student in. Galileo feels constrained to make a confession to Andrea. His science is in no very good state, its most important concerns must be concealed from the authorities, and for the moment they are only hypotheses. 'I want to become an astronomer,' Andrea says quickly. At this answer Galileo looks at him with an almost tender smile. Usually actors do not rehearse such details separately, or often, enough to render them quickly in the performance.

[Dismissal of Andrea]

The dismissal of Andrea during the conversation with Ludovico is a piece of stage business for which time must be allowed. Galileo now drinks his milk as if it were the only pleasure to be had, and one which will not last very long. He is fully aware of Andrea's presence. Ill-humouredly he sends him away. One of those unavoidable everyday compromises!

Galileo Underestimates the New Invention

Ludovico Marsili describes a new spyglass which he has seen in Holland and cannot understand. Galileo asks for detailed information and makes a sketch which solves the problem. He holds the cardboard with the sketch without showing it to his pupil, who expected to have a look. (L. insisted that the actor playing Ludovico should expect this.) The sketch itself he drew casually, just to solve a problem that offered some relief from the conversation. Then, his way of asking the housekeeper to send Andrea for lenses and borrowing a scudo from the entering procurator—all that had an automatic and routine quality. The whole incident seemed only to demonstrate that Galileo too was capable of ploughing water.

A New Commodity

The birth of the telescope as a commodity took a long time to emerge clearly in the rehearsals. We found out why: L. had reacted too quickly and arrogantly to the university's refusal of a grant. All was well as soon as he accepted the blow in hurt silence and then went on, almost sadly, to speak like a poor man. As a natural result, Galileo's 'Mr. Priuli, I may have something for you,' came out in a way to make Galileo's dismissal of the new spyglass as 'bosh' perfectly clear.

[Interruption of Work]

When Andrea returns with the lenses he finds Galileo deep in his work. (L. has shown, during a by no means brief interval, how the scholar handles his books.) He has already forgotten the lenses, he lets the boy wait, then proceeds, almost guiltily because he has no desire to take up the lucrative bosh, to arrange the two lenses on a piece of cardboard. Finally he takes the 'thing' away, not without a little demonstration of his showmanship.

The senators surround and congratulate Galileo and draw him to the rear, but the tiny exchange with Ludovico Marsili, with its imputation of plagiarism, must as it were still hover in the air; for when the half-curtain closes behind them [Ludovico and Virginia] and in front of Galileo and the others, they continue and conclude the conversation while exiting along the footlights. And Ludovico's cynical remark, 'I am beginning to understand science,' serves as a springboard for the ensuing third scene—that of the great discoveries.

3

[Confidence in Objective Judgment]

Galileo lets his friend Sagredo look through the telescope at the moon and Jupiter. L. sat down, his back to the instrument, relaxed, as though his work was done and he only wanted his friend to pass impartial judgment on what he saw, and that this was all he needed to do since his friend was now seeing for himself. By this means he established that the new possibilities of observation must bring all controversy about the Copernican system to an end.

This attitude explains at the very beginning of the scene the boldness of his application for the lucrative position at the court of Florence.

The Historical Moment

L. conducted the exchange with his friend at the telescope without any emphasis. The more casually he acted, the more clearly one could sense the historic night; the more soberly he spoke, the more solemn the moment appeared.

An Embarrassment

When the procurator of the university comes in to complain about the fraud of the telescope, L.'s Galileo shows noticeable embarrassment by studiously looking through the telescope, obviously less to observe the sky than to avoid looking the procurator in the eye. Shamelessly he exploits the 'higher' function of the instrument which the Venetians have found not to be very profitable.

It is true that he also shows his behind to the angry man who has trusted him. But, far from trying to put him off with the discoveries of 'pure' science, he at once offers him another profitable item, the astronomical clock for ships. When the procurator has left, he sits glumly before the telescope, scratching his neck and telling Sagredo about his physical and intellectual needs which must be satisfied in one way or another. Science is a milch cow for all to milk, he himself of course included. While at this point in time Galileo's attitude is still helpful to science, later on, in his fight with Rome, it is going to push science to the brink of the abyss, in other words, deliver it into the hands of the rulers.

The Wish Is Father to the Thought

Looking up from their calculations of the movements of Jupiter's moons, Sagredo voices his concern for the man about to publish a discovery so embarrassing to the church. Galileo mentions the seductive power of evidence. He fishes a pebble from his pocket and lets it fall from palm to palm, following gravity: 'Sooner or later everybody must succumb to it' [the evidence]. As he argued along these lines, L. never forgot for a moment to do it in such a way that the audience would remember it later when he announced his decision to hand over his dangerous discoveries to the Catholic court of Florence.

[Rejection of Virginia]

L.'s Galileo used the little scene with his daughter Virginia to indicate how far he might be blamed for Virginia's subsequent behaviour as a spy for the Inquisition. He does not take her interest in the telescope seriously and sends her off to matins. L. scrutinised his daughter after her question, 'May I look through it?' before replying, 'What for? It's not a toy.'

The Fun in Contradictions

Saying, 'I am going to Florence,' Galileo carefully signs his letter of application. In this hasty capitalization of his discoveries as well as in his discourse on the seductive power of evidence and the representative value of great discoveries, L. left the spectator completely at liberty to study, criticise, admire Galileo's contradictory personality.

4

The Acting of Anger

Vis-à-vis the court scholars who refuse to look through the telescope, because to do so would either confirm Aristotle's doctrine or show up

Galileo as a swindler, what L. acted was not so much anger as the attempt to dominate anger.

Servility

After Galileo, erupting at last, has threatened to take his new science to the dockyards, he sees the court depart abruptly. Deeply alarmed and disturbed, he follows the departing prince in cringing servility, stumbling, all dignity gone. In such a case an actor's greatness can be seen in the degree to which he can make the character's behaviour incomprehensible or at least objectionable.

4 and 6*

The Fight and the Particular Manner of Fighting

L. insisted that throughout the two following scenes, 4 and 6, the sketch of Jupiter's moons from Galileo's original report should remain projected on the backdrop screen. It was a reminder of the fight. To show one of its aspects, the heel-cooling for the sake of truth, L., at the end of scene 4, when the chamberlain stays behind after the hasty departure of the court to inform him of the appeal to Rome, let himself be driven out of the space that stood for his house and stood in front of the half-curtain. He stood there between scenes 4 and 6 and again between scenes 6 and 7, waiting, and occasionally verifying that the pebble from his pocket continued to fall from one raised hand to the other stretched out below.

6

[Observation of the Clergy]

Galileo is not entirely devoid of appreciation when he observes the jeering monks at the Collegium Romanum—after all, by pretending to stand on a rolling globe they are trying to *prove* the absurdity of his propositions. The very old cardinal fills him with pity.

After the astronomer Clavius has confirmed Galileo's findings, Galileo shows his pebble to the hostile cardinal who retreats in dismay; L. did this by no means triumphantly, rather as if he wanted to offer his adversary a last chance to convince himself.

*Scene 5 was not played in this production.

Fame

Invited to the masked ball of Cardinals Bellarmin and Barberini Galileo lingers for a moment in the anteroom, alone with the clerical secretaries who later turn out to be secret agents. He has been greeted on his arrival by distinguished masked guests with great respect: obviously he stands in high favour. From the halls a boys' choir is heard, and Galileo listens to one of these melancholic stanzas which are sung amid the joy of life. L. needed no more than this brief listening and the word 'Rome!' to express the pride of the conqueror who has the capital of the world at his feet.

The Duel of Quotations

In the brief duel of Bible quotations with Cardinal Barberini, L.'s Galileo shows, beside the fun he has with such intellectual sport, that the possibility of an unfavourable outcome to his affairs is dawning on him. For the rest, the effectiveness of the scene depends on the elegance of its performance; L. made full use of his heavy body.

Two Things at Once

The brief argument about the capacity of the human brain (which the playwright was delighted to have heard formulated by Albert Einstein) furnished L. the opportunity to show two traits: 1) a certain arrogance of the professional when his field is invaded by laymen, and 2) an awareness of the difficulty of such a problem.

[Disarmed by Lack of Logic]

When the decree is read out forbidding the guest to teach a theory acknowledged to have been proven, L.'s Galileo reacts by twice turning abruptly from the reading secretaries to the liberal Barberini. Thunderstruck, he lets the two cardinals drag him to the ball as if he were a steer stunned by the axe. L. was able, in a manner the playwright cannot describe, to give the impression that what mainly disarmed Galileo was the lack of logic.

8

[*Indomitable Urge to Research*]

If in the seventh scene Galileo experiences the *No* of the church, in the eighth he is confronted with the *No* of the people. It comes from the lips of the little monk, himself a physicist. Galileo is disturbed, then recognises the situation: in the fight against science it is not the church that defends the peasant, but the peasant who defends the church. It was L.'s theatrical conception to let Galileo be so profoundly upset that he delivers his counter-arguments in a spirit of defence, even of angry self-defence, and makes the throwing down of the manuscript into a gesture of helplessness. He blamed his indomitable urge to research like a sex offender blaming his glands.

Laughton Does Not Forget to Tell the Story

In the eighth scene one of Galileo's lines contains a sentence which continues the story: 'Should I condone this decree . . .' L. distilled this small but important detail with great care.

9

[*The Impatience of Galileo the Scientist*]

Whereas L. insisted he must be allowed to give Galileo's character a markedly criminal evolution after the recantation in scene 13, he did not feel a similar need at the beginning of scene 9. Here too, to oblige the church, Galileo has for many years abstained from publicising his discoveries, but this cannot be considered a betrayal like the later one. At this point the people know very little about the new science, the cause of the new astronomy has not yet been taken up by the North Italian bourgeoisie, the battle fronts are not yet political. There may not be an open declaration on his part, but there is no recantation either. In this scene therefore it is still the scientist's personal impatience and dissatisfaction which must be portrayed.

When Does Galileo Become Antisocial?

The issue in Galileo's case is not that a man must stand up for his opinion as long as he holds it to be true; that would entitle him to be called a 'character'. The man who started it all, Copernicus, did not stand up for his opinion; it would be truer to say that he lay down for it inasmuch as he had it published only after his death; and yet, quite rightly, no one has ever reproached him for this. Something had been laid down to be picked up by anybody.

The man who had laid it down had gone, out of range of blame or thanks. Here was a scientific achievement which allowed simpler, shorter and more elegant calculations of celestial motions; so let humanity make use of it. Galileo's life's work is on the whole of the same order, and humanity used it. But unlike Copernicus who had avoided a battle, Galileo fought it and betrayed it. If Giordano Bruno, of Nola, who did not avoid the battle and had been burned twenty years earlier, had recanted, no great harm might have come of it; it could even be argued that his martyrdom deterred scientists more than it aroused them. In Bruno's time the battle was still a feeble one. But time did not stand still: a new class, the bourgeoisie with its new industries, had assertively entered the scene; no longer was it only scientific achievements that were at stake, but battles for their large-scale general exploitation. This exploitation had many aspects because the new class, in order to pursue its interests, had to come to power and smash the prevailing ideology that obstructed it. The church, which defended the privileges of princes and landowners as God-given and therefore natural, did not rule by means of astronomy, but it ruled within astronomy, as in everything else. And in no field could it allow its rule to be smashed. The new class, clearly, could exploit a victory in any field including that of astronomy. But once it had singled out a particular field and concentrated the battle in it, the new class became broadly vulnerable there. The maxim, 'A chain is as strong as its weakest link,' applies to chains that bind (such as the ideology of the church) as well as to transmission chains (such as the new class's new ideas about property, law, science, etc.). Galileo became antisocial when he led his science into this battle and then abandoned the fight.

Teaching

Words cannot do justice to the lightness and elegance with which L. conducted the little experiment with the pieces of ice in the copper basin. A fairly long reading from books was followed by the rapid demonstration. Galileo's relationship with his pupils is like a duel in which the fencing master uses all his feints—using them against the pupil to serve the pupil. Catching Andrea out in a hasty conclusion, Galileo crosses out his wrong entry in the record book with the same matter-of-fact patience as he displays in correcting the ice's position in the submersion experiment.

Silence

With his pupils he uses his tricks mainly to quell their dissatisfaction with him. They are offended by his keeping silent in the European controversy about sunspots, where his views are constantly being solicited as those of the greatest authority in the field. He knows he owes his authority to the church, and hence owes the clamour for his views to his silence. His authority was given him on condition that he should not use it. L. shows how Galileo suffers by the episode of the book on sunspots, which has been brought along and is discussed by his pupils. He pretends complete indifference, but how badly he does it! He is not allowed to leaf through the book, probably full of errors and thus twice as attractive. In little things he supports their revolt, though not himself revolting. When the lens grinder Federzoni angrily drops the scales on the floor because he cannot read Latin, Galileo himself picks them up— casually, like a man who would pick up anything that fell down.

Resumption of Research—a Sensual Pleasure

L. used the arrival of Ludovico Marsili, Virginia's fiancé, to show his disgust at the routine nature of his work. He organised the reception of his guest in such a way that it interrupted the work and made his pupils shake their heads. On being told that the reactionary pope was on his deathbed Galileo visibly began to enjoy his wine. His bearing changed completely. Sitting at the table, his back to the audience, he experienced a rebirth; he put his hands in his pockets, placed one leg on the bench in a delicious sprawl. Then he rose slowly and walked up and down with his glass of wine. At the same time he let it be seen how his future son-in-law, the landowner and reactionary, displeased him more with every sip. His instructions to the pupils for the new experiment were so many challenges to Ludovico. With all this, L. still took care to make it plain that he was seizing the opportunity for new research not by the forelock, but just by a single little hair.

The Gest of Work

The speech about the need for caution with which Galileo resumes a scientific activity that defies all caution shows L. in a rare gest of creative, very vulnerable softness.

Even Virginia's fainting spell on finding her fiancé gone barely interests Galileo. As the pupils hover over her, he says painfully: 'I've got to know.' And in saying it he did not seem hard.

10

Political Attitude on Dramatic Grounds

L. took the greatest interest in the tenth (carnival) scene, where the Italian people are shown relating Galileo's revolutionary doctrine to their own revolutionary demands. He helped sharpen it by suggesting that representatives of the guilds, wearing masks, should toss a rag doll representing a cardinal in the air. It was so important to him to demonstrate that property relationships were being threatened by the doctrine of the earth's rotation that he declined a New York production where this scene was to be omitted.

11

Decomposition

The eleventh scene is the decomposition scene. L. begins it with the same authoritative attitude as in the ninth scene. He does not permit his increasing blindness to detract one iota from his virility. (Throughout, L. strictly refused to exploit this ailment which Galileo had contracted in the pursuit of his profession, and which of course could easily have won him the sympathy of the audience. L. did not want Galileo's surrender to be ascribable to his age or physical defects. Even in his last scene he was a man who was spiritually, not physically broken.)

The playwright would sooner have Galileo's recantation in this scene, rather than let it take place before the Inquisition. Galileo executes it when he rejects the offer of the progressive bourgeoisie, in the person of the iron founder Vanni, to support him in his fight against the church, and insists that what he has written is an unpolitical scientific work. L. acted this rejection with the utmost abruptness and strength.

Two Versions

In the New York production L. changed his gest for the meeting with the cardinal inquisitor as he emerges from the inner chambers. In the California production he remained seated, not recognising the cardinal, while his daughter bowed. This created the impression of something ominous passing through, unrecognisable but bowing. In New York L. rose and himself acknowledged the cardinal's bow. The playwright finds no merit in the change, since it establishes a relationship between Galileo and the cardinal inquisitor which is irrelevant, and turns Galileo's ensuing remark, 'His attitude was respectful, I think,' into a statement rather than a question.

The Arrest

As soon as the chamberlain appears at the head of the stairs, Galileo hastily puts the book under his arm and runs upstairs, passing the startled chamberlain. Stopped short by the chamberlain's words, he leafs through the book as though its quality was all that mattered. Left standing on the lower part of the staircase, he must now retrace his steps. He stumbles. Almost at the footlights—his daughter has run to meet him—he completely pulls himself together and gives his instructions firmly and to the point. It becomes clear that he has taken certain precautions. Holding his daughter close and supporting her, he sets out to leave the hall at a rapid, energetic pace. When he reaches the wings the chamberlain calls him back. He receives the fateful decision with great composure. Acting thus, L. shows that this is neither a helpless nor an ignorant man who is being caught, but one who has made great mistakes.

13

A Difficulty for the Actor: Some Effects Become Apparent Only When the Play Is Seen a Second Time

In preparing for the recantation scene L. never neglected in the preceding scenes to exhibit in all their fine shades the compliance and noncompliance in Galileo's conduct vis-à-vis the authorities, even those instances which would only mean anything to a spectator who had already seen the entire play once. Both he and the playwright recognised that in this type of play certain details unavoidably depend on a knowledge of the whole.

The Traitor

In the book there is a stage direction for Galileo when he returns to his pupils after he recanted to the Inquisition: 'He is changed, almost unrecognisable.' The change in L. was not of a 'physical nature' as the playwright had intended. There was something infantile, bedwetting in his loose gait, his grin, indicating a self-release of the lowest order, as if restraints had been thrown off that had been very necessary.

This, like what follows, can best be seen in photographs of the California production.

Andrea Sarti is feeling sick; Galileo has asked for a glass of water for him, and now the little monk passes by him, his face averted. Galileo's gaze is answered by Federzoni, the artisan-scholar, and for some time the two stare at each other until the monk returns with the water. This is Galileo's punishment: it will be the Federzonis of future centuries who will have to pay for his betrayal at the very inception of their great career.

'Unhappy the Land'

The pupils have abandoned the fallen man. Sarti's last word had been: 'Unhappy is the land that breeds no hero.' Galileo has to think of an answer, then calls after them, too late for them to hear: 'Unhappy is the land that needs a hero.' L. says it soberly, as a statement by the physicist who wants to take away nature's privilege to ordain tragedies and mankind's need to produce heroes.

14

The Goose

Galileo spends the last years of his life on an estate near Florence as a prisoner of the Inquisition. His daughter Virginia, whom he has neglected to instruct, has become a spy for the Inquisition. He dictates his *Discorsi* to her, in which he lays down his main teachings. But to conceal the fact that he is making a copy of the book he exaggerates the extent of his failing eyesight. Now he pretends not to recognise a goose which she shows him, the gift of a traveller. His wisdom has been degraded to cunning. But his zest for food is undiminished: he instructs his daughter carefully how he wants the liver prepared. His daughter conceals neither her disbelief in his inability to see nor her contempt for his gluttony. And Galileo, aware that she defends him vis-à-vis the Inquisition's guards, sharpens the conflicts of her troubled conscience by hinting that he may be deceiving the Inquisition. Thus in the basest manner he experiments with her filial love and her devotion to the church. Nonetheless L. succeeded brilliantly in eliciting from the spectator not only a measure of contempt but also a measure of horror at degradations that debase. And for all this he had only a few sentences and pauses at his disposal.

Collaboration

Anxious to show that crime makes the criminal more criminal, L. insisted, during the adaptation of the original version, on a scene in which Galileo collaborates with the authorities in full view of the audience. There was another reason for this: during the scene Galileo makes the most dignified use of his well-preserved intellectual powers by analysing his betrayal for the benefit of his former pupil. So he now dictates to his daughter, to whom he had for many weeks been dictating his main work, the *Discorsi*, an abject letter to the archbishop in which he advises him how the Bible may be used for the suppression of starving artisans. In this he quite frankly shows his daughter his cynicism without being entirely able to conceal the effort this ignominious exercise costs him. L. was fully aware of the recklessness with which he swam against the stream by thus throwing away his character—no audience can stand a thing like that.

The Voice of the Visitor

Virginia has laid down the manuscript of the letter to the archbishop and gone out to receive a belated visitor. Galileo hears the voice of Andrea Sarti, formerly his favourite pupil, who had broken with him after the recantation. To those readers of the play who complained that it gave no description of the spiritual agonies to which our nuclear physicists were subjected by the authorities ordering the bombs, L. could show that no first-rate actor needs more than a fleeting moment to indicate such spiritual discomfort. It is of course right to compare Galileo's submissiveness towards his authorities with that of our physicists towards rulers whom they distrust, but it would be wrong to go all the way into their stomach pains. What would be gained by that? L. was simply making this the moment to display his bad conscience, which could not have been shown later in the scene when his betrayal is analysed, without getting in his way.

The Laughter

The laughter in the picture [in the Model Book] was not suggested by the text, and it was frightening. Sarti, the former favourite pupil, calls and Virginia overhears the strained conversation. When Galileo inquires about his former collaborators, Sarti answers with utter frankness calculated to hurt his master. They get to Federzoni, a lens grinder whom Galileo had made his scientific collaborator even though he had no Latin. When Sarti reports he is back in a shop grinding lenses Galileo answers: 'He can't read the books': Then L. makes him laugh. The laugh however does not contain bitterness about a society that treats science as something secret reserved for the well-to-do, but a disgraceful mocking of Federzoni's inadequacies together with a brazen complicity in his degradation, though this is simply (and completely) explained by his being inadequate. L. thus intended to make the fallen man a provocateur. Sarti, naturally, responds with indignation and seizes the opportunity to inflict a blow on the shameless recanter when Galileo cautiously inquires about Descartes's further work. Sarti coldly reports that Descartes shelved his investigations into the nature of light when he heard that Galileo had recanted. And Galileo once had exclaimed that he would willingly be 'imprisoned a thousand feet beneath the earth, if in exchange he could find out what light is'. L. inserted a long pause after this unpleasant information.

The Right to Submit

During the first sentences of his exchange with Sarti he listens inconspicuously for the footsteps of the Inquisition's official in the anteroom, who stops every now and then, presumably in order to eavesdrop. Galileo's inconspicuous listening is difficult to act since it must remain concealed from Sarti but not from the audience; concealed from Sarti because otherwise he would not take the prisoner's repentant remarks at face value. But Galileo must convey them to him at face value so that his visitor can cash them when he reaches foreign parts; it would not do at all if it were rumoured abroad that the prisoner was recalcitrant. Then the conversation reaches a point where Galileo abandons this way of speaking for the benefit of hostile ears, and proclaims, authoritatively and forcefully, that it is his right to submit. Society's command to its members to produce is but vague and accompanied by no manner of guarantee; a producer produces at his own risk, and Galileo can prove any time that being productive endangers his comfort.

Handing over the Book

L. made the disclosure about the existence of the *Discorsi* quickly and with exaggerated indifference; but in a way suggesting that the old man was only trying to get rid of the fruits of a regrettable lapse, with yet another implication beneath this: anxiety lest the visitor reject the imposition together with the risk involved in taking the book with him. As he was protesting ill-humouredly that he wrote the book only as a slave of habit—the thoroughly vicious habit of thinking—the spectator could see that he was also listening. (Having made his eyesight worse by secretly copying the book which is endangered by the Inquisition, when he wants to gauge Sarti's reaction he is wholly dependent on his ears.) Toward the end of his appeal he virtually abandons his attitude of 'condescending grandeur' and comes close to begging. The remark about having continued his scientific work simply to kill time, uttered when Sarti's exclamation 'The *Discorsi*!' had made him aware of his visitor's enthusiasm, came so falsely from L.'s lips that it could deceive no one.

It is furthermore important to realise that when Galileo so strongly emphasises his own condemnation of the teaching activities which are now forbidden to him he is mainly trying to deceive himself. Since working, let alone sharing the results with the outside world, would threaten whatever was left of his comfort, he himself is passionately against this 'weakness' which makes him like a cat that cannot stop catching mice. Indeed the audience is witnessing his defeat when it sees him yield so reluctantly yet helplessly to an urge fostered in him by society. He must consider the risks to be larger than ever because now he is wholly in the hands of the Inquisition; his punishment would no longer be a public one; and the body of people who formerly would have protested has dispersed—thanks to his own fault. And not only has the danger increased, but he would be too late now with any contribution anyway, since astronomy has become apolitical, the exclusive concern of scientists.

Watchfulness

After the young physicist has found the book for which the scientific community no longer dares to hope, he at once changes his opinion about his former teacher and launches, with great passion, into a rationalisation of Galileo's motives for the betrayal; motives, he finds, which exonerate him completely. Galileo has recanted so that he can go on with his work and find more evidence for the truth. Galileo listens for a while, interjecting monosyllables. What he is hearing now may well be all that he can expect posterity to say in recognition of his difficult and dangerous endeavour. First he seems to be testing his pupil's improvised theory, just in the same way as any other theory must be tested for its validity. But presently he discovers that it is not tenable. At this point, immersed in the world of his scientific concerns, he forgets his watchfulness vis-à-vis a possible eavesdropper: he stops listening for steps.

The Analysis

Galileo's great counterattack against the golden bridge opens with a scornful outburst that abandons all grandeur: 'Welcome to my gutter, dear colleague in science and brother in treason! I sold out, you are a buyer.' This is one of the few passages which gave L. trouble. He doubted whether the spectator would get the meaning of the words, apart from the fact that the words are not taken from Galileo's usual, purely logical vocabulary. L. could not accept the playwright's argument that there must be some gest simply showing how the opportunist damns himself by damning all who accept the rewards of opportunism; what he understood even less was that the playwright would be quite satisfied with the exhibition of a state of mind that defies rational analysis. The omission of a spiteful and strained grin at this point robbed the opening of the great instructional speech of its malice. It was not fully brought out that deriding the ignorant is the lowest form of instruction and that it is an ugly light that is shed solely for the purpose of letting one's own light shine. Because the lowest starting point was missing some spectators were unable to gauge the full height which L. undoubtedly reached in the course of the great speech, nor was it entirely possible to see the collapse of Galileo's vain and violently authoritarian attitude that coloured even his scientific statements. The theatrical content of the speech, in fact, is not directly concerned with the ruthless demonstration of bourgeois science's fall from grace at the beginning of its rise—its surrender of scientific knowledge to the rulers who are authorised 'to use it, not use it, abuse it, as it suits their ends'. The theatrical content derives from the whole course of the action, and the speech should show how well this perfect brain functions when it has to judge its owner. That man, the spectator should be able to conclude, is sitting in a hell more terrible than Dante's, where the true function of intellect has been gambled away.

Background of the Performance

It is important to realise that our performance took place at the time and in the country of the atom bomb's recent production and military application: a country where nuclear physics was then shrouded in deepest secrecy. The day the bomb was dropped will not easily be forgotten by anyone who spent it in the United States.

The Japanese war had cost the United States real sacrifices. The troop ships left from the west coast, and the wounded and the victims of tropical diseases returned there. When the news reached Los Angeles it was at once clear that this was the end of the hateful war, that sons and brothers would soon come home. But the great city rose to an astonishing display of mourning. The playwright heard bus drivers and saleswomen in fruit markets express nothing but horror. It was victory, but it was the shame of defeat. Next came the suppression of the tremendous energy source by the military and politicians, and this upset the intellectuals. Freedom of investigation, the exchange of scientific discoveries, the international community of scholars: all were jettisoned by authorities that were strongly distrusted. Great physicists left the service of their bellicose government in headlong flight; one of the best known took an academic position where he was forced to waste his working time in teaching rudimentary essentials solely to escape working for the government. It had become ignominious to make new discoveries.

[From *Aufbau eier Rolle/Laughtons Galilei*, East Berlin, Henschel, 1956.]

Appendices to 'Building Up a Part'
Sense and sensuality

The demonstrative style of acting, which depicts life in such a way that it is laid open to intervention by the human reason, and which strikes Germans as thoroughly doctrinaire, presented no special difficulty to the Englishman L. What makes the sense seem so striking and insistent once it is 'lugged in' is our particular lack of sensuality. To lack sensuality in art is certainly senseless, nor can any sense remain healthy if it is not sensual. Reason, for us, immediately implies something cold, arbitrary, mechanical, presenting us with such pairs of alternatives as ideas and life, passion and thinking, pleasure and utility. Hence when we stage a performance of our *Faust*—a regular occurrence for educational reasons—we strip it of all sensuality and thus transport the audience into an indefinite atmosphere where they feel themselves confronted with all sorts of thoughts, no single one of which they can grasp clearly. L. didn't even need any kind of theoretical information about the required 'style'. He had enough taste not to make any distinction between the supposedly lofty and the supposedly base, and he detested preaching. And so he was able to unfold the great physicist's contradictory personality in a wholly corporeal form, without either suppressing his own thoughts about the subject or forcing them on us.

Beard or no beard

In the California production L. acted without a beard, in the New York with one. This order has no significance, nor were there any fundamental discussions about it. It is the sort of case where the desire for a change can be the deciding factor. At the same time it does of course lead to modifications in the character. People who had seen the New York production confirmed what can be seen from the pictures [in the Model Book], namely that L. acted rather differently. But everything essential was still there, and the experiment can be taken as evidence to show how much room is left for the 'personal' element.

The leavetaking

Certainly nothing could have been more horrible than the moment when L. has finished his big speech and hastens to the table saying 'I must eat now', as though in delivering his insights Galileo has done everything that can be expected of him. His leavetaking from Sarti is cold. Standing absorbed in the sight of the goose he is about to eat, he replies to Sarti's repeated attempt to express his regard for him with a formal 'Thank you, sir'. Then, relieved of all further responsibility, he sits down pleasurably to his food.

Concluding remark

Though it resulted from several years of preparation and was brought about by sacrifices on the part of all concerned, the production of *Galileo* was seen by a bare ten thousand people. It was put on in two small theatres, a dozen times in each: first in Beverly Hills, Los Angeles, and then with a completely new cast in New York. Though all the performances were sold out the notices in the main papers were bad. Against that could be set the favourable remarks of such people as Charles Chaplin and Erwin Piscator, as well as the interest of the public, which looked like being enough to fill the theatre for some considerable time. But the size of the cast meant that the potential earnings were low even if business was really good, and when an artistically interested producer made an offer it had to be rejected because L., having already turned down a number of film engagements and made considerable sacrifices, could not afford to turn down another. So the whole thing remained a private operation by a great artist who, while earning his keep outside the theatre, indulged himself by displaying a splendid piece of work to a (not very large) number of interested parties.

Though this is something that needed to be said, it does not however convey the complete picture. Given the way the American theatre was organised in those years, it was impossible that such plays and such productions should reach their audience. Productions like this one, therefore, should be treated as examples of a kind of theatre that might become possible under other political and economic conditions. Their achievements, like their mistakes, make them object lessons for anyone who is looking for a theatre of great themes and rewarding acting.

[From Werner Hecht (ed.), *Materialien zu Brechts 'Leben des Galilei'*, pp. 78–80. In the last of these notes Brecht is perhaps being undeservedly kind to Laughton, since the actor's wariness of Communist associations, at a time when Brecht and Hanns Eisler were being heard by the Un-American Activities Committee, appears to have been another strong factor in deciding him to close the play.]

NOTE OF TWO CONVERSATIONS WITH CASPAR NEHER ABOUT *LIFE OF GALILEO*

After the Italian fashion, a lightly built stage that is recognisable as having been lightly built. Nothing stony, weighty, massive. No interior decoration.

Colour to emerge from the costumes, i.e. in movement.

The stage shows Galileo's background, making use of contemporary evidence (Leonardo's technical drawings, Romulus and Remus with the she-wolf, a man of war from the Venice arsenal and so on).

No projections, since this would prevent the full illumination of the stage. Giant photographs, maybe, nobly suspended. A flagged floor.

[Dated October 3 and 5, 1955. From Werner Hecht (ed.), *ibid.*, p. 88. The eventual stage set for the Berliner Ensemble's production, completed by Erich Engel after Brecht's death and first performed on January 15, 1957, was somewhat different from this.]

Editorial Notes

Much of the information that follows, including some of the quotations from Brecht, is derived from Ernst Schumacher's *Drama und Geschichte. Bertolt Brecht's 'Leben des Galilei' und andere Stücke,* Henschel, East Berlin 1965, whose usefulness is gratefully acknowledged.

I. GENERAL

Judging by the proportion of Brecht's papers devoted to it in the Brecht Archive in Berlin, *Galileo* is much the most heavily worked-over of all his plays. None of the others went through such stages, for not only did *Galileo* occupy him during the last nineteen years of his life, but its linguistic, theatrical, and thematic bases all changed drastically during that period, as did the dramatist's own circumstances. Thus it was written in German, then entirely rewritten in English (with Brecht himself contributing in a mixture of English and German), then rewritten in German once more largely on the basis of the English-language version. Again, it was first written with no clear prospect of production, then rewritten for a specific actor, Laughton, and a specific production before an American audience, then rewritten once more for Brecht's own Berliner Ensemble to play in East Berlin. During Brecht's work on the first version, it became known that Niels Bohr had split the uranium atom; then while he and Laughton were preparing the second, the first atom bomb dropped on Hiroshima, on August 6, 1945. Finally, Brecht himself was at first living as an exile, close to Germany, on the eve of an impending war; he rewrote the play once in the aura of Hollywood, when an Allied victory was at last certain, then the second time after his own successful reestablishment in his country, within a bitterly divided world.

There are thus three principal versions of the play whose differences will be described in what follows. The first is the German version whose earliest typescript was entitled *The Earth Moves* and which was originally written in November 1938. What appear to be early sketches lay down a structure as follows:

Life of Galileo

1. PADUA/Welcoming the new age/Copernicus's hypothesis/authoritarian economy in Italy.
2. SIGNORIA/Landscape.
3. RESEARCH/Danger of the truth/speech about reason and its seductions.
4. DEMONSTRATIONS/The addicts of authority exhorted to see.
5. PLAGUE.
6. COLLEGIUM ROMANUM/The Copernican system ridiculed.
7. THE DECREE/On the church's responsibilities/the ch. system too all-embracing.
7a. CONVERSATION/The monk's parents/Horace.
8. THE SUNSPOTS/On science/Keunos.
9. The new age without fear/strict research/hope in working people.
9a. BALLAD
10. THE INQUISITION'S SUMMONS.
11. INQUISITION/Condemnation of doubt.
12. RECANTATION/Praise of steadfastness.
13. THE PRISONER/Passage from the *Discorsi*/On the scientist's duty/On expropriation/The new age, a harridan.
14. SMUGGLING.

It did not take long to complete. On November 17 his secretary-collaborator Margarete Steffin wrote to Walter Benjamin:

Ten days ago Brecht began getting *Galileo* down in dramatic form, after it had been plaguing his mind for some while. He has already finished nine of the fourteen scenes, and very fine they are.

A mere six days after that, according to his diary, he had completed it, commenting that

The only scene to present difficulties was the last one. As in *St. Joan* [*of the Stockyards*] I needed some sort of twist at the end to make absolutely certain of the necessary detachment on the part of the audience. At any rate, now even a man subject to unthinking empathy must experience the A-effect in the course of identifying himself with Galileo. A legitimate degree of empathy occurs, given strictly epic presentation.

On January 6, 1939, the *Berlingske Tidende* published an interview in which he said that the play was 'really written for New York'; this referred no doubt to his discussions with Ferdinand Reyher. A few weeks later he carefully revised it under the title *Life of Galileo* and had a number of duplicated copies run off, of which Walter Benjamin and Fritz Sternberg each appear to have been given one. This was also to all intents and purposes the version sent to Zurich and staged there in the middle of the war.

But already Brecht was dissatisfied with it:

Technically, *Life of Galileo* is a great step backwards, far too opportunistic, like *Señora Carrar's Rifles*. The play would need to be completely rewritten to convey that 'breath of wind that cometh from new shores', that rosy dawn of science. It would all have to be more direct, without the interiors, the atmospherics, the empathy. And all switched to planetary demonstration. The division into scenes can be kept, Galileo's characterisation likewise, but work, the pleasures of work, would need to be realised in practical form, through contact with a theatre. The first thing would be to study the *Fatzer* and *Breadshop* fragments [two unfinished plays dating from before 1933]. Technically those represent the highest standard.

So he noted on February 25. On the 27th he heard a Danish radio interview with three of Niels Bohr's assistants, one of whom, Professor C. Møller, knew Brecht and later recalled discussing Galileo and the *Discorsi* with him early the previous year. This interview described the splitting of the uranium atom, which (so Ernst Schumacher suggests) may have prompted the passage in the revised text about 'the greatest discoveries . . . being made at one or two places'. The revision, however, certainly did nothing to change the play 'technically'. Though an early but undated note speaks of a *Life of Galileo* version for workers, there appears to be no indication that a start was ever made on this.

The second or American version dates from April 1944, when Brecht took up the play again as a result of a meeting with Jed Harris, the producer of Thornton Wilder's *Our Town*. A translation of the

first version had already been made by Desmond Vesey; in addition
Brecht now got a rough interlinear translation made by one of his own
collaborators, followed by a new acting version by two of Orson
Welles's associates, Brainerd Duffield and Emerson Crocker. The two
last-named had been recommended to him by Charles Laughton, who
seems to have become interested in the play some time that autumn
and to have used their version for his own work with Brecht on the
adaptation. 'Now working systematically with Laughton on the translation and stage version of *The Life of the Physicist Galileo*' said a diary note of December 10. In the course of this activity, which lasted
off and on until December 1945, Brecht redrafted many passages in a
remarkable mixture of German and English; thus his sketch for the
beginning of scene 4 runs:

Rede des Mathematikers
Das Universum des göttlichen Aristoteles mit seinen
mystisch musizierenden Sphären und Kristallnen Gewöl-
circles   heavenly bodies
ben sowie den Kreisläufen seiner Himmelskörper,
obliquity of the ecliptic
seinem Schiefenwinkel der Sonnenbahn/den Geheimnissen
Sternen
der Table of Cords, dem/Reichtum des Catalogue
inspirierten
for the southern hemisphere/der/construction of a
celestial globe is ein Gebäude von grosser Ordnung
und Schönheit.
The Universe of divine Classics.

For the New York production, which took place after Brecht's return
to Europe, there were, according to its director Joseph Losey, 'Different words, thanks in part to the collaboration of George Tabori in
rewriting with Laughton and me from notes left behind in New York
by Brecht.'

The text as we reproduce it in the appendix (pp. 195ff) was published by Indiana University Press in 1953 in *From the Modern
Repertoire, Series Two*, edited by Eric Bentley, then in *Seven Plays by
Bertolt Brecht*, Grove Press, New York, 1961, and separately by
Grove Press again in 1966. The play still struck Brecht himself as formally conventional, to judge from a note of January 1945 which
found that

with its interiors and atmospheric effects the construction of the scenes, derived from the epic theatre, makes a singularly theatrical impact.

He also told an interviewer somewhat apologetically that summer that 'Galileo is anyway interesting as a contrast to my parables. Where they embody ideas, it extracts ideas from a subject'. And on July 30 he noted that 'I wouldn't go to the stake for the formal aspects of this play.'

In 1953, he got Elisabeth Hauptmann and Benno Besson of the Berliner Ensemble, with some advice from Ruth Berlau to draft a third version in German, using the best parts of the previous texts. This he himself revised to form the play which was given its German première at Cologne in April 1955, published as *Versuche 14* and subsequently rehearsed by him for some three months with his own company. With minor amendments it is the text of the *Gesammelte Werke* on which our edition is based. It differs substantially from the second version, not least by being very much longer.

2. THE FIRST VERSION, 1938–1943

From Brecht's first completed typescript, dating presumably from November 1938, to the text used for the Zurich production of 1943, the play remained essentially the same, the only changes of real substance being those in the last scene but one, which define the nature of Galileo's crime. The general structure of this first version was already very similar to that of the text which we have followed, and certain scenes, or large parts of them, were taken into the latter without drastic rewriting, for instance the first half of scene 1, scene 3, the start of scene 4, scene 5b (Plague), scene 6 (Collegium Romanum), much of scene 8, scene 11 (The Pope) and the last (Smuggling) scene. Even the carnival scene (10) had the same place, gist and purpose, though the ballad round which it centres was later rewritten. There were, however, some striking differences among the characters. To sum these up briefly:

Mrs. Sarti originally died of the plague in scene 5b. The character in 9 was 'the housekeeper'. This was altered after the first typescript.

Ludovico, Virginia's fiancé, did not appear till scene 7 (The Ball). He was then called Sitti, and was not a member of the landowning aristocracy; indeed in scene 9 (Sunspots) he lamented that he had no fortune of his own. His function of introducing Galileo to the principle of the telescope (scenes 1 and 2) was performed by a silly-ass character called Doppone, son of a wool merchant, whose only other appearance was, briefly, as a papal chamberlain in the ball scene.

Virginia was much less contemptuously treated by her father. Her relations with Andrea were friendlier, though her role in the penultimate scene was the same.

Federzoni the lens grinder did not figure in the play at all. Some of his lines were spoken by an 'elderly scholar'.

Vanni the iron founder did not figure in the play either.

A stove-fitter and a doctor appeared in the penultimate scene.

In the first typescript the play was called *The Earth Moves* (*Die Erde bewegt sich*) and the scenes bore no titles. The title *Life of Galileo*, together with the individual scene titles, more or less in their final form, are to be found in the revised scripts of early 1939. The verses before each scene are absent from this version.

The following is a scene-by-scene account of it.

I

GALILEO GALILEI, TEACHER OF MATHEMATICS
IN PADUA, SETS OUT TO DEMONSTRATE
THE NEW COPERNICAN SYSTEM

Galileo's long speech about the 'new age' (pp. 6–8) was about ten lines shorter, omitting inter alia the passages about the ships previously hugging the shores and about the masons in Siena, but taking in the lines about 'those old constructions that people have believed for the last thousand years' which come at the close of the scene in the final text (p. 17). Andrea's age was not originally specified, but the revised versions make him thirteen (as opposed to eleven in the final text).

The whole episode with Ludovico is absent. Instead Galileo explains to Andrea the nature of a hypothesis. Copernicus, he says, knows that the earth rotates

only because he has worked it out. Actually he doesn't know it at all. He's assuming it. It's simply what is called a hypothesis. No facts. No proofs. They're being looked for. A few people in Prague and in England are looking for the proofs. It's the greatest hypothesis there has ever been, but it's no more than that. Hence the great flaw in the new system is that nobody who isn't a mathematician *can* understand why it's like that and can't be any other way. All I've showed you is that it can be that way. There's no reason why not, if you see what I mean.

ANDREA: Can't I become a mathematician and find out the reason why it should?

GALILEO: And how am I going to pay the butcher and the milkman and the bookseller if I start giving you lessons for nothing? Off you go, now; I must get on with my work.

In the revised versions Andrea asks 'What's a hypothesis?' and gets the answer which the final text puts at the end of the scene, down to 'that can hardly see at all' (p. 17), concluding 'Copernicus's hypothesis is the greatest hypothesis there has ever been, but it's no more than that.'

ANDREA: Then what about what the church is saying? What's that?

GALILEO: Oh, that's a hypothesis too, but not such a good one. Lots of flaws that don't explain very much. But the great flaw of the new system . . .

—and so on, as above.

The episode with the procurator of the university, which follows, is close to the final text, though the reference to the scientific implications of 'the cry for better looms' is lacking. Doppone appears *after* this, and is taken on as a private pupil for thirty scudi a month; his father wants him to become a theologian, since he likes arguing. Before leaving, he tells Galileo about the telescope, which Galileo then constructs from two lenses bought for him by Andrea. The scene ends with them looking through it.

GALILEO: You didn't eat the apple—which shows you've got the makings of a mathematician. A taste for unrewarding art. I'll teach you. It won't break me. This flimflam is worth five hundred scudi.

ANDREA (*after Galileo has allowed him another look*): How clearly one sees. Here's Signor Gambione the bailiff coming up to our house.

GAMBIONE: Quick, shove those forty-five scudi in your pocket!

2

GALILEO PRESENTS A NEW INVENTION TO THE
REPUBLIC OF VENICE

Federzoni and Ludovico do not figure in this scene, which is dated August 24, 1609. Nor does Virginia. The telescope is handed over by Andrea, who however has nothing to say. The scene starts with Galileo's telling Sagredo that he has used it to look at the moon. Then his presentation speech is read for him by the procurator, including as Galileo's own the emphasis on the instrument's military usefulness; he adds a comment that Galileo hopes to continue serving the Venetians. During this speech Doppone appears and tries to catch the eye of Galileo, who is annoyed and embarrassed: 'It's one of my pupils, an unbelievable idiot. I can't imagine what he wants.' As the city fathers try the instrument Galileo goes on talking to Sagredo about its relevance to Copernican theory.

> GALILEO (*without looking at him*): How about this? Flecks of light on the dark portion of the disk, dark patches on the bright sickle. It fits almost too well. Of course, I'm very sceptical, extremely sceptical.

The scene ends with Doppone breaking through the Doge's guards and saying breathlessly:

> Signor Galilei, why wouldn't you listen to me before the presentation? It's all wrong. The cover ought to be green. It was green; trust Doppone.

3

JANUARY 10, 1610: BY MEANS OF THE TELESCOPE GALILEO
DISCOVERS CELESTIAL PHENOMENA WHICH PROVE
THE COPERNICAN SYSTEM. WARNED BY HIS FRIEND OF
THE POSSIBLE CONSEQUENCES OF HIS INVESTIGATIONS,
GALILEO AFFIRMS HIS FAITH IN REASON

Up to Mrs. Sarti's exit two-thirds of the way through (p. 28) this scene is very close to the final text, the main differences being the omission of Galileo's six lines on the value of star charts for navigation (p. 24);

the fact that Sarti appears 'in night attire'; and the doubling of Galileo's eventual salary (one thousand scudi in this version, as against the final five hundred). The episode with Virginia is then shifted to the end of the scene, after Sagredo's second 'Don't go to Florence, Galileo!' (p. 31), which leads to a cross-fade, thus:

GALILEO: You'd do better helping me write my letter to the Floren-
tines.
SAGREDO: You really mean to go there?
GALILEO: Certainly. And with the tube. And with the truth. And with my belief in human reason.
SAGREDO: Then there's nothing more to say, is there? *He leaves hurriedly without speaking.*
GALILEO: *laughs as he sits down at the telescope and starts making notes. It gets dark. When the lights come on again it is morning. Galileo is still sitting at this table writing by two candles. He has his coat on, as the fire has evidently gone out. A bell is ringing for early mass. Enter Galileo's very young daughter Virginia, warmly dressed.*

As in the final text she announces that she is going to matins, though without mention of Ludovico. In her dialogue with her father, which is rather differently phrased here, he does not snub her with such words as 'It's not a toy' (p. 29) and 'Nothing in your line', though she complains of never being allowed to look through the telescope. He then tells her to read his letter to Duke Cosimo to see if it is humble enough, and she reads out the text which is now at the end of the scene. They discuss it, and in conclusion he sleepily comments:

The only way an unpopular and embarrassing man can get a job that gives him enough free time is by crawling on his belly.
VIRGINIA *hugging him*: Shall we have a big house there?
GALILEO: Time, that's the main thing, my dear, time!

Virginia expresses no particular joy about going to court.

4

GALILEO HAS EXCHANGED THE VENETIAN REPUBLIC FOR THE COURT OF FLORENCE. THE DISCOVERIES HE HAS MADE WITH THE HELP OF THE TELESCOPE ARE MET WITH DISBELIEF BY THE COURT SCHOLARS

The first part, up to the quarrel between the two boys, is close to the final text, apart from the substitution of the court chamberlain for Cosimo's tutor and the fact that in the earliest typescript Mrs. Sarti's opening speech was about a third of its subsequent length. After that, however, the scene was, in the main, differently written (again, without Federzoni) and incorporated scene 5a, thus reducing the plague scene to 5b only. In this version the reason given for Cosimo's sudden departure was not the court ball but 'a particularly important message', leading the three representatives of orthodox physics to continue the speculations with which they made their original appearance.

I wonder what sort of a message His Highness got? I don't like those cases of illness in the old town—The message couldn't possibly have anything to do with that! The medical faculty is quite certain that . . . *There is a knock on the door downstairs. Mrs. Sarti opens it. Virginia comes in with a travelling bag* (p. 41).

And so into 5a.

The preceding argument between Galileo and the three scholars (who in the typescript were simply Professors A, B, and C, before being distinguished in the revised versions as astronomer, mathematician and theologian) is the same in substance, but largely different in form. There is no formal dispute, no attempt to use Latin, no accompanying court ladies; the dialogue is slacker and more repetitive. Galileo's references to his work with the employees of the Venice arsenal and to the sailors are not yet included (p. 40). On the other hand, he begins his immediately preceding speech with:

You must realise that it is up to you to set an example and trust your reason. That the meanest stableboy is waiting to be encouraged and challenged to trust your reason.

The next lines about 'doctrines believed to be unshakeable are beginning to totter' were already there in the first typescript.

The cannibalised 5a is somewhat differently arranged, since Galileo appears at the top of the stairs, chuckling at the scholars' panicky departure, sees Virginia and asks what she is doing here (when she should be at her convent school). Virginia's presence in this scene was in fact an amendment to the first typescript, which originally gave her lines to the neighbour's wife. Mrs. Sarti then announced that the neighbour had arranged a carriage to take them all away, but Brecht changed this to 'The court is sending a carriage' and added the lackey's speech which in this version finished with a friendly message from Cosimo to Andrea.

After Mrs. Sarti's 'But it's not exactly sensible' (p. 43) Galileo adds:

> And I can tell you another reason. In times like these nobody can say how long he's going to remain alive. *He smiles.* So let's go and paint more stars on the lens. *Goes into his study.*

The first two of these sentences were added in pen to the original typescript.

5b [5]

UNDETERRED EVEN BY THE PLAGUE, GALILEO CARRIES ON WITH HIS RESEARCHES

Originally, after the old woman's 'Your mother may be there', Andrea replied 'No, she's dead'. Brecht, however, amended this on the typescript to read as now. Otherwise the differences from the final text are insignificant. Conceivably this scene was a last-minute addition to the first typescript. The numbering and typing seem to suggest it.

6 [5 *on first typescript*, 6 *in revised versions*]

1616: THE VATICAN RESEARCH INSTITUTE, THE COLLEGIUM ROMANUM, CONFIRMS GALILEO'S FINDINGS

Virtually the same as the final text, apart from the ending, which in the first typescript (later reworded) read:

> *The astronomer escorts him in.*
> THE ASTRONOMER: That was him, Your Eminence.
> THE INQUISITOR *very politely*: May I look through the tube?
> I find this tube extremely interesting.

7 [6 *in first typescript only*]

BUT THE INQUISITION PLACES COPERNICUS'S TEACHINGS ON THE INDEX (MARCH 5, 1616)

Though the structure and general gist of this, the ball scene, are the same as in the final version, there are considerable differences in the dialogue. Partly this is due to the fact that Ludovico, who makes his first appearance here, is not specifically identified with the aristocracy or even, in the first typescript, given a surname; hence the absence of the First Secretary's reference to 'All the great families of Italy', with their resounding names. Doppone also makes a last brief entry, speaking jerkily like Mr. Jingle:

GALILEO: I've concluded my business here.
DOPPONE: Yes, I know—known to one and all—brilliant triumph—sat at your feet myself—epicircle and all that.

Neither Galileo's verse ('Fret not, daughter') nor the Lorenzo de' Medici madrigal are included. The old cardinal does not appear, and Bellarmin and Barberini are in different disguises, the former as a fox, the latter as a donkey.

In Galileo's argument with these two cardinals some of the key phrases are already there, such as Barberini's reference to astronomy as 'the itch', Galileo's pronouncement 'I believe in men's reason' (only uttered once however), Bellarmin's account of the Campagna peasants whose situation can only be justified by positing a Higher Being, and Barberini's objection that Galileo is accusing God of 'the most elementary errors in astronomy' (p. 56). Bellarmin's reference to star charts and navigation, however, is once again missing, as is the subsequent bandying of Biblical texts and Barberini's 'Welcome to Rome...' (p. 55) to which it leads. Instead the dialogue runs (after 'the itch'):

BELLARMIN: Unfortunately not only have the new theories displaced our good earth, which the Almighty designated as our dwelling place, from the centre of the cosmos, in an almost contemptuous way, but the assumption of utterly incredible distances in the cosmos makes the world seem so tiny that the interest which God evidently takes in the human race becomes almost impossible to understand.

GALILEO: As the Collegium Romanum has at last admitted . . .

BELLARMIN: What we feel is, that to say it's easier to explain phenomena by positing that the earth moves and the sun stands still, than by accepting the Ptolemaic cycles and epicycles, is a wholly admirable thing, risks nothing and is all right for mathematicians. But suppose one tried to suggest that the sun is really at the centre of our world and rotates only round itself without moving across from east to west while the earth circles round the sun at immense speed, then that would be a very risky affair, don't you think, because it would upset philosophy and the theologians, who are awkward customers and what's more it would make the scriptures untrue.

BARBERINI: But don't you see, Bellarmin, the scriptures don't satisfy his reason? Whereas Copernicus does . . .

After Barberini, leading Bellarmin aside, has asked Galileo about the possibility of God giving the stars irregular movements, Galileo makes much the same reply as in the final text, but forgets himself and calls the future pope 'my dear man'. Then the instruction to the secretaries not to take the discussion down comes some two dozen lines later than in the final text, just before Bellarmin formally tells Galileo of the Holy Office's decision. This is not repeated by the secretary, but in the revised versions Bellarmin on leaving instructs the secretaries to 'Make a note of the fact that I have today informed Signor Galileo of the degree of the Holy Office concerning the Copernican doctrine'.

The remainder of the scene, with the inquisitor, is almost as in the final text, except that he enters with two ladies, saying:

> Oh, truly I don't know half what you do. You're so much crueller than I ever could be.

and in asking Virginia about her engagement omits the words 'your future husband comes from a distinguished family' (p. 58).

8 [*Transformation scene*]

This conversation with the little monk has no title, and is presumably intended to be played before the curtain. Its general direction, and much of its dialogue, have remained constant since the first typescript, though Brecht continually added to it. Notable differences in the first version are:

(1) The start:

THE LITTLE MONK: You're right.
GALILEO: Haven't you read the Index Congregation's decree?
THE LITTLE MONK: I have read it.
GALILEO: After that you can't go on saying I'm right, wearing the
   habit you wear.
THE LITTLE MONK: I have been unable to sleep for four nights
(etc.).

(2) In the first typescript Galileo's next speech ran:

> See that man down there hiding behind the oleanders and peep-
> ing up now and again? Since the cardinal inquisitor looked
> through my tube I've never lacked for company. They're very
> interested in criminals in Rome. I'll give him one of my tubes to
> help him observe me better.
> THE LITTLE MONK: Please believe me when I say that I have
> nothing to do with that man and the people who sent him. I'm a
> mathematician.
> GALILEO: And I'm a criminal.

This was removed in revision. Then, after the little monk's long speech
about his peasant family, ending 'a vast goodness of soul?' (p. 63),
Galileo originally went straight to the speech about the Priapus (p. 64).
The first part of his comment on the situation of the peasants was
added on the first typescript, but not the passage about the oyster and
the pearls. The important exchange about whether the truth will out
('The only truth that gets through will be what we force through',
p. 65) was added in the process of revision. The ensuing sentence about
'divine patience' is not in this version.

9 [8 or 7 in first typescript]

AFTER KEEPING SILENT FOR EIGHT YEARS GALILEO
IS ENCOURAGED BY THE ACCESSION OF A NEW POPE,
WHO IS HIMSELF A SCIENTIST, TO RESUME HIS RESEARCHES
INTO THE FORBIDDEN AREA. THE SUNSPOTS

Apart from the penultimate scene, this is the most heavily amended of
them all. In place of Federzoni there is the 'elderly scholar', while, in
the first typescript only, 'the housekeeper' figured instead of Mrs.
Sarti. The exchanges with Ludovico are entirely different, as well as
shorter; again Ludovico is no aristocrat, and his nervousness about his

prospective father-in-law's theories seems to stem from hints dropped at the university where he is a student without private means. The order of events also underwent subsequent changes.

Thus the scene opens with Galileo demonstrating the behaviour of floating bodies. He begins with an extended version of the remarks later put after the experiment with the needle (p. 70):

> GALILEO: The aim of science is not to open the door to everlasting wisdom, but to set a limit to everlasting error. Philosophy for the most part is limitless, wild and indefinite, but truth is restricted and contained in small examples. A main cause of poverty in the sciences is the illusion of wealth. We only conquer nature by obeying her. Whatever counts as a cause when we are observing counts as a rule when we are putting something into effect. By observing the small errors on which the great philosophies are erected we arrived in the course of the summer at all kinds of concepts which have been obstructing the advance of science ever since Aristotle's time. Such as cold and thinness, dampness and length, from which some people think they can construct a whole world if they put the words together the right way.

Andrea then puts the Aristotelian case, about the ice and the needle, going on to describe Galileo's disproof of it while Galileo demonstrates. When he succeeds they all laugh, leading the women to make their remarks about laughter (p. 71) up to Sarti's 'I don't know'.

Mucius then appears, and is dealt with very much as in the final text. Then after Galileo has gone into his study Virginia and Mrs. Sarti have their chat about horoscopes (p. 68), in its final from—an episode which was not, however, in the first typescript—before Andrea starts asking Galileo about sunspots, saying he has read Fabricius's book. The dialogue here is largely different. Thus when the elderly scholar asks Galileo 'Is it really right to keep one's mouth shut?' Galileo replies with the Keuner story about the man who was asked if he would serve his enemy, served him for seven years till he died, and then bundled up his corpse, scrubbed out the room, breathed deeply and replied 'No'. Only Galileo tells it, in the first typescript, of 'Mr. Sarrone, a philosopher in Modena', amended to 'the Cretan philosopher Keunos, who was much loved by the Cretans for his libertarian views'. As the others laugh Andrea shakes his head and (in the revised versions) says he doesn't care for the story.

Gaffone the rector makes his brief appearance, as on p. 68, followed by some twenty lines of dialogue between the two women, including

Virginia's remark about 'a very high church person' (p. 66), some references to signs of official surveillance, and an inquiry to Andrea about his fiancée:

> VIRGINIA: How's Jessica? Are you still quarrelling?
> ANDREA *laughing*: No, I've found out now why she didn't want to marry me. Pangs of conscience. Because astronomers are unholy people, you know. Of course that wasn't a very serious obstacle. We're together again. *Goes upstairs.*
> MRS. SARTI [in the revised versions]: She knows she's doing well for herself. Her father's just an ordinary artisan . . .

Ludovico enters in travelling clothes, followed by a servant, saying he has got to speak to Galileo, about a rumour. Is he writing a book on sunspots? Galileo says what nonsense; did Ludovico come all the way to ask that?

> LUDOVICO: I hope you understand. They're all talking about Copernicus again in connection with these sunspots. And I was hoping you weren't getting involved. I've already had hints dropped at the university.
> GALILEO: Oh, so you're frightened?

Like the final Ludovico, this one brings the news that Barberini may soon be pope. Much of Galileo's speech in the first typescript about what his election might mean for science—e.g.

> This means nothing less than the start of a new century of the arts and sciences. No more fear. Knowledge will be a passion and research a self-indulgence. What a dreadful age, where saying what is, is considered a crime. But now people will say, what a dreadful age it was. Who's scared of discoveries now, they'll ask. Who's got reason to be?

—was shifted to immediately in front of his 'Put a grid of squares on the screen' (p. 74), so that his order to focus the telescope on the sun follows instantly on the news, without any of the teasing of Ludovico which is found in the final text. Ludovico begs him not to join in the sunspot controversy, to which Galileo answers:

> . . . Are they to say Galileo hasn't got the courage to open his mouth? People are looking at me, man. The earth rotates—it's I who say that, do you get me? If I keep silent it'll stop!

LUDOVICO: Virginia, I know I love you. But I can't marry you if this is how things are, I haven't any money of my own.

Andrea suggests Galileo should help them. 'My Jessica has come to terms with her conscience, but after all she's only risking hell. I don't know what she'd do if the city clergy stopped getting their communion vessels from her father the silversmith. A threat of that sort is far worse.' But Galileo turns away to his collaborators.

LUDOVICO: Virginia, I love you, and I love your father the way he is. But his concerns are not mine; I don't understand them and I haven't got the courage.

And because Galileo remains silent, Virginia gives Ludovico back his ring.

Thus virtually everything in the final text from Mrs. Sarti's 'Almost!' (p. 74) to Andrea's interruption (p. 76) is missing in this version. Galileo goes straight on to his big speech (p. 76), including already such key phrases as 'My object is not to establish that I have been right all along but to find out if I am' and 'And whatever we wish to find we shall regard, once found, with particular mistrust.' As Ludovico embraces Virginia and leaves, Galileo continues (from 'go on talking all the same')

Then we'll crush this stupidity underfoot, eh, my boy? We'll peel off its skin to carry as our banner. And we'll write on it in blood: look out! Or, rather, in ink—which is more dangerous. At last we're going to bang those narrow-minded heads together till they burst like eggshells. Yes, we're going to make cruel use of our arguments. Perhaps it'll be the first time in history that cruelty has been directed against ignorance. A historic date!

ANDREA: And are you going to write the book on the world systems?

GALILEO: Yes, and not in Latin for the few but in Tuscan for the many. Because this book has got to be understood by everybody. For that I need people who work with their hands. Who else is going to want to know the causes of everything? [Then, in the revised versions, as on p. 76 to 'will probably laugh'.] And the peasants who force their plough into the earth, and the weavers at their looms, the people now stirring in every street, are all going to point at the sun and say: it's not a golden coat of arms but a motor. We move it, because it moves us.

Virginia repacks her trousseau, and Andrea closes the scene with his four-line epigram from p. 73.

10 [*9 or 8 in first typescript*]

THE COPERNICAN DOCTRINE CIRCULATES AMONG
THE COMMON PEOPLE

The setting is a street, with a street singer and his wife singing to a hurdy-gurdy and the populace listening from windows. The ballad differs, above all structurally, from that in the final text, and goes roughly as follows:

> Great Galileo told the sun
> (Or so the story says)
> To give up turning around the earth
> On which it casts its rays.
> What a to-do!
> The sun has started turning around itself
> Not around me and you.
>
> And immediately the sun had ceased
> Reserving all its light for us
> The verger gave up following after the priest
> The apprentice after his boss.
> No doubt you've guessed:
> They all want to turn around themselves
> And do what suits them best.
>
> The bricklayer who was building the house
> Is now its occupier.
> The woodcutter who chops down trees
> Puts the wood on his own fire.
> What a to-do!
> The woodcutter was telling his wife
> His feet were frozen through.
>
> I saw two housewives shopping for fish
> The clock was striking twelve.
> The fishwife took out a piece of bread
> And ate the fish herself

What a to-do!
The fishwife thought she'd have fish for once
Very nutritious too.

The master appears, the maids don't get up
The footmen omit to bow.
The master observes to his great surprise
Nothing turns around him now.
No doubt you've guessed:
The footmen have their hands too full
The maids give them no rest.

THE WOMAN
I too had been dancing out of line
And said to my husband, 'My dear
What you do for me might well be done
By any other star.'

THE MAN
What a to-do!
My wife ought to turn around no one but me—
That's always been my view.

The princes clean their boots with their own hands.
The emperor bakes his own bread.
The soldiers no longer obey commands
But stroll in the streets instead.
No doubt you've guessed:
There was too much work for too many to do.
In the end they had to protest.

(*In a confidential undertone*)
The cardinals all stood in St. Peter's Square
When the pope showed himself to the crowd
The cardinals acted as if he weren't there
And went on talking too loud.
What a to-do!
Their eminences have taken to kissing their own feet—
You know who that's due to.

Three archangels came down to earth, to complain
It should praise God more audibly.
But the earth said; 'There are so many worlds in space

Why do they have to pick on me?'
No doubt you've guessed:
If our earth is just one of a whole lot of worlds
It can share such chores with the rest.

At the end of the ballad '*a Jesuit crosses the square. He crouches when he hears the song, and goes off like a drenched poodle. The people laugh and throw down coins.*'

A note then says that the scene can develop into a ballet. '*A popular carnival celebration can be shown in the style of Brueghel's* The Battle Between Carnival and Lent. *Following the first verse of the ballad a carnival procession can move across the square, including a man dressed as a BIBLE with a hole in it, and a cart with a monk stretching out, trying with both hands to hold back a collapsing ST. PE-TER'S THRONE. Then after the last verse the MOON, SUN, EARTH and PLANETS can appear and demonstrate the new system of motion in a dance, to a severe musical setting.*'

11 [*10 or 9 in first typescript*]

1633. THE INQUISITION SUMMONS THE WORLD-FAMOUS SCIENTIST TO ROME

This short scene in the Medici palace is close to the final text, except that the episode with Vanni the iron founder from Virginia's 'Here's Mr. Vanni' on p. 83 to Galileo's 'you risk losing your arm' on p. 84 is not in this version. Instead a man passes to whom Galileo vainly calls out 'Galliardo! Galliardo!', commenting:

That was the director of artillery equipment. He must have seen me. He usually eats out of my hand. Today he's running away as if he thought I was infectious.

Then a student passes, who wants to stop and talk to Galileo but is called away by his tutor. Just before Cosimo's entrance Galileo comments:

After all, we're not here to get polite attentions paid us. I crawled into this position years ago on all fours, since anybody wanting to introduce the truth—or even a morsel of it—into a place like this can only enter through the lowest hole of all, the one for dogs.

But it was a good thing to do, as now they'll have to protect me. There's something in the air. If I hadn't got the pope's imprimatur for it I'd think it was the book. But they know the book has passed the censors. The pope would flatly reject any attempt to make a trap for me out of it. And after all the grand duke is my pupil. I shall complain to him.

The passage about Sagredo's invitation (p. 85) and the appearance of the cardinal inquisitor were added before this in revision. Galileo's resolve to escape in Volpi's wine cart is not in this version; nor is the last sentence of the final text.

12 [11 or 10 in first typescript]

THE POPE

This scene is divided by a 'transformation' into two halves, of which the second is not in the later versions and is given in full below. The first half, in the pope's own room, is a slightly shorter version of the final text. It excludes notably the reference to Galileo's star charts and the maritime cities' need for them, the mention of his powerful friends, leading to the pope's order 'Hands off him!' (p. 89) with the inquisitor's cynical reply and the pope's comment that 'His thinking springs from sensuality.' This half accordingly ends with 'Not the whole of it, but its best part.' Then, after the transformation:

> *Another room. At the window, Galileo, waiting. Here too the stamping and shuffling of many feet of the gathering congregation is heard. In the foreground two officials of the Inquisition.*
> OFFICIAL *sotto voce to his companion*: He's got good nerves. He's having a look at all his enemies.
> GALILEO: I hope the interview with His Holiness will take place before the session. It's important for me, as I want to ask for my evidence and proofs to be investigated before any decision is come to. It is of course quite impossible for me to make any kind of statement in a matter of such importance for the world of science without my evidence and proofs first getting a most scrupulous hearing and examination. I'd be glad of a little water. *The first official pours him some water from a carafe on the table. Galileo reaches for it uncertainly and spills some.*
> SECOND OFFICIAL *when the first returns*: Having a look at his enemies, but at nothing else. Had you forgotten he's half blind?

GALILEO: I suppose His Holiness really does want to see me?

FIRST OFFICIAL: Definitely.

GALILEO: Then I'd prefer to wait in another room if that's possible.

SECOND OFFICIAL: It's not possible. You wouldn't like His Holiness to arrive and find you weren't here, because you couldn't stand the shuffling.

GALILEO *looks at him blankly.*

SECOND OFFICIAL: Yes, you must be beginning to realise it isn't just a handful of people gathering there to testify against you. It's the most distinguished minds in Italy, the most learned scholars, the stars of all the universities, in short it's everybody.

GALILEO: Yes. *He turns to his window again.*

FIRST OFFICIAL: He must feel rather like someone before the flood who was expecting a spring shower, then the real rain came, then came an endless downpour and that turned into the flood, don't you think?

A high official appears. Galileo turns to face him and makes a deep bow. He thinks it is the pope.

THE HIGH OFFICIAL: Has this person eaten?

FIRST OFFICIAL: He was served a substantial meal.

THE HIGH OFFICIAL: The session later may go on a long time. *Goes out.*

GALILEO *has risen to his feet in confusion*: Gentlemen, I know His Holiness personally, having met him once at Cardinal Bellarmin's. But my eyesight is not what it was, and I must beg you to tell me when he is coming.

FIRST OFFICIAL: Shall be done, even though you wouldn't oblige us by making a proper meal.

GALILEO: The fact that the gentleman who just left used the word 'later' when speaking about the Inquisition's session today is surely a definite sign that His Holiness wants to speak to me first?

FIRST OFFICIAL *shrugs his shoulders.*

GALILEO: Did you say something?

FIRST OFFICIAL: I shrugged my shoulders.

13 [*12 or 11 in first typescript*]

Apart from the fact that Federzoni's subsequent lines are given to the elderly scholar, that the end of the scene (after the blackout) was at first conceived as a short scene on its own, and that Andrea's insults

('Wine-pump!' etc., p. 94) are missing, this version is not much different from the final one. In the first typescript a speech for the elderly scholar was written in; it appears to belong after Andrea's 'He couldn't write his book there' (p. 91) but was omitted in revision.

Clearly he didn't pay enough attention to that part. It's true that he said: it's not enough to know something, you have to be able to prove it. And he held his tongue till he was forty-six years old, and only spoke when he was able to prove his knowledge. But then he talked about his proofs to people with bunged-up ears, not to those who were dissatisfied with what had been believed in up to then but to those who were content with it. His mistake was to think that the choice between speaking in a republic and speaking in a grand duchy wasn't an astronomical problem.

14 [*13 or 12 in first typescript*]

1633–1642. A PRISONER OF THE INQUISITION, GALILEO CONTINUES HIS SCIENTIFIC STUDIES UP TO HIS DEATH. HE MANAGES TO SMUGGLE HIS PRINCIPAL WORK OUT OF ITALY

Like 9, this is a heavily altered scene with substantial differences from the final text. To sum them up briefly: (a) Galileo has conspired with a stove-fitter to conceal and smuggle out his writings; (b) Virginia reads him aphorisms by Montaigne, not scribbled texts provided by the archbishop; (c) his big speech (pp. 103–5) is differently conceived, though containing one or two phrases that recur in its final form; it omits all but the most general references to science's social implications, accuses himself only of failure to speak up for reason, and includes neither the warning of a 'universal cry of horror', nor the proposal for a scientists' Hippocratic oath; (d) it is only *after* this speech that Virginia leaves the room and Galileo admits to having written the *Discorsi*; (e) Andrea's enthusiastic reaction in praise of the 'new ethics' is missing, as also is Galileo's counter-speech of self-abasement ('Welcome to the gutter', p. 103); thus there are no dramatic reversals of feeling between the handing-over of the *Discorsi* and the end of the scene.

In the opening stage direction Galileo is described as '*old and ill, and moves like a blind man.*' Virginia solicitously serves him his supper ('Now let's eat up our good soup, and try not to spill a drop of it'). He then complains that the stove isn't working properly, and asks when the stove-fitter is coming. The official in the antechamber (the monk of the final text) complains to Virginia that manuscripts have been leaking out:

> Don't forget that the *Dialogue Concerning the Two Chief World Systems* was smuggled to Holland from here. And now they've intercepted a letter to Strasbourg, saying a manuscript will be coming. It must already have got out. Who took it? *Enter a big, broad-shouldered man, the stove-fitter. He has his tools with him.*

The stove-fitter is indeed the agent responsible, but this time he has brought the manuscript back because 'They are after us. Villagio has been arrested'. The doctor then appears, to check on Galileo's eyesight.

THE OFFICIAL: Can he or can he not see?
THE DOCTOR *shrugs his shoulders*: I don't know; very little, I'd say. I'll be making my report.

Virginia then comes in again to read to her father. The following passage was published in 1957 in *Versuche 15* as an addendum to the play:

VIRGINIA: Shall I read to you?
GALILEO: Yes, those inscriptions on the beams of M. de Montaigne's library. But only the ones I've marked.
VIRGINIA *gets the book and reads*: 54th inscription: Without leaning.
GALILEO: Is that all?
VIRGINIA: Yes.
GALILEO: But that depends on at least three things: the force of the thrust applied to one, the visibility of the objective and the solidity of the base. Some advice! Go on.
VIRGINIA: 52nd inscription: I do not understand.
GALILEO: That's good. It's a starting point.
VIRGINIA: 13: It is possible and it is not possible.[1]
GALILEO: Good, so long as he gives reasons.
VIRGINIA: 5: It's no more like this than like that or like neither.[2]
GALILEO: Provided one goes on looking.
VIRGINIA: 21: He who knows that he knows doesn't know how he knows.[3]

(1) Sextus Empiricus, *Hypotyposes*, 1, 21.
(2) *Ibid.*, 1, 19, cited Montaigne *Essays*, 2, 12.
(3) 1 Corinthians 8:2. The A.V. quotation is 'And if any man think that he knoweth anything, he knoweth nothing yet as he ought to know.'

GALILEO: Again, that's very good. But it all tastes of defeatism.

VIRGINIA: 10: What are heaven and earth and sea, with all they embrace, against the sum of sums of the immeasurable whole?[4]

GALILEO: One has to start, though. Make a note.

VIRGINIA: 2: He gave them curiosity, that he might torment them.[5]

GALILEO: Rubbish.

VIRGINIA: 15: Man is too fragile.[6]

GALILEO: Not fragile enough.

VIRGINIA: 20: Be wise in moderation, that you may not grow stupid.[7]

GALILEO: Go on.

VIRGINIA: 43: Men are not confused by things but by opinions about things.[8]

GALILEO: That could be wrong too. Who confuses the opinions?

VIRGINIA: Should I make a note of that?

GALILEO: No.

VIRGINIA: 19: I am a human; nothing human is alien to me.[9]

GALILEO: Good.

VIRGINIA: 37: God has created man like a shadow. Who can judge him once the sun has set?[10]

Galileo is silent.

VIRGINIA: 17: You should neither fear your last day nor yearn for it.[11]

GALILEO: I used to find the first point difficult: now it's the second.

VIRGINIA: 14: A wondrous thing is goodness.[12]

---

(4) Lucretius, *De Rerum Natura*, 6, cited Montaigne *Essays* 2, 12.

(5) Ecclesiastes 1, of which verse 13 in A. V. reads 'And I gave my heart to seek and search out by wisdom concerning all things that are done under heaven: this sore travail hath God given to the sons of man to be exercised therewith' (*Essays* 2, 17).

(6) Keramos anthropos. Wrongly attributed to Romans 9.

(7) Ecclesiastes 7: '. . . neither make thyself over wise: why shouldest thou destroy thyself?'

(8) Epictetus, cited by Stobaeus (*Essays* 1, 14).

(9) Terence, *Heautontimoroumenos* Act 1 (*Essays* 2, 2). This was Karl Marx's favourite saying.

(10) Ecclesiastes 7. Or more probably 6:12, which reads 'For who knoweth what is good for man in this life, all the days of his vain life which he spendeth as a shadow? For who can tell a man what shall be after him under the sun?' (*Essays* 2, 12).

(11) *Essays* 2, 37, after Martial, 10.

(12) Plato, *Cratylus*.

GALILEO: Louder!
VIRGINIA *louder*: A wondrous thing is goodness.

A much shorter alternative to the whole passage, which is also given in
the first typescript, with Galileo and Virginia going over proofs, re-
places it in the revised versions. In this Virginia reads Galileo the extract from the *Discorsi* which appears at the end of the previous scene
in the final text.

At this point Andrea enters, and the dialogue is fairly close to the final
text, up to where Galileo asks about his scientific friends 'Did they
learn anything from my recantation?' (p. 100). Andrea hardly answers
the question; he says nothing about Fulganzio, or, of course, Federzoni; the immediately preceding exchange about Descartes is also
missing. Instead the text continues:

ANDREA: For a time there was a considerable difference of opin-
    ion about you. Some of your former friends insisted that you
    had recanted because of services you still hoped to render
    physics by remaining alive. Because of such works as only you
    could write.
GALILEO *brusquely*: There are no such works.
ANDREA: How do you mean? If you hadn't written the *Dia-
    logue* . . .
GALILEO: Then someone else would have written it.
ANDREA: So that wasn't your motive?
GALILEO: Shortly after my trial various people who had known me
    earlier were good enough to credit me with all kinds of noble in-
    tentions. I wouldn't have this. To me it simply signified a decline
    of the critical faculties, brought about by the fact that they found
    drastic physical changes in me.
    After carefully considering all the circumstances, extenuating
    and otherwise, it is impossible to conclude that a man could ar-
    rive at this state of—call it obedience, from any other motive
    than an undue fear of death. *Pause.* That is not to deny *address-
    ing Virginia* the profound regret which I, as a son of the church,
    felt when my superiors induced me, by the most weighty of all
    arguments, to see the error of my ways. As a rule nothing less
    than threatening a man with death will serve to dissuade him
    from something of which his reason, that most dangerous of all
    God's gifts, has persuaded him. I fully understood that I could
    now only expect that hell which, so the poet tells, is inhabited by

people who have gambled away the gifts of the mind and are accordingly without hope.

He tells Andrea that science should be able to get along without authority (including his own). 'Authority and absence of truth doubtless go together, and so do truth and absence of authority.' Andrea then sums up the case against him, as it emerges in this version:

> ... a lot of people everywhere were hanging on your words and actions because they felt what you stood for was not a particular theory about the movements of the stars but the freedom to theorise in any field. Not just for any particular thoughts, in other words, but for the right to think in the first place, which was now being threatened. So as soon as these people heard you recanting all you had said they concluded that it was not merely certain thoughts about celestial motions that were being discredited but thinking itself that was being regarded as unholy, since it operates by means of causes and proofs.

Virginia replies that the church has not forbidden science, but has even absorbed Galileo's main discoveries. 'Only he mustn't attack the opinions of theology, which is an entirely different science.' The big speech follows, starting very much as it does in the final text (p. 103):

GALILEO: In my free time, and I've got plenty of that, I have asked myself how the world of science, of which I no longer consider myself a member, even if I still know a thing or two about its pursuits, will judge my conduct. *In lecture style, hands folded over his paunch.* It will have to take into account whether it is good enough for its members to provide it with a given number of principles, for instance about the tendencies of falling bodies or the motions of certain stars. I have, as I said, excluded myself from the scientific way of thinking; however, I take it that when faced with the threat of destruction that world will be in no position to lay down more far-reaching duties for its members, e.g., that of collaborating in its own maintenance as science. Even a wool merchant, in addition to buying cheap and providing good wool, has to worry about his trade being permitted at all and without restriction. On that principle no member of the scientific world is logically entitled to point to his own possible contributions to research if he has failed to honour his profession as such and to defend it against any use of force. This, however, is a business of vast scope. For science consists, not in a licence to subordinate facts to opinions, but in an obligation to subordinate opinions to facts. It is not in any position to permit restriction of these principles or to establish them only for 'certain views' and 'those particular facts'. In order to make sure that it can apply these principles unrestrictedly at any one time, science has to fight to be respected in every sphere. For science and humanity as a whole happen to be in the same boat. So it can't say 'What business is it of mine if the boat springs a leak at the other end?' [A passage cut from the original typescript here is repeated between two asterisks on p. 184 below.] Science has no use for people who fail to stick up for reason. It must expel them in ignominy, because, however many truths science knows, it could have no future in a world of lies. If the hand that feeds it occasionally seizes it unpredictably by the throat then humanity will have to chop it off. That is why science cannot tolerate a person like me in its ranks.

VIRGINIA *with passion*: But you are accepted in the ranks of the faithful. (cf. p. 105)

GALILEO: That is the position. In my view I have wrecked every experiment that might have been injurious to blind faith. Only my ingrained habit of making allowances for improbabilities would lead me to say 'nearly every experiment'. Plainly nothing but the irresistible arguments put forward by the Inquisition could have convinced me of the harmfulness of my researches.

ANDREA *in a strangled voice*: Yes.

Virginia leaves the room, and Galileo at once slyly admits that he has had relapses (p. 100). The dialogue then roughly anticipates that in the final text, up to where Andrea takes up the manuscript of the *Discorsi*, with the difference that Andrea never assumes that the work has been irrevocably handed over to 'the monks' as occurs, with consequently heightened tension, in the final text. Nor does Galileo simply tell him to 'Stuff it under your coat' (p. 102), but makes more elaborate and self-protective hints as to how he might take it away. Then as Andrea leaves, there is a significantly different exchange, to which the section in square brackets was added in the course of revision:

ANDREA *who has concealed the manuscript on him*: Yes, I'm going now. [I realise it's as if a tower had collapsed which was enormously tall and thought to be unshakeable. The noise it made collapsing was louder than the noise of the builders and their machines during the whole period of its construction, and the column of dust which its collapse caused was even higher than it had been. But conceivably when the dust disperses it may turn out that although the top twelve stories fell down the bottom thirty are still standing. In which case the building could be developed further. Is that what you mean? It would be supported by the fact that the inconsistencies in our science are still all in evidence and have been sifted. The difficulty seems to have increased, but at the same time the necessity has become greater.] I'm glad I came. *He holds out his hand to him.*

GALILEO *does not take it; hesitantly*: My eyesight is bad, Andrea. I can't see any more, I only stare. You had better go. *He walks slowly to* [*the globe and sees if it is shut.* I'm not unresponsive to the kindnesses I'm always being shown. Travellers passing through remember me, and so on. I don't misinterpret such things.] I'm glad too to have talked to you, and to have found you as you are. You have had experiences which could have given you a quite wrong view of what we've always termed the future of reason. But of course, no single man could either bring it to pass or discredit it.*It is too big an affair ever to be contained inside a single head. Reason is something people can be divided into. It can be described as the egoism of all humanity.* Such egoism is not strong enough. But even a person like myself can still see that reason is not coming to an end but beginning. And I still believe that this is a new age. It may look like a bloodstained old harridan, but if so that must be the way new ages look. When light breaks in it does so in the uttermost darkness. While a few places are the scene of the most immense discoveries, which must contribute immeasurably to humanity's resources for happiness, great areas of this world still lie entirely in the dark. In fact the blackness has actually deepened there. Look out for yourself when you travel through Germany with the truth under your coat.

Andrea goes out.

Andrea says nothing about a 'devastating analysis' (p. 105). The scene quickly closes, somewhat as in the final text, though not on the word 'Clear' but on Galileo's ensuing comment: 'That's good. Then he'll be able to see his way'.

15 [*14*]

1637. GALILEO'S BOOK THE *DISCORSI* CROSSES
THE ITALIAN FRONTIER.

Very close to the final text.

3. THE AMERICAN VERSION, 1944–1947

This English-language version, which Brecht and Laughton worked on from the end of 1944 up to the Hollywood production of July 1947, maintains the general structure of the play, but shortens and very largely rewrites it. The main structural changes are the omission of the first half of scene 4; the cutting of scene 5a off the end of scene 4 and the elimination of it and 5b (the plague scenes); also the cutting of the second half of scene 12 (pp. 177–178 above), with Galileo waiting for the pope. An element of social interest was introduced by making Ludovico an aristocrat and creating two new characters: Federzoni the lens grinder, who helps bring out the point of Galileo's use of the vernacular language, and the iron founder here called Matti, whose function is to appear in scenes 1 and 11 and show that the embryo bourgeoisie is on Galileo's side. Ludovico takes over Doppone's role in scenes 1 and 2; not surprisingly he becomes a little unconvincing. Federzoni too gets some of the elderly scholar's lines in scene 9. In this scene Mucius is cut, in scene 14 the stove-fitter and the doctor. According to Brecht it was Laughton who insisted on transposing the handing-over of the *Discorsi* in this scene so that Galileo's big self-accusatory speech should come after it.

The carnival scene (10) was rewritten entirely, with a new English-language ballad, though the gist of this remained much the same. The actions of the masqueraders and the crowd, while not exactly amounting to the 'ballet' proposed in the first version, were described in some detail, finishing with the appearance of the enormous dummy figure of 'Galileo, the Bible-buster'.

Finally there are no scene titles in the text as published, but short English verses were put at the beginning of each scene, and at the end of the play, which now finished with the warning:

> May you now guard science's light,
> Kindle it and use it right,

> Lest it be a flame to fall
> Downward to consume us all.

The full text of this version is given on pp. 195ff. The following is a brief scene-by-scene commentary on the changes. Scene numbers are those of the final text, with the American versions numbering in square brackets.

1.

The scene begins with the arrival of the Ptolemaic model which was previously already there. Galileo's speech on the 'new age' is shorter and simpler and more sloppily worded ('A new age was coming. I was on to it years ago'), but includes the ships and the Sienese masons. His second demonstration to Andrea, with the apple (which is in both the first and the final versions), is cut from Andrea's 'But it isn't true' (p. 10) to Galileo's 'Ha' on p. 11. Ludovico then appears, the gist of the dialogue being much the same as in the final text, but very much shortened. Galileo's discussion with Andrea about hypotheses is cut. The procurator, who follows Ludovico's exit, is for some reason a museum curator; again the dialogue is shortened and simplified, even vulgarised:

CURATOR: You've never let me down yet, Galilei.
GALILEO: You are always an inspiration to me, Priuli.

The ending of the scene is likewise shorter.

2.

The form of the scene is as in the final text, except that Virginia makes the presentation, that Matti the (Florentine) ironfounder appears, and that the Doge has nothing to say. Note the curator's '*best chamber-of-commerce manner*' and the allusion to him as a businessman, also the new silliness of Virginia as exemplified in the closing exchange.

3.

This is the same scene as in the final version, but shortened. It intro-duces Galileo's remarks about star charts, but cuts the episode with Mrs. Sarti (p. 28) who does not appear at all. Virginia enters earlier—there is no cross-fade as before—and stays long enough to hear Sagredo read out the end of the letter to the grand duke. The scene now ends approximately as in the final text, though rather more abruptly.

4.

The first half of the scene has been cut: Mrs. Sarti's speech, the grand duke's arrival and the episode with the two boys, also Galileo's open-ing speech and the beginning of the scientific argument up to where Cosimo's three professors are invited to look through the telescope for themselves (p. 35 in the final version). Instead it begins with the phi-losopher talking Latin and the exchange (p. 36) about the need to use the vernacular for Federzoni's sake. The argument which follows, now interrupted by the court ladies with jarringly improbable comments, follows the same pattern as the final version, though again in shortened form. It introduces notably Galileo's remark, 'Why defend shaken teachings? You should be doing the shaking,' and the speech that fol-lows about the arsenal workers and the sailors. The professors leave without speculating about Cosimo's hurried departure, now attributed to the state ball.

5.

[is cut]

6. [5]

Apart from the ending, this is a shortened form of the Collegium Ro-manum scene as we have it. The episode with the two astronomers is cut (from their entry p. 48 to their exit p. 49), apart from the very thin (or in this version infuriated) monk's first remark. His ensuing speech (starting 'They degrade humanity's dwelling place') is likewise cut.

The scene ends on the little monk's remark about Galileo's having won. Galileo's answer and the appearance of the cardinal inquisitor are omitted. The inscription about astronomical charts which is lowered after the curtain is not found in the other versions.

7. [6]

Again, this is a slightly shortened form of the final text. The great families attending the ball are named, Doppone is omitted, the two cardinals are now lamb and dove, the reference to star charts is new, Barberini swaps Biblical texts with Galileo and welcomes him to Rome, Bellarmin's speech about the Campagna peasants and the 'great plan' is cut, the inquisitor greets Virginia with the comment that her fiancé comes 'from a fine family'. The Lorenzo de' Medici madrigal is still missing.

8. [7]

The scene with the little monk is virtually as in the final version. Most of Galileo's speech about the Priapus is cut, but the beginning is as we now have it, and the phrases about the oyster and the pearl, and the peasants' 'divine patience' are included.

9. [8]

The order of events is as in the final text, though the episode with Mucius has been cut. The scene thus starts with Virginia's dialogue with Mrs. Sarti, including the talk about horoscopes. The Keunos story has gone, as have all allusions to Andrea's Jessica. Instead there is the dialogue between the collaborators as the experiment is prepared, including the little monk's remark about 'happiness in doubting' but omitting Andrea's account of how he has been observing the sun's rays in the attic. The whole episode with Ludovico corresponds closely to the final text, from his entrance on p. 71 to his exit on p. 76, apart from the omission of Mrs. Sarti's long speech (p. 74) and the little monk's immediately preceding remark about God and physics. The end of the scene too is the same, except that it stops at the end of Galileo's important speech.

10. [9]

The rewriting of this scene has already been mentioned (p. 161).

11. [10]

Close to the final text. Half the Vanni episode is here, though he is called Matti (as in scene 2) and it ends at the equivalent of 'please remember you've friends in every branch of business' (p. 83). (The rest appears to have been written at the same time, but not included in the published text.) Galliardo and the student do not appear. The passages about Sagredo's invitation and the possibility of escape were not in the earlier version.

12. [11]

The inquisitor's long speech is shortened by half, notably by the references to papal politics and the abolition of top and bottom, with the ensuing quotation from Aristotle. The exchange about Galileo's self-indulgence is new. That about the conclusion of his book is omitted. The ending, after 'but its best part' (p. 90) is new; the final stage instruction (which does not read like Brecht) being found only in this version. Otherwise this part of the scene is as we now have it. As already noted, the second part of the scene is cut.

13. [12]

From Andrea's cry 'someone who doesn't know the truth' (p. 92) to his imitation of Galileo is cut. The rest is as in the final version except for Federzoni's remark about Andrea not getting paid, and the shifting of Andrea's 'Unhappy is the land that breeds no hero' to immediately before Galileo's answer.

14. [13]

The order of events has been shifted, and is the same as in the final text. There is now nothing about the Inquisition's suspicions that manuscripts are being smuggled out, and the episodes with the doctor and the stove-fitter are cut. The 'weekly letter to the archbishop', whose discussion replaces that of the Montaigne inscriptions, is about half as long as in the final text. Andrea's ensuing dialogue with Galileo is as in the final text up to the point where Virginia leaves the room (which now comes very much earlier), that is to say it discusses what has happened to his former collaborators. The revelation of the *Discorsi* then comes before the analysis of Galileo's motives and conduct, which is now without the passages quoted on pp. 181 ff., but introduces Andrea's gradually waning praise of Galileo's behaviour, from Andrea's 'Two new branches of science' (p. 101) to Galileo's 'It was not' (p. 103). The 'welcome to the gutter' speech which follows is new, though shorter than its final version. The big speech is likewise about one-third shorter than in the final text, omitting notably the phrases 'But can we deny ourselves to the crowd and still remain scientists?' and 'Science, Sarti, is involved in both these battles', as well as the suggestion of a Hippocratic oath and the picture of scientists as 'inventive dwarfs'. The shift of emphasis from intellectual to social betrayal, the stressing of the liberating popular effects of the new science, finally the introduction of allusions to the horrors of the atom bomb, can all best be seen by comparing the actual text with that of the earlier version (p. 183).

Galileo's view of 'the new age', in the final exchanges, is expressed in the same terms as in the previous version. Again he ignores Andrea's hand, without comment. There is no mention of Andrea's journey through Germany, and the scene ends with Virginia's final remark.

15. [14]

The scene is broadly similar to its earlier version, but has been wholly rewritten, including the song. Among other things, the witch's house is shown, and the children steal her milk jug and kick it over.

4. THE BERLIN VERSION, 1953–1956

We can now summarise what happened when Brecht decided to make a new German version of the play after his return to Berlin. Two principal texts are involved: that published in his *Versuche 14* in 1955, and the final revised text of the collected *Stücke* (1957), which incorporates minor changes made in the course of Brecht's rehearsals and as a result of the Cologne production in the former year. This version follows the general structure of the American version, giving more or less the same account of characters, incidents, motivations and social substructure. However, it brings back important stretches of dialogue (from the first version, eliminating many of the crudities of the American text and giving more elbow-room to the arguments at the cost, of course, of making a considerably longer play).

The characters remain the same as in the American version, apart from the bringing back of Mucius at the beginning of scene 9, and the renaming of Vanni, who no longer figures in scene 2. So do their social roles. The plague scene is restored in a new form by running together 5a and 5b; this, presumably, being something that Brecht had wished to have 'in the book' even though, like Laughton, he was excluding it from the acting version. Scene 4 is restored to its full length, scene 15 put back into its old form. The original German text of the ballad in scene 10 has not been restored; instead it has been (freely) re-translated from the English, so as to fit Eisler's setting, though with the addition of the singer's remarks to the crowd. The same applies to the between-scene verses, which were not done in time for the *Versuche* edition. The Lorenzo de' Medici madrigal in scene 7 (which appears to derive from the sixtieth and last stanzas of his Eclogue 'La Ritrozia') now makes its appearance for the first time.

The play again begins as in the first version, though Galileo's speech on the 'new age' has been slighly expanded; the second demonstration with Andrea and the full conversation with the procurator are restored. In scene 3 the episode with Mrs. Sarti is brought back, leading to the (shortened) conclusion, 'they grab at it' (p. 28), while immediately before her entry Galileo's speech is given a new last sentence: 'Thinking is one of the chief pleasures of the human race' (p. 27). Virginia is now made to leave before the reading of the letter to the grand duke. In scene 4 some of the fatuous remarks of the court ladies (e.g., 'Perfect poise!' and 'What diction!') are eliminated; the professors' proposal for a formal disputation is new, as is Federzoni's call for new textbooks.

In the plague scene the second half (b) is virtually as in the (revised) first version, but the first half has been revised, notably cutting Galileo's last remarks, with their reference to the uncertainty of remaining alive 'in times like these.' In the ball scene (7) a new poem for Galileo, which could be a quasi-Horatian variant on Herrick's 'Delight in Disorder', re-places the English one which we give, and Bellarmin's remarks about the Campagna peasants and the (social) need to attribute all the world's horrors to a 'great plan' are restored. In the sunspot scene (9) the episode with Mucius now comes near the start of the scene, which has been cor-respondingly rewritten; Mrs. Sarti's speech (p. 74) has also been restored, as has Galileo's call for 'people who work with their hands' (p. 76), in lieu of the American version's too simple view that scientific work is not worth doing 'for less than the population at large'. The end of this scene ('I've got to know') is quite new.

In the carnival scene (10) the procession is now described briefly in a single stage direction at the end. In scene 11 the episode with Vanni is extended to emphasise Galileo's sense of security (and of his own comforts). Scene 12 restores the inquisitor's comments on papal politics and introduces the graffito about the Barberinis' love of art, as well as the exchange about condemning the doctrine and keeping its practical applications. For the slight changes in scenes 13 and 14 see pp. 189–190 above. There is in the Brecht-Archive a sketch for the notion of a Hippocratic oath for scientists which was evidently noted down in America (in Brecht's homemade English) but for some reason not then worked into the play. It goes thus:

ingenious dwarfs

Hypocratic
hypocrades Oath

    Had I resisted, the natural sciences might have

          something like the   of the physicians.

    develloped their own Hypöcratic oath
      mankind

Now, the most we can hope for will be a race of ingenious dwarfs who can be hired for any purpose who will, as on islands, produce whatever their masters demand.

        means

        what's the use of progress, if it is a

        leaving behind of mankind? There even

        a state of things could develop, when our

        inventions

[Spelling and spacing as on Brecht's typescript, but not showing his corrections and deletions. From BBA 609/91, reproduced in Schumacher: *Drama and Geschichte*, 1965, p. 208.]

Appendix

GALILEO

By BERTOLT BRECHT

Translated by Charles Laughton

It is my opinion that the earth is very noble and admirable by
reason of so many and so different alterations and generations
which are incessantly made therein.

—GALILEO GALILEI

CHARACTERS

GALILEO GALILEI

ANDREA SARTI (*two actors: boy and man*)

MRS. SARTI

LUDOVICO MARSILI

PRIULI, THE CURATOR

SAGREDO, *Galileo's friend*

VIRGINIA GALILEI

TWO SENATORS

MATTI, *an iron founder*

PHILOSOPHER (*later, Rector of the University*)

ELDERLY LADY

YOUNG LADY

FEDERZONI, *assistant to Galileo*

MATHEMATICIAN

LORD CHAMBERLAIN

FAT PRELATE

TWO SCHOLARS

TWO MONKS

INFURIATED MONK

OLD CARDINAL

ATTENDANT MONK

CHRISTOPHER CLAVIUS

LITTLE MONK

TWO SECRETARIES

CARDINAL BELLARMIN

CARDINAL BARBERINI

CARDINAL INQUISITOR

YOUNG GIRL

HER FRIEND

GIUSEPPE

STREET SINGER

HIS WIFE REVELLER

A LOUD VOICE

INFORMER

TOWN CRIER

OFFICIAL

PEASANT

CUSTOMS OFFICER

BOY

SENATORS, OFFICIALS, PROFESSORS, LADIES, GUESTS, CHILDREN

There are two wordless roles: The DOGE *in Scene Two and* PRINCE COSIMO DE MEDICI *in Scene Four. The ballad of Scene Nine is filled out by a pantomime: among the individuals in the pantomimic crowd are three extras (including the* "KING OF HUNGARY"*),* COBBLER'S BOY, THREE CHILDREN, PEASANT WOMAN, MONK, RICH COUPLE, DWARF, BEGGAR, *and* GIRL.

Scene One

In the year sixteen hundred and nine
Science' light began to shine.
At Padua City, in a modest house
Galileo Galilei set out to prove
The sun is still, the earth is on the move.

Galileo's scantily furnished study. Morning. Galileo is washing himself.
A bare-footed boy, Andrea, son of his housekeeper, Mrs. Sarti, enters
with a big astronomical model.

GALILEO: Where did you get that thing?

ANDREA: The coachman brought it.

GALILEO: Who sent it?

ANDREA: It said "From the Court of Naples" on the box.

GALILEO: I don't want their stupid presents. Illuminated manuscripts,
    a statue of Hercules the size of an elephant—they never send money.

ANDREA: But isn't this an astronomical instrument, Mr. Galilei?

GALILEO: That is an antique too. An expensive toy.

ANDREA: What's it for?

GALILEO: It's a map of the sky according to the wise men of ancient
    Greece. Bosh! We'll try and sell it to the university. They still teach
    it there.

ANDREA: How does it work, Mr. Galilei?

GALILEO: It's complicated.

ANDREA: I think I could understand it.

GALILEO (*interested*): Maybe. Let's begin at the beginning. Descrip-
    tion!

ANDREA: There are metal rings, a lot of them.

GALILEO: How many?

ANDREA: Eight.

GALILEO: Correct. And?

ANDREA: There are words painted on the bands.

GALILEO: What words?

ANDREA: The names of stars.

GALILEO: Such as?

ANDREA: Here is a band with the sun on it and on the inside band is the moon.

GALILEO: Those metal bands represent crystal globes, eight of them.

ANDREA: Crystal?

GALILEO: Like huge soap bubbles one inside the other and the stars are supposed to be tacked on to them. Spin the band with the sun on it. (*Andrea does*) You see the fixed ball in the middle?

ANDREA: Yes.

GALILEO: That's the earth. For two thousand years man has chosen to believe that the sun and all the host of stars revolve about him. Well. The Pope, the Cardinals, the princes, the scholars, captains, merchants, housewives, have pictured themselves squatting in the middle of an affair like that.

ANDREA: Locked up inside?

GALILEO (*triumphant*): Ah!

ANDREA: It's like a cage.

GALILEO: So you sensed that. (*Against the model*) I like to think the ships began it.

ANDREA: Why?

GALILEO: They used to hug the coasts and then all of a sudden they left the coasts and spread over the oceans. A new age was coming. I was on to it years ago. I was a young man, in Siena. There was a group of masons arguing. They had to raise a block of granite. It was hot. To help matters, one of them wanted to try a new arrangement of ropes. After five minutes' discussion, out went a method which had been employed for a thousand years. The millenium of faith is ended, said I, this is the millenium of doubt. And we are pulling out of that contraption. The sayings of the wise men won't wash anymore. Everybody, at last, is getting nosey. I predict that in our time astronomy will become the gossip of the market place and the sons of fishwives will pack the schools.

ANDREA: You're off again, Mr. Galilei. Give me the towel. (*He wipes some soap from Galileo's back.*)

GALILEO: By that time, with any luck, they will be learning that the earth rolls round the sun, and that their mothers, the captains, the scholars, the princes and the Pope are rolling with it.

ANDREA: That turning-round-business is no good. I can see with my own eyes that the sun comes up in one place in the morning and goes down in a different place in the evening. It doesn't stand still, I can see it move.

GALILEO: You see nothing, all you do is gawk. Gawking is not seeing. (*He puts the iron washstand in the middle of the room.*) Now: that's the sun. Sit down. (*Andrea sits on a chair. Galileo stands behind him.*) Where is the sun, on your right or on your left?

ANDREA: Left.

GALILEO: And how will it get to the right?

ANDREA: By your putting it there, of course.

GALILEO: Of course? (*He picks Andrea up, chair and all, and carries him round to the other side of the washstand.*) Now where is the sun?

ANDREA: On the right.

GALILEO: And did it move?

ANDREA: I did.

GALILEO: Wrong. Stupid! The chair moved.

ANDREA: But I was on it.

GALILEO: Of course. The chair is the earth, and you're sitting on it.
(*Mrs. Sarti, who has come in with a glass of milk and a roll, has been watching.*)

MRS. SARTI: What are you doing with my son, Mr. Galilei?

ANDREA: Now, mother, you don't understand.

MRS. SARTI: You understand, don't you? Last night he tried to tell me that the earth goes round the sun. You'll soon have him saying that two times two is five.

GALILEO (*eating his breakfast*): Apparently we are on the threshold of a new era, Mrs. Sarti.

MRS. SARTI: Well, I hope we can pay the milkman in this new era. A young gentleman is here to take private lessons and he is well-dressed and don't you frighten him away like you did the others. Wasting your time with Andrea! (*To Andrea*) How many times have I told you not to wheedle free lessons out of Mr. Galilei? (*Mrs. Sarti goes.*)

GALILEO: So you thought enough of the turning-round-business to tell your mother about it.

ANDREA: Just to surprise her.

GALILEO: Andrea, I wouldn't talk about our ideas outside.

ANDREA: Why not?

GALILEO: Certain of the authorities won't like it.

ANDREA: Why not, if it's the truth?

GALILEO (*laughs*): Because we are like the worms who are little and have dim eyes and can hardly see the stars at all, and the new astronomy is a framework of guesses or very little more—yet.
(*Mrs. Sarti shows in Ludovico Marsili, a presentable young man.*)

GALILEO: This house is like a marketplace. (*Pointing to the model*) Move that out of the way! Put it down there! (*Ludovico does.*)

LUDOVICO: Good morning, sir. My name is Ludovico Marsili.

GALILEO (*reading a letter of recommendation be has brought*): You came by way of Holland and your family lives in the Campagna? Private lessons, thirty scudi a month.

LUDOVICO: That's all right, of course, sir.

GALILEO: What is your subject?

LUDOVICO: Horses.

GALILEO: Aha.

LUDOVICO: I don't understand science, sir.

GALILEO: Aha.

LUDOVICO: They showed me an instrument like that in Amsterdam. You'll pardon me, sir, but it didn't make sense to me at all.

GALILEO: It's out of date now.

(*Andrea goes.*)

LUDOVICO: You'll have to be patient with me, sir. Nothing in science makes sense to me.

GALILEO: Aha.

LUDOVICO: I saw a brand new instrument in Amsterdam. A tube affair. "See things five times as large as life!" It had two lenses, one at each end, one lens bulged and the other was like that. (*Gesture*) Any normal person would think that different lenses cancel each other out. They didn't! I just stood and looked a fool.

GALILEO: I don't quite follow you. What does one see enlarged?

LUDOVICO: Church steeples, pigeons, boats. Anything at a distance.

GALILEO: Did you yourself—see things enlarged?

LUDOVICO: Yes, sir.

GALILEO: And the tube had two lenses? Was it like this? (*He has been making a sketch.*)

(*Ludovico nods.*)

GALILEO: A recent invention?

LUDOVICO: It must be. They only started peddling it on the streets a few days before I left Holland.

GALILEO (*starts to scribble calculations on the sketch; almost friendly*): Why do you bother your head with science? Why don't you just breed horses?

(*Enter Mrs. Sarti. Galileo doesn't see her. She listens to the following.*)

LUDOVICO: My mother is set on the idea that science is necessary nowadays for conversation.

GALILEO: Aha. You'll find Latin or philosophy easier. (*Mrs. Sarti catches his eye.*) I'll see you on Tuesday afternoon.

LUDOVICO: I shall look forward to it, sir.

GALILEO: Good morning. (*He goes to the window and shouts into the street.*) Andrea! Hey, Redhead, Redhead!

MRS. SARTI: The curator of the museum is here to see you.

GALILEO: Don't look at me like that. I took him, didn't I?

MRS. SARTI I caught your eye in time.

GALILEO: Show the curator in.

(*She goes. He scribbles something on a new sheet of paper. The Curator comes in.*)

CURATOR: Good morning, Mr. Galilei.

GALILEO: Lend me a scudo. (*He takes it and goes to the window, wrapping the coin in the paper on which he has been scribbling.*) Redhead, run to the spectacle-maker and bring me two lenses; here are the measurements. (*He throws the paper out of the window. During the following scene Galileo studies his sketch of the lenses.*)

CURATOR: Mr. Galilei, I have come to return your petition for an honorarium. Unfortunately I am unable to recommend your request.

GALILEO: My good sir, how can I make ends meet on five hundred scudi?

CURATOR: What about your private students?

GALILEO: If I spend all my time with students, when am I to study? My particular science is on the threshold of important discoveries. (*He throws a manuscript on the table.*) Here are my findings on the laws of falling bodies. That should be worth 200 scudi.

CURATOR: I am sure that any paper of yours is of infinite worth, Mr. Galilei. . . .

GALILEO: I was limiting it to 200 scudi.

CURATOR (*cool*): Mr. Galilei, if you want money and leisure, go to Florence. I have no doubt Prince Cosimo de Medici will be glad to subsidize you, but eventually you will be forbidden to think—in the name of the Inquisition. (*Galileo says nothing.*) Now let us not make a mountain out of a molehill. You are happy here in the Republic of Venice but you need money. Well, that's human, Mr. Galilei, may I suggest a simple solution? You remember that chart you made for the army to extract cube roots without any knowledge of mathematics? Now that was practical!

GALILEO: Bosh!

CURATOR: Don't say bosh about something that astounded the Chamber of Commerce. Our city elders are businessmen. Why don't you invent something useful that will bring them a little profit?

GALILEO (*playing with the sketch of the lenses; suddenly*): I see. Mr. Priuli, I may have something for you.

CURATOR: You don't say so.

GALILEO: It's not quite there yet, but . . .

CURATOR: You've never let me down yet, Galilei.

GALILEO: You are always an inspiration to me, Priuli.

CURATOR: You are a great man: a discontented man, but I've always said you are a great man.

GALILEO (*tartly*): My discontent, Priuli, is for the most part with myself. I am forty-six years of age and have achieved nothing which satisfies me.

CURATOR: I won't disturb you any further.

GALILEO: Thank you. Good morning.

CURATOR: Good morning. And thank you.

(He goes. Galileo sighs. Andrea returns, bringing lenses.)

ANDREA: One scudo was not enough. I had to leave my cap with him before he'd let me take them away.

GALILEO: We'll get it back some day. Give them to me. (*He takes the lenses over to the window, holding them in the relation they would have in a telescope.*)

ANDREA: What are those for?

GALILEO: Something for the senate. With any luck, they will rake in 200 scudi. Take a look!

ANDREA: My, things look close! I can read the copper letters on the bell in the Campanile. And the washerwomen by the river, I can see their washboards!

GALILEO: Get out of the way. (*Looking through the lenses himself.*) Aha!

Scene Two

No one's virtue is complete:
Great Galileo liked to eat.
You will not resent, we hope,
The truth about his telescope.

The great arsenal of Venice, overlooking the harbor full of ships.
Senators and Officials on one side, Galileo, his daughter Virginia and
his friend Sagredo, on the other side. They are dressed in formal, festive
clothes. Virginia is fourteen and charming. She carries a velvet cushion
on which lies a brand new telescope. Behind Galileo are some Artisans
from the arsenal. There are onlookers, Ludovico amongst them.

CURATOR (*announcing*): Senators, Artisans of the Great Arsenal of
   Venice; Mr. Galileo Galilei, professor of mathematics at your University of Padua.
   (Galileo steps forward and starts to speak.)
GALILEO: Members of the High Senate! Gentlemen: I have great pleasure, as director of this institute, in presenting for your approval
   and acceptance an entirely new instrument originating from this our
   great arsenal of the Republic of Venice. As professor of mathematics
   at your University of Padua, your obedient servant has always
   counted it his privilege to offer you such discoveries and inventions
   as might prove lucrative to the manufacturers and merchants of our
   Venetian Republic. Thus, in all humility, I tender you this, my optical tube, or telescope, constructed, I assure you, on the most scientific and Christian principles, the product of seventeen years patient
   research at your University of Padua.
   (Galileo steps back. The senators applaud.)
SAGREDO (*aside to Galileo*): Now you will be able to pay your bills.
GALILEO: Yes. It will make money for them. But you realize that it is
   more than a money-making gadget?—I turned it on the moon last
   night . . .
CURATOR (*in his best chamber-of-commerce manner*): Gentlemen: Our
   Republic is to be congratulated not only because this new acquisition

will be one more feather in the cap of Venetian culture . . . (*Polite applause*) . . . not only because our own Mr. Galilei has generously handed this fresh product of his teeming brain entirely over to you, allowing you to manufacture as many of these highly saleable articles as you please. . . . (*Considerable applause*) But Gentlemen of the Senate, has it occurred to you that—with the help of this remarkable new instrument—the battlefleet of the enemy will be visible to us a full two hours before we are visible to him? (*Tremendous applause*)

GALILEO (*aside to Sagredo*): We have been held up three generations for lack of a thing like this. I want to go home.

SAGREDO: What about the moon?

GALILEO: Well, for one thing, it doesn't give off its own light.

CURATOR (*continuing his oration*): And now, Your Excellency, and Members of the Senate, Mr. Galilei entreats you to accept the instrument from the hands of his charming daughter Virginia.

(*Polite applause. He beckons to Virginia who steps forward and presents the telescope to the Doge.*)

CURATOR (*during this*): Mr. Galilei gives his invention entirely into your hands, Gentlemen, enjoining you to construct as many of these instruments as you may please.

(*More applause. The Senators gather round the telescope, examining it, and looking through it.*)

GALILEO (*aside to Sagredo*): Do you know what the Milky Way is made of?

SAGREDO: No.

GALILEO: I do.

CURATOR (*interrupting*): Congratulations, Mr. Galilei. Your extra five hundred scudi a year are safe.

GALILEO: Pardon? What? Of course, the five hundred scudi! Yes!

(*A prosperous man is standing beside the Curator.*)

CURATOR: Mr. Galilei, Mr. Matti of Florence.

MATTI: You're opening new fields, Mr. Galilei. We could do with you at Florence.

CURATOR: Now, Mr. Matti, leave something to us poor Venetians.

MATTI: It is a pity that a great republic has to seek an excuse to pay its great men their right and proper dues.

CURATOR: Even a great man has to have an incentive. (*He joins the Senators at the telescope.*)

MATTI: I am an iron founder.

GALILEO: Iron founder!

MATTI: With factories at Pisa and Florence. I wanted to talk to you about a machine you designed for a friend of mine in Padua.

GALILEO: I'll put you on to someone to copy it for you, I am not going to have the time.—How are things in Florence?
(They wander away.)

FIRST SENATOR *(peering)*: Extraordinary! They're having their lunch on that frigate. Lobsters! I'm hungry!
(Laughter)

SECOND SENATOR: Oh, good heavens, look at her! I must tell my wife to stop bathing on the roof. When can I buy one of these things?
(Laughter. Virginia has spotted Ludovico among the onlookers and drags him to Galileo.)

VIRGINIA *(to Ludovico)*: Did I do it nicely?

LUDOVICO: I thought so.

VIRGINIA: Here's Ludovico to congratulate you, father.

LUDOVICO *(embarrassed)*: Congratulations, sir.

GALILEO: I improved it.

LUDOVICO: Yes, sir. I am beginning to understand science.
(Galileo is surrounded.)

VIRGINIA: Isn't father a great man?

LUDOVICO: Yes.

VIRGINIA: Isn't that new thing father made pretty?

LUDOVICO: Yes, a pretty red. Where I saw it first it was covered in green.

VIRGINIA: What was?

LUDOVICO: Never mind. *(A short pause)* Have you ever been to Holland?
(They go. All Venice is congratulating Galileo, who wants to go home.)

Scene Three

January ten, sixteen ten:
Galileo Galilei abolishes heaven.

Galileo's study at Padua. It is night. Galileo and Sagredo at a telescope.

SAGREDO (*softly*): The edge of the crescent is jagged. All along the dark part, near the shiny crescent, bright particles of light keep coming up, one after the other and growing larger and merging with the bright crescent.

GALILEO: How do you explain those spots of light?

SAGREDO: It can't be true . . .

GALILEO: It is true: they are high mountains.

SAGREDO: On a star?

GALILEO: Yes. The shining particles are mountain peaks catching the first rays of the rising sun while the slopes of the mountains are still dark, and what you see is the sunlight moving down from the peaks into the valleys.

SAGREDO: But this gives the lie to all the astronomy that's been taught for the last two thousand years.

GALILEO: Yes. What you are seeing now has been seen by no other man beside myself.

SAGREDO: But the moon can't be an earth with mountains and valleys like our own any more than the earth can be a star.

GALILEO: The moon *is* an earth with mountains and valleys,—and the earth *is* a star. As the moon appears to us, so we appear to the moon. From the moon, the earth looks something like a crescent, sometimes like a half-globe, sometimes a full-globe, and sometimes it is not visible at all.

SAGREDO: Galileo, this is frightening.

(An urgent knocking on the door)

GALILEO: I've discovered something else, something even more astonishing.

(More knocking. Galileo opens the door and the Curator comes in.)

CURATOR: There it is—your "miraculous optical tube." Do you know that this invention he so picturesquely termed "the fruit of seventeen years research" will be on sale tomorrow for two scudi apiece at every street corner in Venice? A shipload of them has just arrived from Holland.

SAGREDO: Oh, dear!

(*Galileo turns his back and adjusts the telescope.*)

CURATOR: When I think of the poor gentlemen of the senate who believed they were getting an invention they could monopolize for their own profit. . . . Why, when they took their first look through the glass, it was only by the merest chance that they didn't see a peddler, seven times enlarged, selling tubes exactly like it at the corner of the street.

SAGREDO: Mr. Priuli, with the help of this instrument, Mr. Galilei has made discoveries that will revolutionize our concept of the universe.

CURATOR: Mr. Galilei provided the city with a first rate water pump and the irrigation works he designed function splendidly. How was I to expect this?

GALILEO (*still at the telescope*): Not so fast, Priuli. I may be on the track of a very large gadget. Certain of the stars appear to have regular movements. If there were a clock in the sky, it could be seen from anywhere. That might be useful for your shipowners.

CURATOR: I won't listen to you. I listened to you before, and as a reward for my friendship you have made me the laughingstock of the town. You can laugh—you got your money. But let me tell you this: you've destroyed my faith in a lot of things, Mr. Galilei. I'm disgusted with the world. That's all I have to say. (*He storms out.*)

GALILEO (*embarrassed*): Businessmen bore me, they suffer so. Did you see the frightened look in his eyes when he caught sight of a world not created solely for the purpose of doing business?

SAGREDO: Did you know that telescopes had been made in Holland?

GALILEO: I'd heard about it. But the one I made for the Senators was twice as good as any Dutchman's. Besides, I needed the money. How can I work, with the tax collector on the doorstep? And my poor daughter will never acquire a husband unless she has a dowry, she's not too bright. And I like to buy books—all kinds of books. Why not? And what about my appetite? I don't think well unless I eat well. Can I help it if I get my best ideas over a good meal and a bottle of wine? They don't pay me as much as they pay the butcher's boy. If only I could have five years to do nothing but research! Come on. I am going to show you something else.

SAGREDO: I don't know that I want to look again.

GALILEO: This is one of the brighter nebulae of the Milky Way. What do you see?

SAGREDO: But it's made up of stars—countless stars.

GALILEO: Countless worlds.

SAGREDO (*hesitating*): What about the theory that the earth revolves round the sun? Have you run across anything about that?

GALILEO: No. But I noticed something on Tuesday that might prove a step towards even that. Where's Jupiter? There are four lesser stars near Jupiter. I happened on them on Monday but didn't take any particular note of their position. On Tuesday I looked again. I could have sworn they had moved. They have changed again. Tell me what you see.

SAGREDO: I only see three.

GALILEO: Where's the fourth? Let's get the charts and settle down to work.

(*They work and the lights dim. The lights go up again. It is near dawn.*)

GALILEO: The only place the fourth can be is round at the back of the larger star where we cannot see it. This means there are small stars revolving around a big star. Where are the crystal shells now that the stars are supposed to be fixed to?

SAGREDO: Jupiter can't be attached to anything: there are other stars revolving round it.

GALILEO: There is no support in the heavens. (*Sagredo laughs awkwardly.*) Don't stand there looking at me as if it weren't true.

SAGREDO: I suppose it is true. I'm afraid.

GALILEO: Why?

SAGREDO: What do you think is going to happen to you for saying that there is another sun around which other earths revolve? And that there are only stars and no difference between earth and heaven? Where is God then?

GALILEO: What do you mean?

SAGREDO: God? Where is God?

GALILEO (*angrily*): Not there! Any more than he'd be here—if creatures from the moon came down to look for him!

SAGREDO: Then where is He?

GALILEO: I'm not a theologian: I'm a mathematician.

SAGREDO: You are a human being! (*Almost shouting*) Where is God in your system of the universe?

GALILEO: Within ourselves. Or—nowhere.

SAGREDO: Ten years ago a man was burned at the stake for saying that.

GALILEO: Giordano Bruno was an idiot: he spoke too soon. He would never have been condemned if he could have backed up what he said with proof.

SAGREDO (*incredulously*): Do you really believe proof will make any difference?

GALILEO: I believe in the human race. The only people that can't be reasoned with are the dead. Human beings are intelligent.

SAGREDO: Intelligent—or merely shrewd?

GALILEO: I know they call a donkey a horse when they want to sell it, and a horse a donkey when they want to buy it. But is that the whole story? Aren't they susceptible to truth as well? (*He fishes a small pebble out of his pocket.*) If anybody were to drop a stone . . . (*Drops the pebble*) . . . and tell them that it didn't fall, do you think they would keep quiet? The evidence of your own eyes is a very seductive thing. Sooner or later everybody must succumb to it.

SAGREDO: Galileo, I am helpless when you talk.

(*A church bell has been ringing for some time, calling people to mass. Enter Virginia, muffled up for mass, carrying a candle, protected from the wind by a globe.*)

VIRGINIA: Oh, father, you promised to go to bed tonight, and it's five o'clock again.

GALILEO: Why are you up at this hour?

VIRGINIA: I'm going to mass with Mrs. Sarti. Ludovico is going too. How was the night, father?

GALILEO: Bright.

VIRGINIA: What did you find through the tube?

GALILEO: Only some little specks by the side of a star. I must draw attention to them somehow. I think I'll name them after the Prince of Florence. Why not call them the Medicean planets? By the way, we may move to Florence. I've written to His Highness, asking if he can use me as Court Mathematician.

VIRGINIA: Oh, father, we'll be at the court!

SAGREDO (*amazed*): Galileo!

GALILEO: My dear Sagredo, I must have leisure. My only worry is that His Highness after all may not take me. I'm not accustomed to writing formal letters to great personages. Here, do you think this is the right sort of thing?

SAGREDO (*reads and quotes*): "Whose sole desire is to reside in Your Highness' presence—the rising sun of our great age." Cosimo de Medici is a boy of nine.

GALILEO: The only way a man like me can land a good job is by crawling on his stomach. Your father, my dear, is going to take his share of the pleasures of life in exchange for all his hard work, and about time too. I have no patience, Sagredo, with a man who doesn't use his brains to fill his belly. Run along to mass now.

(Virginia goes.)

SAGREDO: Galileo, do not go to Florence.

GALILEO: Why not?

SAGREDO: The monks are in power there.

GALILEO: Going to mass is a small price to pay for a full belly. And there are many famous scholars at the court of Florence.

SAGREDO Court monkeys.

GALILEO: I shall enjoy taking them by the scruff of the neck and making them look through the telescope.

SAGREDO: Galileo, you are traveling the road to disaster. You are suspicious and skeptical in science, but in politics you are as naive as your daughter! How can people in power leave a man at large who tells the truth, even if it be the truth about the distant stars? Can you see the Pope scribbling a note in his diary: "10th of January, 1610, Heaven abolished?" A moment ago, when you were at the telescope, I saw you tied to the stake, and when you said you believed in proof, I smelt burning flesh!

GALILEO: I am going to Florence.

(Before the next scene a curtain with the following legend on it is lowered.)

By setting the name of Medici in the sky, I am bestowing immortality upon the stars. I commend myself to you as your most faithful and devoted servant, whose sole desire is to reside in Your Highness' presence, the rising sun of our great age.

—GALILEO GALILEI

Scene Four

Galileo's house at Florence. Well-appointed. Galileo is demonstrating his telescope to Prince Cosimo de Medici, a boy of nine, accompanied by his Lord Chamberlain, Ladies and Gentlemen of the Court and an assortment of university Professors. With Galileo are Andrea and Federzoni, the new assistant (an old man). Mrs. Sarti stands by. Before the scene opens the voice of the Philosopher can be heard.

VOICE OF THE PHILOSOPHER: Quaedam miracula universi. Orbes mystice canorae, arcus crystallini, circulatio corporum coelestium. Cyclorum epicyclorumque intoxicatio, integritas tabulae chordarum et architectura elata globorum coelestium.

GALILEO: Shall we speak in everyday language? My colleague Mr. Federzoni does not understand Latin.

PHILOSOPHER Is it necessary that he should?

GALILEO: Yes.

PHILOSOPHER: Forgive me. I thought he was your mechanic.

ANDREA: Mr. Federzoni is a mechanic and a scholar.

PHILOSOPHER: Thank you, young man. If Mr. Federzoni insists . . .

GALILEO: I insist.

PHILOSOPHER: It will not be as clear, but it's your house. Your Highness . . . (*The Prince is ineffectually trying to establish contact with Andrea.*) I was about to recall to Mr. Galilei some of the wonders of the universe as they are set down for us in the Divine Classics. (*The Ladies "ah."*) Remind him of the "mystically musical spheres, the crystal arches, the circulation of the heavenly bodies—"

ELDERLY LADY: Perfect poise!

PHILOSOPHER: "—the intoxication of the cycles and epicycles, the integrity of the tables of chords and the enraptured architecture of the celestial globes."

ELDERLY LADY: What diction!

PHILOSOPHER: May I pose the question: Why should we go out of our way to look for things that can only strike a discord in this ineffable harmony?

(The Ladies applaud.)

FEDERZONI: Take a look through here—you'll be interested.

ANDREA: Sit down here, please.

(The Professors laugh.)

MATHEMATICIAN: Mr. Galilei, nobody doubts that your brain child—or is it your adopted brain child?—is brilliantly contrived.

GALILEO: Your Highness, one can see the four stars as large as life, you know.

(The Prince looks to the Elderly Lady for guidance.)

MATHEMATICIAN: Ah. But has it occurred to you that an eyeglass through which one sees such phenomena might not be a too reliable eyeglass?

GALILEO: How is that?

MATHEMATICIAN: If one could be sure you would keep your temper, Mr. Galilei, I could suggest that what one sees in the eyeglass and what is in the heavens are two entirely different things.

GALILEO *(quietly)*: You are suggesting fraud?

MATHEMATICIAN: No! How could I, in the presence of His Highness?

ELDERLY LADY: The gentlemen are just wondering if Your Highness' stars are really, really there!

(Pause)

YOUNG LADY *(trying to be helpful)*: Can one see the claws on the Great Bear?

GALILEO: And everything on Taurus the Bull.

FEDERZONI: Are you going to look through it or not?

MATHEMATICIAN: With the greatest of pleasure.

(Pause. Nobody goes near the telescope. All of a sudden the boy Andrea turns and marches pale and erect past them through the whole length of the room. The Guests follow with their eyes.)

MRS. SARTI *(as he passes her)*: What is the matter with you?

ANDREA *(shocked)*: They are wicked.

PHILOSOPHER: Your Highness, it is a delicate matter and I had no intention of bringing it up, but Mr. Galilei was about to demonstrate the impossible. His new stars would have broken the outer crystal sphere—which we know of on the authority of Aristotle. I am sorry.

MATHEMATICIAN: The last word.

FEDERZONI: He had no telescope.

MATHEMATICIAN: Quite.

GALILEO *(keeping his temper)*: "Truth is the daughter of Time, not of Authority." Gentlemen, the sum of our knowledge is pitiful. It has been my singular good fortune to find a new instrument which brings a small patch of the universe a little bit closer. It is at your disposal.

PHILOSOPHER: Where is all this leading?

GALILEO: Are we, as scholars, concerned with where the truth might lead us?

PHILOSOPHER: Mr. Galilei, the truth might lead us anywhere!

GALILEO: I can only beg you to look through my eyeglass.

MATHEMATICIAN (*wild*): If I understand Mr. Galilei correctly, he is asking us to discard the teachings of two thousand years.

GALILEO: For two thousand years we have been looking at the sky and didn't see the four moons of Jupiter, and there they were all the time. Why defend shaken teachings? You should be doing the shaking. (*The Prince is sleepy.*) Your Highness! My work in the Great Arsenal of Venice brought me in daily contact with sailors, carpenters, and so on. These men are unread. They depend on the evidence of their senses. But they taught me many new ways of doing things. The question is whether these gentlemen here want to be found out as fools by men who might not have had the advantages of a classical education but who are not afraid to use their eyes. I tell you that our dockyards are stirring with that same high curiosity which was the true glory of Ancient Greece.

(*Pause*)

PHILOSOPHER: I have no doubt Mr. Galilei's theories will arouse the enthusiasm of the dockyards.

CHAMBERLAIN: Your Highness, I find to my amazement that this highly informative discussion has exceeded the time we had allowed for it. May I remind Your Highness that the State Ball begins in three-quarters of an hour?

(*The Court bows low.*)

ELDERLY LADY: We would really have liked to look through your eyeglass, Mr. Galilei, wouldn't we, Your Highness? (*The Prince bows politely and is led to the door. Galileo follows the Prince, Chamberlain and Ladies towards the exit. The Professors remain at the telescope.*)

GALILEO (*almost servile*): All anybody has to do is look through the telescope, Your Highness.

(*Mrs. Sarti takes a plate with candies to the Prince as he is walking out.*)

MRS. SARTI: A piece of homemade candy, Your Highness?

ELDERLY LADY: Not now. Thank you. It is too soon before His Highness' supper.

PHILOSOPHER: Wouldn't I like to take that thing to pieces.

MATHEMATICIAN: Ingenious contraption. It must be quite difficult to keep clean. (*He rubs the lens with his handkerchief and looks at the handkerchief.*)

FEDERZONI: We did not paint the Medicean stars on the lens.

ELDERLY LADY (*to the Prince, who has whispered something to her*): No, no, no, there is nothing the matter with your stars!

CHAMBERLAIN (*across the stage to Galileo*): His Highness will of course seek the opinion of the greatest living authority: Christopher Clavius, Chief Astronomer to the Papal College in Rome.

Scene Five

Things take indeed a wondrous turn
When learned men do stoop to learn.
Clavius, we are pleased to say,
Upheld Galileo Galilei.

A burst of laughter is heard and the curtains reveal a ball in the Collegium Romanum. High Churchmen, monks and Scholars standing about talking and laughing. Galileo by himself in a corner.

FAT PRELATE (*shaking with laughter*): Hopeless! Hopeless! Hopeless! Will you tell me something people won't believe?

A SCHOLAR: Yes, that you don't love your stomach!

FAT PRELATE: They'd believe that. They only do not believe what's good for them. They doubt the devil, but fill them up with some fiddle-de-dee about the earth rolling like a marble in the gutter and they swallow it hook, line, and sinker. Sancta simplicitas!
(*He laughs until the tears run down his cheeks. The others laugh with him. A group has formed whose members boisterously begin to pretend they are standing on a rolling globe.*)

A MONK: It's rolling fast, I'm dizzy. May I hold on to you, Professor? (*He sways dizzily and clings to one of the scholars for support.*)

THE SCHOLAR: Old Mother Earth's been at the bottle again. Whoa!

MONK Hey! Hey! We're slipping off! Help!

SECOND SCHOLAR: Look! There's Venus! Hold me, lads. Whee!

SECOND MONK: Don't, don't hurl us off on to the moon. There are nasty sharp mountain peaks on the moon, brethren!

VARIOUSLY: Hold tight! Hold tight! Don't look down! Hold tight! It'll make you giddy!

FAT PRELATE: And we cannot have giddy people in Holy Rome. (*They rock with laughter. An infuriated Monk comes out from a large door at the rear holding a Bible in his hand and pointing out a page with his finger.*)

INFURIATED MONK: What does the Bible say—"Sun, stand thou still on Gideon and thou, moon, in the valley of Ajalon." Can the sun come to a standstill if it doesn't ever move? Does the Bible lie?

FAT PRELATE: How did Christopher Clavius, the greatest astronomer we have, get mixed up in an investigation of this kind?

INFURIATED MONK: He's in there with his eye glued to that diabolical instrument.

FAT PRELATE (*to Galileo, who has been playing with his pebble and has dropped it*): Mr. Galilei, something dropped down.

GALILEO: Monsignor, are you sure it didn't drop up?

INFURIATED MONK: As astronomers we are aware that there are phenomena which are beyond us, but man can't expect to understand everything!

(*Enter a very old Cardinal leaning on a Monk for support. Others move aside.*)

OLD CARDINAL: Aren't they out yet? Can't they reach a decision on that paltry matter? Christopher Clavius ought to know his astronomy after all these years. I am informed that Mr. Galilei transfers mankind from the center of the universe to somewhere on the outskirts. Mr. Galilei is therefore an enemy of mankind and must be dealt with as such. Is it conceivable that God would trust this most precious fruit of His labor to a minor frolicking star? Would He have sent His Son to such a place? How can there be people with such twisted minds that they believe what they're told by the slave of a multiplication table?

FAT PRELATE (*quietly to Cardinal*): The gentleman is over there.

OLD CARDINAL: So you are the man. You know my eyes are not what they were, but I can see you bear a striking resemblance to the man we burned. What was his name?

MONK Your Eminence must avoid excitement, the doctor said . . .

OLD CARDINAL (*disregarding him*): So you have degraded the earth despite the fact that you live by her and receive everything from her. I won't have it! I won't have it! I won't be a nobody on an inconsequential star briefly twirling hither and thither. I tread the earth, and the earth is firm beneath my feet, and there is no motion to the earth, and the earth is the center of all things, and I am the center of the earth, and the eye of the creator is upon me. About me revolve, affixed to their crystal shells, the lesser lights of the stars and the great light of the sun, created to give light upon me that God might see me—Man, God's greatest effort, the center of creation. "In the image of God created He him." Immortal . . . (*His strength fails him and he catches for the Monk for support.*)

MONK: You musn't overtax your strength, Your Eminence. (*At this moment the door at the rear opens and Christopher Clavius enters followed by his Astronomers. He strides hastily across the hall, looking neither to right nor left. As he goes by we hear him say—*)

CLAVIUS: He is right.
  (Deadly silence. All turn to Galileo.)
OLD CARDINAL: What is it? Have they reached a decision?
  (No one speaks.)
MONK: It is time that Your Eminence went home.
  (The hall is emptying fast. One little Monk who had entered with Clavius speaks to Galileo.)
LITTLE MONK: Mr. Galilei, I heard Father Clavius say: "Now it's for the theologians to set the heavens right again." You have won.
  (Before the next scene a curtain with the following legend on it is lowered.)

. . . . . . As these new astronomical charts enable us to determine longitudes at sea and so make it possible to reach the new continents by the shortest routes, we would beseech Your Excellency to aid us in reaching Mr. Galilei, mathematician to the Court of Florence, who is now in Rome. . . . . .
  —From a letter written by a member of the Genoa Chamber of Commerce and Navigation to the Papal Legation.

Scene Six

When Galileo was in Rome
A Cardinal asked him to his home
He wined and dined him as his guest
And only made one small request.

Cardinal Bellarmin's house in Rome. Music is heard and the chatter of many guests. Two Secretaries are at the rear of the stage at a desk. Galileo, his daughter Virginia, now 21, and Ludovico Marsili, who has become her fiancé, are just arriving. A few Guests, standing near the entrance with masks in their hands, nudge each other and are suddenly silent. Galileo looks at them. They applaud him politely and bow.

VIRGINIA: O father! I'm so happy. I won't dance with anyone but you, Ludovico.

GALILEO (*to a Secretary*): I was to wait here for His Eminence.

FIRST SECRETARY: His Eminence will be with you in a few minutes.

VIRGINIA: Do I look proper?

LUDOVICO: You are showing some lace.

(Galileo puts his arms around their shoulders.)

GALILEO (*quoting mischievously*):
Fret not, daughter, if perchance
You attract a wanton glance.
The eyes that catch a trembling lace
Will guess the heartbeat's quickened pace.
Lovely woman still may be
Careless with felicity.

VIRGINIA (*to Galileo*): Feel my heart.

GALILEO (*to Ludovico*): It's thumping.

VIRGINIA: I hope I always say the right thing.

LUDOVICO: She's afraid she's going to let us down.

VIRGINIA: Oh, I want to look beautiful.

GALILEO: You'd better. If you don't they'll start saying all over again that the earth doesn't turn.

LUDOVICO (*laughing*): It *doesn't* turn, sir.

(Galileo laughs.)

GALILEO: Go and enjoy yourselves. *(He speaks to one of the Secretaries.)* A large fête?

FIRST SECRETARY: Two hundred and fifty guests, Mr. Galilei. We have represented here this evening most of the great families of Italy, the Orsinis, the Villanis, the Nuccolis, the Soldanieris, the Canes, the Lecchis, the Estensis, the Colombinis, the . . .

(Virginia comes running back.)

VIRGINIA: Oh father, I didn't tell you: you're famous.

GALILEO: Why?

VIRGINIA The hairdresser in the Via Vittorio kept four other ladies waiting and took me first. *(Exit)*

GALILEO *(at the stairway, leaning over the well)*: Rome!

(Enter Cardinal Bellarmin, wearing the mask of a lamb, and Cardinal Barberini, wearing the mask of a dove)

SECRETARIES: Their Eminences, Cardinals Bellarmin and Barberini.

(The Cardinals lower their masks.)

GALILEO *(to Bellarmin)*: Your Eminence.

BELLARMIN: Mr. Galilei, Cardinal Barberini.

GALILEO: Your Eminence.

BARBERINI: So you are the father of that lovely child!

BELLARMIN: Who is inordinately proud of being her father's daughter. *(They laugh.)*

BARBERINI *(points his finger at Galileo)*: "The sun riseth and setteth and returneth to its place," saith the Bible. What saith Galilei?

GALILEO: Appearances are notoriously deceptive, Your Eminence. Once when I was so high, I was standing on a ship that was pulling away from the shore and I shouted, "The shore is moving!" I know now that it was the ship which was moving.

BARBERINI *(laughs)*: You can't catch that man. I tell you, Bellarmin, his moons around Jupiter are hard nuts to crack. Unfortunately for me I happened to glance at a few papers on astronomy once. It is harder to get rid of than the itch.

BELLARMIN: Let's move with the times. If it makes navigation easier for sailors to use new charts based on a new hypothesis let them have them. We only have to scotch doctrines that contradict Holy Writ. *(He leans over the balustrade of the well and acknowledges various Guests.)*

BARBERINI: But Bellarmin, you haven't caught on to this fellow. The scriptures don't satisfy him. Copernicus does.

GALILEO: Copernicus? "He that withholdeth corn the people shall curse him." Book of Proverbs.

BARBERINI: "A prudent man concealeth knowledge." Also Book of Proverbs.

GALILEO: "Where no oxen are, the stable is clean, but much increase is by the strength of the ox."

BARBERINI "He that ruleth his spirit is better than he that taketh a city."

GALILEO: "But a broken spirit drieth up the bones." (*Pause*) "Doth not wisdom cry?"

BARBERINI: "Can one walk on hot coals and his feet not be scorched?"—Welcome to Rome, Friend Galileo. You recall the legend of our city's origin? Two small boys found sustenance and refuge with a she-wolf and from that day we have paid the price for the she-wolf's milk. But the place is not bad. We have everything for your pleasure—from a scholarly dispute with Bellarmin to ladies of high degree. Look at that woman flaunting herself. No? He wants a weighty discussion! All right! (*To Galileo*) You people speak in terms of circles and ellipses and regular velocities—simple movements that the human mind can grasp—very convenient—but suppose Almighty God had taken it into his head to make the stars move like that . . . (*He describes an irregular motion with his fingers through the air.*) . . . then where would you be?

GALILEO: My good man—the Almighty would have endowed us with brains like that . . . (*Repeats the movement*) . . . so that we could grasp the movements . . . (*Repeats the movement*) . . . like that. I believe in the brain.

BARBERINI: I consider the brain inadequate. He doesn't answer. He is too polite to tell me he considers *my* brain inadequate. What is one to do with him? Butter wouldn't melt in his mouth. All he wants to do is to prove that God made a few boners in astronomy. God didn't study his astronomy hard enough before he composed Holy Writ. (*To the Secretaries*) Don't take anything down. This is a scientific discussion among friends.

BELLARMIN (*to Galileo*): Does it not appear more probably—even to you—that the Creator knows more about his work than the created?

GALILEO: In his blindness man is liable to misread not only the sky but also the Bible.

BELLARMIN: The interpretation of the Bible is a matter for the ministers of God. (*Galileo remains silent.*) At last you are quiet. (*He gestures to the Secretaries. They start writing.*) Tonight the Holy Office has decided that the theory according to which the earth goes around the sun is foolish, absurd, and a heresy. I am charged, Mr. Galilei, with cautioning you to abandon these teachings. (*To the First Secretary*) Would you repeat that?

FIRST SECRETARY: (*reading*) "His Eminence, Cardinal Bellarmin, to the aforesaid Galilei: The Holy Office has resolved that the theory according to which the earth goes around the sun is foolish, absurd, and a heresy. I am charged, Mr. Galilei, with cautioning you to abandon these teachings."

GALILEO (*rocking on his base*): But the facts!

BARBERINI (*consoling*): Your findings have been ratified by the Papal Observatory, Galilei. That should be most flattering to you . . .

BELLARMIN (*cutting in*): The Holy Office formulated the decree without going into details.

GALILEO (*to Barberini*): Do you realize, the future of all scientific research is . . .

BELLARMIN (*cutting in*): Completely assured, Mr. Galilei. It is not given to man to know the truth: it is granted to him to seek after the truth. Science is the legitimate and beloved daughter of the Church. She must have confidence in the Church.

GALILEO (*infuriated*): I would not try confidence by whistling her too often.

BARBERINI (*quickly*): Be careful what you're doing—you'll be throwing out the baby with the bath water, friend Galilei. (*Serious*) We need you more than you need us.

BELLARMIN: Well, it is time we introduced our distinguished friend to our guests. The whole country talks of him!

BARBERINI: Let us replace our masks, Bellarmin. Poor Galilei hasn't got one.

(*He laughs. They take Galileo out.*)

FIRST SECRETARY: Did you get his last sentence?

SECOND SECRETARY: Yes. Do you have what he said about believing in the brain?

(*Another cardinal—the Inquisitor—enters.*)

INQUISITOR: Did the conference take place?

(*The First Secretary hands him the papers and the Inquisitor dismisses the Secretaries. They go. The Inquisitor sits down and starts to read the transcription. Two or three Young Ladies skitter across the stage; they see the Inquisitor and curtsy as they go.*)

YOUNG GIRL: Who was that?

HER FRIEND: The Cardinal Inquisitor.

(*They giggle and go. Enter Virginia. She curtsies as she goes. The Inquisitor stops her.*)

INQUISITOR: Good evening, my child. Beautiful night. May I congratulate you on your betrothal? Your young man comes from a fine family. Are you staying with us here in Rome?

VIRGINIA: Not now, Your Eminence. I must go home to prepare for the wedding.

INQUISITOR: Ah. You are accompanying your father to Florence. That should please him. Science must be cold comfort in a home. Your youth and warmth will keep him down to earth. It is easy to get lost up there. (*He gestures to the sky.*)

VIRGINIA: He doesn't talk to me about the stars, Your Eminence.

INQUISITOR: No. (*He laughs.*) They don't eat fish in the fisherman's house. I can tell you something about astronomy. My child, it seems that God has blessed our modern astronomers with imaginations. It is quite alarming! Do you know that the earth—which we old fogies supposed to be so large—has shrunk to something no bigger than a walnut, and the new universe has grown so vast that prelates—and even cardinals—look like ants. Why, God Almighty might lose sight of a Pope! I wonder if I know your Father Confessor.

VIRGINIA: Father Christopherus, from Saint Ursula's at Florence, Your Eminence.

INQUISITOR: My dear child, your father will need you. Not so much now perhaps, but one of these days. You are pure, and there is strength in purity. Greatness is sometimes, indeed often, too heavy a burden for those to whom God has granted it. What man is so great that he has no place in a prayer? But I am keeping you, my dear. Your fiancé will be jealous of me, and I am afraid your father will never forgive me for holding forth on astronomy. Go to your dancing and remember me to Father Christopherus.

(*Virginia kisses his ring and runs off. The Inquisitor resumes his reading.*)

Scene Seven

Galileo, feeling grim,
A young monk came to visit him.
The monk was born of common folk.
It was of science that they spoke.

Garden of the Florentine Ambassador in Rome. Distant hum of a great city. Galileo and the Little Monk of Scene Five are talking.

GALILEO: Let's hear it. That robe you're wearing gives you the right to say whatever you want to say. Let's hear it.

LITTLE MONK: I have studied physics, Mr. Galilei.

GALILEO: That might help us if it enabled you to admit that two and two are four.

LITTLE MONK: Mr. Galilei, I have spent four sleepless nights trying to reconcile the decree that I have read with the moons of Jupiter that I have seen. This morning I decided to come to see you after I had said Mass.

GALILEO: To tell me that Jupiter has no moons?

LITTLE MONK: No, I found out that I think the decree a wise decree. It has shocked me into realizing that free research has its dangers. I have had to decide to give up astronomy. However, I felt the impulse to confide in you some of the motives which have impelled even a passionate physicist to abandon his work.

GALILEO: Your motives are familiar to me.

LITTLE MONK: You mean, of course, the special powers invested in certain commissions of the Holy Office? But there is something else. I would like to talk to you about my family. I do not come from the great city. My parents are peasants in the Campagna, who know about the cultivation of the olive tree, and not much about anything else. Too often these days when I am trying to concentrate on tracking down the moons of Jupiter, I see my parents. I see them sitting by the fire with my sister, eating their curded cheese. I see the beams of the ceiling above them, which the smoke of centuries has blackened, and I can see the veins stand out on their toil-worn hands, and

the little spoons in their hands. They scrape a living, and underlying their poverty there is a sort of order. There are routines. The
routine of scrubbing the floors, the routine of the seasons in the
olive orchard, the routine of paying taxes. The troubles that come
to them are recurrent troubles. My father did not get his poor bent
back all at once, but little by little, year by year, in the olive orchard; just as year after year, with unfailing regularity, childbirth
has made my mother more and more sexless. They draw the
strength they need to sweat with their loaded baskets up the stony
paths, to bear children, even to eat, from the sight of the trees
greening each year anew, from the reproachful face of the soil,
which is never satisfied, and from the little church and Bible texts
they hear there on Sunday. They have been told that God relies
upon them and that the pageant of the world has been written
around them that they may be tested in the important or unimpor-
tant parts handed out to them. How could they take it, were I to
tell them that they are on a lump of stone ceaselessly spinning in
empty space, circling around a second-rate star? What, then,
would be the use of their patience, their acceptance of misery?
What comfort, then, the Holy Scriptures, which have mercifully
explained their crucifixion? The Holy Scriptures would then be
proved full of mistakes. No, I see them begin to look frightened. I
see them slowly put their spoons down on the table. They would
feel cheated. "There is no eye watching over us, after all," they
would say. "We have to start out on our own, at our time of life.
Nobody has planned a part for us beyond this wretched one on a
worthless star. There is no meaning in our misery. Hunger is just
not having eaten. It is no test of strength. Effort is just stooping
and carrying. It is not a virtue." Can you understand that I read
into the decree of the Holy Office a noble motherly pity and a
great goodness of the soul?

GALILEO (*embarrassed*): Hm, well at least you have found out that it
is not a question of the satellites of Jupiter, but of the peasants of the
Campagna! And don't try to break me down by the halo of beauty
that radiates from old age. How does a pearl develop in an oyster? A
jagged grain of sand makes its way into the oyster's shell and makes
its life unbearable. The oyster exudes slime to cover the grain of
sand and the slime eventually hardens into a pearl. The oyster nearly
dies in the process. To hell with the pearl, give me the healthy oyster! And virtues are not exclusive to misery. If your parents were
prosperous and happy, they might develop the virtues of happiness
and prosperity. Today the virtues of exhaustion are caused by the

exhausted land. For that my new water pumps could work more wonders than their ridiculous superhuman efforts. Be fruitful and multiply: for war will cut down the population, and our fields are barren! (*A pause*) Shall I lie to your people?

LITTLE MONK: We must be silent from the highest of motives: the inward peace of less fortunate souls.

GALILEO: My dear man, as a bonus for not meddling with your parents' peace, the authorities are tendering me, on a silver platter, persecution-free, my share of the fat sweated from your parents, who, as you know, were made in God's image. Should I condone this decree, my motives might not be disinterested: easy life, no persecution and so on.

LITTLE MONK: Mr. Galileo. I am a priest.

GALILEO: You are also a physicist. How can new machinery be evolved to domesticate the river water if we physicists are forbidden to study, discuss, and pool our findings about the greatest machinery of all, the machinery of the heavenly bodies? Can I reconcile my findings on the paths of falling bodies with the current belief in the tracks of witches on broom sticks? (*A pause*) I am sorry—I shouldn't have said that.

LITTLE MONK: You don't think that the truth, if it is the truth, would make its way without us?

GALILEO: No! No! No! As much of the truth gets through as we push through. You talk about the Campagna peasants as if they were the moss on their huts. Naturally, if they don't get a move on and learn to think for themselves, the most efficient of irrigation systems cannot help them. I can see their divine patience, but where is their divine fury?

LITTLE MONK (*helpless*): They are old!

(*Galileo stands for a moment, beaten; he cannot meet the little monk's eyes. He takes a manuscript from the table and throws it violently on the ground.*)

LITTLE MONK: What is that?

GALILEO: Here is writ what draws the ocean when it ebbs and flows. Let it lie there. Thou shalt not read. (*Little Monk has picked up the manuscript.*) Already! An apple of the tree of knowledge, he can't wait, he wolfs it down. He will rot in hell for all eternity. Look at him, where are his manners?—Sometimes I think I would let them imprison me in a place a thousand feet beneath the earth where no light could reach me, if in exchange I could find out what stuff that is: "Light." The bad thing is that, when I find something, I have to boast about it like a lover or a drunkard or a traitor. That is a hopeless vice and leads to the abyss. I wonder how long I shall be content to discuss it with my dog!

LITTLE MONK (*immersed in the manuscript*): I don't understand this sentence.

GALILEO: I'll explain it to you, I'll explain it to you.

(*They are sitting on the floor.*)

Scene Eight

Eight long years with tongue in cheek
Of what he knew he did not speak.
Then temptation grew too great
And Galileo challenged fate.

Galileo's house in Florence again. Galileo is supervising his Assistants Andrea, Federzoni, and the Little Monk who are about to prepare an experiment. Mrs. Sarti and Virginia are at a long table sewing bridal linen. There is a new telescope, larger than the old one. At the moment it is covered with a cloth.

ANDREA (*looking up a schedule*): Thursday. Afternoon. Floating bodies again. Ice, bowl of water, scales, and it says here an iron needle. Aristotle.

VIRGINIA: Ludovico likes to entertain. We must take care to be neat. His mother notices every stitch. She doesn't approve of father's books.

MRS. SARTI: That's all a thing of the past. He hasn't published a book for years.

VIRGINIA: That's true. Oh Sarti, it's fun sewing a trousseau.

MRS. SARTI: Virginia, I want to talk to you. You are very young, and you have no mother, and your father is putting those pieces of ice in water, and marriage is too serious a business to go into blind. Now you should go to see a real astronomer from the university and have him cast your horoscope so you know where you stand. (*Virginia giggles.*) What's the matter?

VIRGINIA: I've been already.

MRS. SARTI Tell Sarti.

VIRGINIA: I have to be careful for three months now because the sun is in Capricorn, but after that I get a favorable ascendant, and I can undertake a journey if I am careful of Uranus, as I'm a Scorpion.

MRS. SARTI: What about Ludovico?

VIRGINIA: He's a Leo, the astronomer said. Leos are sensual.
(*Giggles*)

(There is a knock at the door, it opens. Enter the Rector of the University, the philosopher of Scene Four, bringing a book.)

RECTOR (*to Virginia*): This is about the burning issue of the moment. He may want to glance over it. My faculty would appreciate his comments. No, don't disturb him now, my dear. Every minute one takes of your father's time is stolen from Italy. (*He goes*)

VIRGINIA: Federzoni! The rector of the university brought this. *(Federzoni takes it.)*

GALILEO: What's it about?

FEDERZONI (*spelling*): De maculis in sole.

ANDREA: Oh, it's on the sun spots! *(Andrea comes one side, and the Little Monk the other, to look at the book.)*

ANDREA: A new one! *(Federzoni resentfully puts the book into their hands and continues with the preparation of the experiment.)*

ANDREA: Listen to this dedication. (*Quotes*) "To the greatest living authority on physics, Galileo Galilei."—I read Fabricius' paper the other day. Fabricius says the spots are clusters of planets between us and the sun.

LITTLE MONK: Doubtful.

GALILEO (*noncommittal*): Yes?

ANDREA Paris and Prague hold that they are vapors from the sun. Federzoni doubts that.

FEDERZONI: Me? You leave me out. I said "hm," that was all. And don't discuss new things before me. I can't read the material, it's in Latin. (*He drops the scales and stands trembling with fury.*) Tell me, can I doubt anything?

(Galileo walks over and picks up the scales silently. Pause.)

LITTLE MONK: There is happiness in doubting. I wonder why.

ANDREA: Aren't we going to take this up?

GALILEO: At the moment we are investigating floating bodies.

ANDREA: Mother has baskets full of letters from all over Europe asking his opinion.

FEDERZONI: The question is whether you can afford to remain silent.

GALILEO: I cannot afford to be smoked on a wood fire like a ham.

ANDREA (*surprised*): Ah. You think the sun spots may have something to do with that again? (*Galileo does not answer.*)

ANDREA: Well, we stick to fiddling about with bits of ice in water. They can't hurt you.

GALILEO: Correct.—Our thesis!

ANDREA: All things that are lighter than water float, and all things that are heavier sink.

GALILEO: Aristotle says—

LITTLE MONK (*reading out of a book, translating*): "A broad and flat disk of ice, although heavier than water, still floats, because it is unable to divide the water."

GALILEO: Well, now I push the ice below the surface. I take away the pressure of my hands. What happens?
(Pause)

LITTLE MONK: It rises to the surface.

GALILEO: Correct. It seems to be able to divide the water as it's coming up, doesn't it?

LITTLE MONK: Could it be lighter than water after all?

GALILEO: Aha!

ANDREA: Then all things that are lighter than water float, and all things that are heavier sink. Q. e. d.

GALILEO: Not at all. Hand me that iron needle. Heavier than water? (*They all nod.*) A piece of paper. (*He places the needle on a piece of paper and floats it on the surface of the water. Pause.*) Do not be hasty with your conclusion. (*Pause*) What happens?

FEDERZONI: The paper has sunk, the needle is floating.

VIRGINIA: What's the matter?

MRS. SARTI Every time I hear them laugh it sends shivers down my spine.
(There is a knocking at the outer door.)

MRS. SARTI: Who's that at the door?
(Enter Ludovico. Virginia runs to him. They embrace. Ludovico is followed by a servant with baggage.)

MRS. SARTI: Well!

VIRGINIA: Oh! Why didn't you write that you were coming?

LUDOVICO: I decided on the spur of the moment. I was over inspecting our vineyards at Bucciole. I couldn't keep away.

GALILEO: Who's that?

LITTLE MONK: Miss Virginia's intended. What's the matter with your eyes?

GALILEO (*blinking*): Oh yes, it's Ludovico, so it is. Well! Sarti, get a jug of that Sicilian wine, the old kind. We celebrate.
(Everybody sits down. Mrs. Sarti has left, followed by Ludovico's Servant.)

GALILEO: Well, Ludovico, old man. How are the horses?

LUDOVICO: The horses are fine.

GALILEO: Fine.

LUDOVICO: But those vineyards need a firm hand. (*To Virginia*) You look pale. Country life will suit you. Mother's planning on September.

VIRGINIA: I suppose I oughtn't, but stay here, I've got something to show you.

LUDOVICO: What?

VIRGINIA: Never mind. I won't be ten minutes. (*She runs out*)

LUDOVICO: How's life these days, sir?

GALILEO: Dull.—How was the journey?

LUDOVICO: Dull.—Before I forget, mother sends her congratulations on your admirable tact over the latest rumblings of science.

GALILEO: Thank her from me.

LUDOVICO: Christopher Clavius had all Rome on its ears. He said he was afraid that the turning around business might crop up again on account of these spots on the sun.

ANDREA: Clavius is on the same track! (*To Ludovico*) My mother's baskets are full of letters from all over Europe asking Mr. Galilei's opinion.

GALILEO: I am engaged in investigating the habits of floating bodies. Any harm in that?

(*Mrs. Sarti re-enters, followed by the Servant. They bring wine and glasses on a tray.*)

GALILEO (*hands out the wine*): What news from the Holy City, apart from the prospect of my sins?

LUDOVICO: The Holy Father is on his death bed. Hadn't you heard?

LITTLE MONK: My goodness! What about the succession?

LUDOVICO: All the talk is of Barberini.

GALILEO: Barberini?

ANDREA: Mr. Galilei knows Barberini.

LITTLE MONK: Cardinal Barberini is a mathematician.

FEDERZONI: A scientist in the chair of Peter!

(*Pause*)

GALILEO (*cheering up enormously*): This means change. We might live to see the day, Federzoni, when we don't have to whisper that two and two are four. (*To Ludovico*) I like this wine. Don't you, Ludovico?

LUDOVICO: I like it.

GALILEO: I know the hill where it is grown. The slope is steep and stony, the grape almost blue. I am fond of this wine.

LUDOVICO: Yes, sir.

GALILEO: There are shadows in this wine. It is almost sweet but just

stops short.—Andrea, clear that stuff away, ice, bowl and needle.—
I cherish the consolations of the flesh. I have no patience with cow
ards who call them weaknesses. I say there is a certain achievement
in enjoying things.

(The Pupils get up and go to the experiment table.)

LITTLE MONK: What are we to do?

FEDERZONI: He is starting on the sun.

(They begin with clearing up.)

ANDREA *(singing in a low voice)*:
  The Bible proves the earth stands still,
  The Pope, he swears with tears:
  The earth stands still. To prove it so
  He takes it by the ears.

LUDOVICO: What's the excitement?

MRS. SARTI: You're not going to start those hellish goings-on again,
  Mr. Galilei?

ANDREA:
  And gentlefolk, they say so too.
  Each learned doctor proves,
  (If you grease his palm): The earth stands still.
  And yet—and yet it moves.

GALILEO: Barberini is in the ascendant, so your mother is uneasy, and
  you're sent to investigate me. Correct me if I am wrong, Ludovico.
  Clavius is right: these spots on the sun interest me.

ANDREA: We might find out that the sun also revolves. How would
  you like that, Ludovico?

GALILEO: Do you like my wine, Ludovico?

LUDOVICO: I told you I did, sir.

GALILEO: You really like it?

LUDOVICO: I like it.

GALILEO: Tell me, Ludovico, would you consider going so far as to
  accept a man's wine or his daughter without insisting that he drop
  his profession? I have no wish to intrude, but have the moons of
  Jupiter affected Virginia's bottom?

MRS. SARTI: That isn't funny, it's just vulgar. I am going for Virginia.

LUDOVICO *(keeps her back)*: Marriages in families such as mine are
  not arranged on a basis of sexual attraction alone.

GALILEO: Did they keep you back from marrying my daughter for
  eight years because I was on probation?

LUDOVICO: My future wife must take her place in the family pew.

GALILEO: You mean, if the daughter of a bad man sat in your family
  pew, your peasants might stop paying the rent?

LUDOVICO: In a sort of way.

GALILEO: When I was your age, the only person I allowed to rap me on the knuckles was my girl.

LUDOVICO: My mother was assured that you had undertaken not to get mixed up in this turning around business again, sir.

GALILEO: We had a conservative Pope then.

MRS. SARTI: Had! His Holiness is not dead yet!

GALILEO (*with relish*): Pretty nearly.

MRS. SARTI: That man will weigh a chip of ice fifty times, but when it comes to something that's convenient, he believes it blindly. "Is His Holiness dead?"—"Pretty nearly!"

LUDOVICO: You will find, sir, if His Holiness passes away, the new Pope, whoever he turns out to be, will respect the convictions held by the solid families of the country.

GALILEO (*to Andrea*): That remains to be seen.—Andrea, get out the screen. We'll throw the image of the sun on our screen to save our eyes.

LITTLE MONK: I thought you'd been working at it. Do you know when I guessed it? When you didn't recognize Mr. Marsili.

MRS. SARTI: If my son has to go to hell for sticking to you, that's my affair, but you have no right to trample on your daughter's happiness.

LUDOVICO (*to his Servant*): Giuseppe, take my baggage back to the coach, will you?

MRS. SARTI: This will kill her. (*She runs out, still clutching the jug.*)

LUDOVICO (*politely*): Mr. Galilei, if we Marsilis were to countenance teachings frowned on by the church, it would unsettle our peasants. Bear in mind: these poor people in their brute state get everything upside down. They are nothing but animals. They will never comprehend the finer points of astronomy. Why, two months ago a rumor went around, an apple had been found on a pear tree, and they left their work in the fields to discuss it.

GALILEO (*interested*): Did they?

LUDOVICO: I have seen the day when my poor mother has had to have a dog whipped before their eyes to remind them to keep their place. Oh, you may have seen the waving corn from the window of your comfortable coach. You have, no doubt, nibbled our olives, and absentmindedly eaten our cheese, but you can have no idea how much responsibility that sort of thing entails.

GALILEO: Young man, I do not eat my cheese absentmindedly. (*To Andrea*) Are we ready?

ANDREA: Yes, sir.

GALILEO (*leaves Ludovico and adjusts the mirror*): You would not confine your whippings to dogs to remind your peasants to keep their places, would you, Marsili?

LUDOVICO (*after a pause*): Mr. Galilei, you have a wonderful brain, it's a pity.

LITTLE MONK (*astonished*): He threatened you.

GALILEO: Yes. And he threatened you too. We might unsettle his peasants. Your sister, Fulganzio, who works the lever of the olive press, might laugh out loud if she heard the sun is not a gilded coat of arms but a lever too. The earth turns because the sun turns it.

ANDREA: That could interest his steward too and even his money lender—and the seaport towns. . . .

FEDERZONI: None of them speak Latin.

GALILEO: I might write in plain language. The work we do is exacting. Who would go through the strain for less than the population at large!

LUDOVICO: I see you have made your decision. It was inevitable. You will always be a slave of your passions. Excuse me to Virginia, I think it's as well I don't see her now.

GALILEO: The dowry is at your disposal at any time.

LUDOVICO: Good afternoon. (*He goes followed by the Servant.*)

ANDREA: Exit Ludovico. To hell with all Marsilis, Villanis, Orsinis, Canes, Nuccolis, Soldanieris. . . .

FEDERZONI: . . . who ordered the earth stand still because their castles might be shaken loose if it revolves . . .

LITTLE MONK: . . . and who only kiss the Pope's feet as long as he uses them to trample on the people. God made the physical world, God made the human brain. God will allow physics.

ANDREA: They will try to stop us.

GALILEO: Thus we enter the observation of these spots on the sun in which we are interested, at our own risk, not counting on protection from a problematical new Pope . . .

ANDREA: . . . but with great likelihood of dispelling Fabricius' vapors, and the shadows of Paris and Prague, and of establishing the rotation of the sun . . .

GALILEO : . . . and with *some* likelihood of establishing the rotation of the sun. My intention is not to prove that I was right but to find out *whether* I was right. "Abandon hope all ye who enter—an observation." Before assuming these phenomena are spots, which would suit us, let us first set about proving that they are not—fried fish. We crawl by inches. What we find today we will wipe from the blackboard tomorrow and reject it—unless it shows up again the day after tomorrow. And if we find anything which would suit us, that thing we will eye with particular distrust. In fact, we will approach this observing of the sun with the implacable determination to prove that the earth stands still and only if hopelessly defeated in this pious undertaking can we allow ourselves to wonder if we may not have been right all the time: the earth revolves. Take the cloth off the telescope and turn it on the sun.

(Quietly they start work. When the corruscating image of the sun is focused on the screen, Virginia enters hurriedly, her wedding dress on, her hair disheveled, Mrs. Sarti with her, carrying her wedding veil. The two women realize what has happened. Virginia faints. Andrea, Little Monk and Galileo rush to her. Federzoni continues working.)

Scene Nine

On April Fool's Day, thirty two,
Of science there was much ado.
People had learned from Galilei:
They used his teaching in their way.

Around the corner from the market place a Street Singer and his Wife,
who is costumed to represent the earth in a skeleton globe made of
thin hands of brass, are holding the attention of a sprinkling of
representative citizens, some in masquerade who were on their way to
see the carnival procession. From the market place the noise of an
impatient crowd.

BALLAD SINGER (*accompanied by his Wife on the guitar*):
  When the Almighty made the universe
  He made the earth and then he made the sun.
  Then round the earth he bade the sun to turn—
  That's in the Bible, Genesis, Chapter One.
  And from that time all beings here below
  Were in obedient circles meant to go:
    Around the pope the cardinals
    Around the cardinals the bishops
    Around the bishops the secretaries
    Around the secretaries the aldermen
    Around the aldermen the craftsmen
    Around the craftsmen the servants
    Around the servants the dogs, the chickens, and the beggars.
  (*A conspicuous reveller—henceforth called the Spinner—has slowly*
  caught on and is exhibiting his idea of spinning around. He does
  not lose dignity, he faints with mock grace.)
BALLAD SINGER:
  Up stood the learned Galileo
  Glanced briefly at the sun
  And said: "Almighty God was wrong
  In Genesis, Chapter One!"

Now that was rash, my friends, it is no matter small
For heresy will spread today like foul diseases.
Change Holy Writ, forsooth? What will be left at all?
Why: each of us would say and do just what he pleases!

(Three wretched Extras, employed by the chamber of commerce, en-
ter. Two of them, in ragged costumes, moodily bear a litter with a
mock throne. The third sits on the throne. He wears sacking, a false
beard, a prop crown, he carries a prop orb and sceptre, and around
his chest the inscription "The King of Hungary." The litter has a
card with "No. 4" written on it. The litter bearers dump him down
and listen to the Ballad Singer.)

BALLAD SINGER:

Good people, what will come to pass
If Galileo's teachings spread?
No altar boy will serve the mass
No servant girl will make the bed.

Now that is grave, my friends, it is no matter small:
For independent spirit spreads like foul diseases!
(Yet life is sweet and man is weak and after all—
How nice it is, for a little change, to do just as one pleases!)

(The Ballad Singer takes over the guitar. His Wife dances around
him, illustrating the motion of the earth. A Cobbler's Boy with a
pair of resplendent lacquered boots hung over his shoulder has been
jumping up and down in mock excitement. There are three more
children, dressed as grownups among the spectators, two together
and a single one with mother. The Cobbler's Boy takes the three
Children in hand, forms a chain and leads it, moving to the music,
in and out among the spectators, "whipping" the chain so that the
last child bumps into people. On the way past a Peasant Woman,
he steals an egg from her basket. She gestures to him to return it. As
he passes her again he quietly breaks the egg over her head. The
King of Hungary ceremoniously hands his orb to one of his bear-
ers, marches down with mock dignity, and chastises the Cobbler's
Boy. The parents remove the three Children. The unseemliness
subsides.)

BALLAD SINGER:

The carpenters take wood and build
Their houses—not the church's pews.
And members of the cobblers' guild
Now boldly walk the streets—in shoes.
The tenant kicks the noble lord
Quite off the land he owned—like that!

The milk his wife once gave the priest
Now makes (at last!) her children fat.

  Ts, ts, ts, ts, my friends, this is no matter small
  For independent spirit spreads like foul diseases
  People must keep their place, some down and some on top!
  (Though it is nice, for a little change, to do just as one pleases!)

(The Cobbler's Boy has put on the lacquered boots he was carrying. He struts off. The Ballad Singer takes over the guitar again. His Wife dances around him in increased tempo. A Monk has been standing near a rich Couple, who are in subdued costly clothes, without masks: shocked at the song, he now leaves. A Dwarf in the costume of an astronomer turns his telescope on the departing Monk, thus drawing attention to the rich Couple. In imitation of the Cobbler's Boy, the Spinner forms a chain of grownups. They move to the music, in and out, and between the rich Couple. The Spinner changes the Gentleman's bonnet for the ragged hat of a Beggar. The Gentleman decides to take this in good part, and a Girl is emboldened to take his dagger. The Gentleman is miffed, throws the Beggar's hat back. The Beggar discards the Gentleman's bonnet and drops it on the ground. The King of Hungary has walked from his throne, taken an egg from the Peasant Woman, and paid for it. He now ceremoniously breaks it over the Gentleman's head as he is bending down to pick up his bonnet. The Gentleman conducts the Lady away from the scene. The King of Hungary, about to resume his throne, finds one of the Children sitting on it. The Gentleman returns to retrieve his dagger. Merriment. The Ballad Singer wanders off. This is part of his routine. His Wife sings to the Spinner.)

WIFE:

Now speaking for myself I feel
That I could also do with a change.
You know, for me . . . *(Turning to a reveller)* . . . *you* have appeal
Maybe tonight we could arrange . . .

(The Dwarf-Astronomer has been amusing the people by focusing his telescope on her legs. The Ballad Singer has returned)

BALLAD SINGER:

No, no, no, no, no, stop, Galileo, stop!
For independent spirit spreads like foul diseases
People must keep their place, some down and some on top!
(Though it is nice, for a little change, to do just as one pleases!)

(The Spectators stand embarrassed. A Girl laughs loudly)

BALLAD SINGER AND HIS WIFE:

Good people who have trouble here below

In serving cruel lords and gentle Jesus
Who bids you turn the other cheek just so . . . (*With mimicry*)
While they prepare to strike the second blow:
Obedience will never cure your woe
So each of you wake up and do just as he pleases!
(The Ballad Singer and his Wife hurriedly start to try to sell pamphlets to the spectators.)

BALLAD SINGER: Read all about the earth going round the sun, two centesimi only. As proved by the great Galileo. Two centesimi only. Written by a local scholar. Understandable to one and all. Buy one for your friends, your children and your aunty Rosa, two centesimi only. Abbreviated but complete. Fully illustrated with pictures of the planets, including Venus, two centesimi only.

(During the speech of the Ballad Singer we hear the carnival procession approaching followed by laughter. A Reveller rushes in.)

REVELLER: The procession!

(The litter bearers speedily joggle out the King of Hungary. The Spectators turn and look at the first float of the procession, which now makes its appearance. It bears a gigantic figure of Galileo, holding in one hand an open Bible with the pages crossed out. The other hand points to the Bible, and the head mechanically turns from side to side as if to say "No! No!")

A LOUD VOICE: Galileo, the Bible killer!

(The laughter from the market place becomes uproarious. The Monk comes flying from the market place followed by delighted Children.)

Scene Ten

The depths are hot, the heights are chill
The streets are loud, the court is still.

Ante-chamber and staircase in the Medicean palace in Florence. Galileo, with a book under his arm, waits with his Daughter to be admitted to the presence of the Prince.

VIRGINIA: They are a long time.

GALILEO: Yes.

VIRGINIA: Who is that funny looking man? (*She indicates the Informer who has entered casually and seated himself in the background, taking no apparent notice of Galileo.*)

GALILEO: I don't know.

VIRGINIA: It's not the first time I have seen him around. He gives me the creeps.

GALILEO: Nonsense. We're in Florence, not among robbers in the mountains of Corsica.

VIRGINIA: Here comes the Rector.

(The Rector comes down the stairs.)

GALILEO: Gaffone is a bore. He attaches himself to you. (*The Rector passes, scarcely nodding.*)

GALILEO: My eyes are bad today. Did he acknowledge us?

VIRGINIA: Barely. (*Pause*) What's in your book? Will they say it's heretical?

GALILEO: You hang around church too much. And getting up at dawn and scurrying to mass is ruining your skin. You pray for me, don't you?

(A Man comes down the stairs.)

VIRGINIA: Here's Mr. Matti. You designed a machine for his Iron Foundries.

MATTI: How were the squabs, Mr. Galilei? (*Low*) My brother and I had a good laugh the other day. He picked up a racy pamphlet against the Bible somewhere. It quoted you.

GALILEO: The squabs, Matti, were wonderful, thank you again.

Pamphlets I know nothing about. The Bible and Homer are my favorite reading.

MATTI: No necessity to be cautious with me, Mr. Galilei. I am on your side. I am not a man who knows about the motions of the stars, but you have championed the freedom to teach new things. Take that mechanical cultivator they have in Germany which you described to me. I can tell you, it will never be used in this country. The same circles that are hampering you now will forbid the physicians at Bologna to cut up corpses for research. Do you know, they have such things as money markets in Amsterdam and in London? Schools for business, too. Regular papers with news. Here we are not even free to make money. I have a stake in your career. They are against iron foundries because they say the gathering of so many workers in one place fosters immorality! If they ever try anything, Mr. Galilei, remember you have friends in all walks of life including an iron founder. Good luck to you.

(He goes.)

GALILEO: Good man, but need he be so affectionate in public? His voice carries. They will always claim me as their spiritual leader particularly in places where it doesn't help me at all. I have written a book about the mechanics of the firmament, that is all. What they do or don't do with it is not my concern.

VIRGINIA *(loud)*: If people only knew how you disagreed with those goings-on all over the country last All Fools day.

GALILEO Yes. Offer honey to a bear, and lose your arm if the beast is hungry.

VIRGINIA *(low)*: Did the prince ask you to come here today?

GALILEO: I sent word I was coming. He will want the book, he has paid for it. My health hasn't been any too good lately. I may accept Sagredo's invitation to stay with him in Padua for a few weeks.

VIRGINIA: You couldn't manage without your books.

GALILEO: Sagredo has an excellent library.

VIRGINIA: We haven't had this month's salary yet—

GALILEO: Yes. *(The Cardinal Inquisitor passes down the staircase. He bows deeply in answer to Galileo's bow.)* What is he doing in Florence? If they try to do anything to me, the new Pope will meet them with an iron NO. And the Prince is my pupil, he would never have me extradited.

VIRGINIA: Psst. The Lord Chamberlain.

(The Lord Chamberlain comes down the stairs.)

LORD CHAMBERLAIN His Highness had hoped to find time for you, Mr. Galilei. Unfortunately, he has to leave immediately to judge the parade at the Riding Academy. On what business did you wish to see His Highness?

GALILEO: I wanted to present my book to His Highness.

LORD CHAMBERLAIN: How are your eyes today?

GALILEO: So, so. With His Highness' permission, I am dedicating the book . . .

LORD CHAMBERLAIN: Your eyes are a matter of great concern to His Highness. Could it be that you have been looking too long and too often through your marvelous tube? (*He leaves without accepting the book*)

VIRGINIA (*greatly agitated*): Father, I am afraid.

GALILEO: He didn't take the book, did he? (*Low and resolute*) Keep a straight face. We are not going home, but to the house of the lens-grinder. There is a coach and horses in his backyard. Keep your eyes to the front, don't look back at that man.

(*They start. The Lord Chamberlain comes back.*)

LORD CHAMBERLAIN: Oh, Mr. Galilei, His Highness has just charged me to inform you that the Florentine Court is no longer in a position to oppose the request of the Holy Inquisition to interrogate you in Rome.

Scene Eleven

THE POPE

A chamber in the Vatican. The Pope, Urban VIII—formerly Cardinal Barberini—is giving audience to the Cardinal Inquisitor. The trampling and shuffling of many feet is heard throughout the scene from the adjoining corridors. During the scene the Pope is being robed for the conclave he is about to attend: at the beginning of the scene he is plainly Barberini, but as the scene proceeds he is more and more obscured by grandiose vestments.

POPE: No! No! No!

INQUISITOR (*referring to the owners of the shuffling feet*): Doctors of all chairs from the universities, representatives of the special orders of the Church, representatives of the clergy as a whole who have come believing with child-like faith in the word of God as set forth in the Scriptures, who have come to hear Your Holiness confirm their faith: and Your Holiness is really going to tell them that the Bible can no longer be regarded as the alphabet of truth?

POPE: I will not set myself up against the multiplication table. No!

INQUISITOR: Ah, that is what these people say, that it is the multiplication table. Their cry is, "The figures compel us," but where do these figures come from? Plainly they come from doubt. These men doubt everything. Can society stand on doubt and not on faith? "Thou art my master, but I doubt whether it is for the best." "This is my neighbor's house and my neighbor's wife, but why shouldn't they belong to me?" After the plague, after the new war, after the unparalleled disaster of the Reformation, your dwindling flock look to their shepherd, and now the mathematicians turn their tubes on the sky and announce to the world that you have not the best advice about the heavens either—up to now your only uncontested sphere of influence. This Galilei started meddling in machines at an early age. Now that men in ships are venturing on the great oceans—I am not against that of course—they are putting their faith in a brass bowl they call a compass and not in Almighty God.

POPE: This man is the greatest physicist of our time. He is the light of Italy, and not just any muddle-head.

INQUISITOR: Would we have had to arrest him otherwise? This bad man knows what he is doing, not writing his books in Latin, but in the jargon of the market place.

POPE (*occupied with the shuffling feet*): That was not in the best of taste. (*A pause*) These shuffling feet are making me nervous.

INQUISITOR: May they be more telling than my words, Your Holiness. Shall all these go from you with doubt in their hearts?

POPE: This man has friends. What about Versailles? What about the Viennese court? They will call Holy Church a cesspool for defunct ideas. Keep your hands off him.

INQUISITOR: In practice it will never get far. He is a man of the flesh. He would soften at once.

POPE: He has more enjoyment in him than any man I ever saw. He loves eating and drinking and thinking. To excess. He indulges in thinking-bouts! He cannot say no to an old wine or a new thought. (*Furious*) I do not want a condemnation of physical facts. I do not want to hear battle cries: Church, church, church! Reason, reason, reason! (*Pause*) These shuffling feet are intolerable. Has the whole world come to my door?

INQUISITOR: Not the whole world, Your Holiness. A select gathering of the faithful.

(*Pause*)

POPE (*exhausted*): It is clearly understood: he is not to be tortured. (*Pause*) At the very most, he may be shown the instruments.

INQUISITOR: That will be adequate, Your Holiness. Mr. Galilei understands machinery.

(*The eyes of Barberini look helplessly at the Cardinal Inquisitor from under the completely assembled panoply of Pope Urban VIII.*)

Scene Twelve

June twenty second, sixteen thirty three,
A momentous date for you and me.
Of all the days that was the one
An age of reason could have begun.

Again the garden of the Florentine Ambassador at Rome, where Galileo's assistants await the news of the trial. The Little Monk and Federzoni are attempting to concentrate on a game of chess. Virginia kneels in a corner, praying and counting her beads.

LITTLE MONK: The Pope didn't even grant him an audience.

FEDERZONI: No more scientific discussions.

ANDREA: The "Discorsi" will never be finished. The sum of his findings. They will kill him.

FEDERZONI (*stealing a glance at him*): Do you really think so?

ANDREA: He will never recant.

(*Silence*)

LITTLE MONK: You know when you lie awake at night how your mind fastens on to something irrelevant. Last night I kept thinking: if only they would let him take his little stone in with him, the appeal-to-reason-pebble that he always carried in his pocket.

FEDERZONI: In the room *they'll* take him to, he won't have a pocket.

ANDREA: But he will not recant.

LITTLE MONK: How can they beat the truth out of a man who gave his sight in order to see?

FEDERZONI: Maybe they can't.

(*Silence*)

ANDREA (*speaking about Virginia*): She is praying that he will recant.

FEDERZONI: Leave her alone. She doesn't know whether she's on her head or on her heels since they got hold of her. They brought her Father Confessor from Florence.

(*The Informer of Scene Ten enters.*)

INFORMER: Mr. Galilei will be here soon. He may need a bed.

FEDERZONI: Have they let him out?

INFORMER: Mr. Galilei is expected to recant at five o'clock. The big bell of Saint Marcus will be rung and the complete text of his recantation publicly announced.

ANDREA: I don't believe it.

INFORMER: Mr. Galilei will be brought to the garden gate at the back of the house, to avoid the crowds collecting in the streets. (*He goes.*)
(*Silence*)

ANDREA: The moon is an earth because the light of the moon is not her own. Jupiter is a fixed star, and four moons turn around Jupiter, therefore we are not shut in by crystal shells. The sun is the pivot of our world, therefore the earth is not the center. The earth moves, spinning about the sun. And he showed us. You can't make a man unsee what he has seen.
(*Silence*)

FEDERZONI: Five o'clock is one minute.
(*Virginia prays louder.*)

ANDREA: Listen all of you, they are murdering the truth.
(*He stops up his ears with his fingers. The two other pupils do the same. Federzoni goes over to the Little Monk, and all of them stand absolutely still in cramped positions. Nothing happens. No bell sounds. After a silence, filled with the murmur of Virginia's prayers, Federzoni runs to the wall to look at the clock. He turns around, his expression changed. He shakes his head. They drop their hands.*)

FEDERZONI: No. No bell. It is three minutes after.

LITTLE MONK: He hasn't.

ANDREA: He held true. It is all right, it is all right.

LITTLE MONK: He did not recant.

FEDERZONI: No.
(*They embrace each other, they are delirious with joy.*)

ANDREA: So force cannot accomplish everything. What has been seen can't be unseen. Man is constant in the face of death.

FEDERZONI: June 22, 1633: dawn of the age of reason. I wouldn't have wanted to go on living if he had recanted.

LITTLE MONK: I didn't say anything, but I was in agony. Oh, ye of little faith!

ANDREA: I was sure.

FEDERZONI: It would have turned our morning to night.

ANDREA: It would have been as if the mountain had turned to water.

LITTLE MONK (*kneeling down, crying*): Oh God, I thank Thee.

ANDREA: Beaten humanity can lift its head. A man has stood up and said "no."

(At this moment the bell of Saint Marcus begins to toll. They stand like statues. Virginia stands up.)

VIRGINIA: The bell of Saint Marcus. He is not damned.

(From the street one hears the Town Crier reading Galileo's recantation.)

TOWN CRIER: I, Galileo Galilei, Teacher of Mathematics and Physics, do hereby publicly renounce my teaching that the earth moves. I foreswear this teaching with a sincere heart and unfeigned faith and detest and curse this and all other errors and heresies repugnant to the Holy Scriptures.

(The lights dim; when they come up again the bell of Saint Marcus is petering out. Virginia has gone but the Scholars are still there waiting.)

ANDREA *(loud)*: The mountain did turn to water.

(Galileo has entered quietly and unnoticed. He is changed, almost unrecognizable. He has heard Andrea. He waits some seconds by the door for somebody to greet him. Nobody does. They retreat from him. He goes slowly and, because of his bad sight, uncertainly, to the front of the stage where he finds a chair, and sits down.)

ANDREA: I can't look at him. Tell him to go away.

FEDERZONI: Steady.

ANDREA *(hysterically)*: He saved his big gut.

FEDERZONI: Get him a glass of water.

(The Little Monk fetches a glass of water for Andrea. Nobody acknowledges the presence of Galileo, who sits silently on his chair listening to the voice of the Town Crier, now in another street.)

ANDREA: I can walk. Just help me a bit.

(They help him to the door.)

ANDREA *(in the door)*: "Unhappy is the land that breeds no hero."

GALILEO: No, Andrea: "Unhappy is the land that needs a hero."

(Before the next scene a curtain with the following legend on it is lowered.)

You can plainly see that if a horse were to fall from a height of three or four feet, it could break its bones, whereas a dog would not suffer injury. The same applies to a cat from a height of as much as eight or ten feet, to a grasshopper from the top of a tower, and to an ant falling down from the moon. Nature could not allow a horse to become as big as twenty horses nor a giant as big as ten men, unless she were to change the proportions of all its members, particularly the bones. Thus the common assumption that great and small structures are equally tough is obviously wrong.

—From the "Discorsi"

Scene Thirteen

1633–1642.
Galileo Galilei remains a prisoner
of the Inquisition until his death.

*A country house near Florence. A large room simply furnished. There is
a huge table, a leather chair, a globe of the world on a stand, and a
narrow bed. A portion of the adjoining anteroom is visible, and the
front door which opens into it. An Official of the Inquisition sits on
guard in the anteroom. In the large room, Galileo is quietly
experimenting with a bent wooden rail and a small ball of wood. He is
still vigorous but almost blind. After a while there is a knocking at the
outside door. The Official opens it to a peasant who brings a plucked
goose. Virginia comes from the kitchen. She is past forty.*

PEASANT (*banding the goose to Virginia*): I was told to deliver this
    here.

VIRGINIA: I didn't order a goose.

PEASANT: I was told to say it's from someone who was passing
    through.

    (*Virginia takes the goose, surprised. The Official takes it from her
    and examines it suspiciously. Then, reassured, he hands it back to
    her. The Peasant goes. Virginia brings the goose in to Galileo.*)

VIRGINIA: Somebody who was passing through sent you something.

GALILEO: What is it?

VIRGINIA: Can't you see it?

GALILEO: No. (*He walks over*) A goose. Any name?

VIRGINIA: No.

GALILEO (*weighing the goose*): Solid.

VIRGINIA (*cautiously*): Will you eat the liver, if I have it cooked with
    a little apple?

GALILEO: I had my dinner. Are you under orders to finish me off with
    food?

VIRGINIA: It's not rich. And what is wrong with your eyes again? You
    should be able to see it.

GALILEO: You were standing in the light.

VIRGINIA: I was not.—You haven't been writing again?

GALILEO: (*sneering*) What do you think?

(*Virginia takes the goose out into the anteroom and speaks to the Official.*)

VIRGINIA: You had better ask Monsignor Carpula to send the doctor. Father couldn't see this goose across the room.—Don't look at me like that. He has not been writing. He dictates everything to me, as you know.

OFFICIAL: Yes?

VIRGINIA: He abides by the rules. My father's repentance is sincere. I keep an eye on him. (*She hands him the goose.*) Tell the cook to fry the liver with an apple and an onion. (*She goes back into the large room.*) And you have no business to be doing that with those eyes of yours, father.

GALILEO: You may read me some Horace.

VIRGINIA: We should go on with your weekly letter to the Archbishop. Monsignor Carpula to whom we owe so much was all smiles the other day because the Archbishop had expressed his pleasure at your collaboration.

GALILEO: Where were we?

VIRGINIA (*sits down to take his dictation*): Paragraph four.

GALILEO: Read what you have.

VIRGINIA: "The position of the Church in the matter of the unrest at Genoa. I agree with Cardinal Spoletti in the matter of the unrest among the Venetian ropemakers . . ."

GALILEO: Yes. (*Dictates*) I agree with Cardinal Spoletti in the matter of the unrest among the Venetian ropemakers: it is better to distribute good nourishing food in the name of charity than to pay them more for their bellropes. It being surely better to strengthen their faith than to encourage their acquisitiveness. St. Paul says: Charity never faileth.—How is that?

VIRGINIA: It's beautiful, father.

GALILEO: It couldn't be taken as irony?

VIRGINIA: No. The Archbishop will like it. It's so practical.

GALILEO: I trust your judgment. Read it over slowly.

VIRGINIA: "The position of the Church in the matter of the unrest . . ."

(*There is a knocking at the outside door. Virginia goes into the anteroom. The Official opens the door. It is Andrea.*)

ANDREA: Good evening. I am sorry to call so late, I'm on my way to Holland. I was asked to look him up. Can I go in?

VIRGINIA: I don't know whether he will see you. You never came.

ANDREA: Ask him.

(Galileo recognizes the voice. He sits motionless. Virginia comes in to Galileo.)

GALILEO: Is that Andrea?

VIRGINIA: Yes. *(Pause)* I will send him away.

GALILEO: Show him in.

(Virginia shows Andrea in. Virginia sits, Andrea remains standing)

ANDREA: *(cool)* Have you been keeping well, Mr. Galilei?

GALILEO: Sit down. What are you doing these days? What are you working on? I heard it was something about hydraulics in Milan.

ANDREA: As he knew I was passing through, Fabricius of Amsterdam asked me to visit you and inquire about your health. *(Pause)*

GALILEO: I am very well.

ANDREA *(formally)*: I am glad I can report you are in good health.

GALILEO Fabricius will be glad to hear it. And you might inform him that, on account of the depth of my repentance, I live in comparative comfort.

ANDREA: Yes, we understand that the church is more than pleased with you. Your complete acceptance has had its effect. Not one paper expounding a new thesis has made its appearance in Italy since your submission.

(Pause)

GALILEO: Unfortunately there are countries not under the wing of the church. Would you not say the erroneous condemned theories are still taught—there?

ANDREA *(relentless)*: Things are almost at a standstill.

GALILEO: Are they? *(Pause)* Nothing from Descartes in Paris?

ANDREA: Yes. On receiving the news of your recantation, he shelved his treatise on the nature of light.

GALILEO: I sometimes worry about my assistants whom I led into error. Have they benefited by my example?

ANDREA: In order to work I have to go to Holland.

GALILEO: Yes.

ANDREA: Federzoni is grinding lenses again, back in some shop.

GALILEO: He can't read the books.

ANDREA: Fulganzio, our little monk, has abandoned research and is resting in peace in the church.

GALILEO: So. *(Pause)* My superiors are looking forward to my spiritual recovery. I am progressing as well as can be expected.

VIRGINIA: You are doing well, father.

GALILEO: Virginia, leave the room.

(Virginia rises uncertainly and goes out.)

VIRGINIA *(to the Official)*: He was his pupil, so now he is his enemy.—Help me in the kitchen.

(She leaves the anteroom with the Official.)

ANDREA: May I go now, sir?

GALILEO: I do not know why you came, Sarti. To unsettle me? I have to be prudent.

ANDREA: I'll be on my way.

GALILEO: As it is, I have relapses. I completed the "Discorsi."

ANDREA: You completed what?

GALILEO: My "Discorsi."

ANDREA: How?

GALILEO: I am allowed pen and paper. My superiors are intelligent men. They know the habits of a lifetime cannot be broken abruptly. But they protect me from any unpleasant consequences: they lock my pages away as I dictate them. And I should know better than to risk my comfort. I wrote the "Discorsi" out again during the night. The manuscript is in the globe. My vanity has up to now prevented me from destroying it. If you consider taking it, you will shoulder the entire risk. You will say it was pirated from the original in the hands of the Holy Office.

(Andrea, as in a trance, has gone to the globe. He lifts the upper half and gets the book. He turns the pages as if wanting to devour them. In the background the opening sentences of the "Discorsi" appear: MY PURPOSE IS TO SET FORTH A VERY NEW SCIENCE DEALING WITH A VERY ANCIENT SUBJECT—MOTION. . . . AND I HAVE DISCOVERED BY EXPERIMENT SOME PROPERTIES OF IT WHICH ARE WORTH KNOWING. . . . *)*

GALILEO: I had to employ my time somehow.

(The text disappears.)

ANDREA: Two new sciences! This will be the foundation stone of a new physics.

GALILEO: Yes. Put it under your coat.

ANDREA: And we thought you had deserted. *(In a low voice)* Mr. Galilei, how can I begin to express my shame. Mine has been the loudest voice against you.

GALILEO: That would seem to have been proper. I taught you science and I decried the truth.

ANDREA: Did you? I think not. Everything is changed!

GALILEO: What is changed?

ANDREA: You shielded the truth from the oppressor. Now I see! In your dealings with the Inquisition you used the same superb common sense you brought to physics.

GALILEO: Oh!

ANDREA: We lost our heads. With the crowd at the street corners we said: "He will die, he will never surrender!" You came back: "I surrendered but I am alive." We cried: "Your hands are stained!" You say: "Better stained than empty."

GALILEO: "Better stained than empty."—It sounds realistic. Sounds like me.

ANDREA: And I of all people should have known. I was twelve when you sold another man's telescope to the Venetian Senate, and saw you put it to immortal use. Your friends were baffled when you bowed to the Prince of Florence: Science gained a wider audience. You always laughed at heroics. "People who suffer bore me," you said. "Misfortunes are due mainly to miscalculations." And: "If there are obstacles, the shortest line between two points may be the crooked line."

GALILEO: It makes a picture.

ANDREA: And when you stopped to recant in 1633, I should have understood that you were again about your business.

GALILEO: My business being?

ANDREA: Science. The study of the properties of motion, mother of the machines which will themselves change the ugly face of the earth.

GALILEO: Aha!

ANDREA: You gained time to write a book that only you could write. Had you burned at the stake in a blaze of glory they would have won.

GALILEO: They have won. And there is no such thing as a scientific work that only one man can write.

ANDREA: Then why did you recant, tell me that!

GALILEO: I recanted because I was afraid of physical pain.

ANDREA: No!

GALILEO: They showed me the instruments.

ANDREA: It was not a plan?

GALILEO: It was not.

(Pause)

ANDREA: But you have contributed. Science has only one commandment: contribution. And you have contributed more than any man for a hundred years.

GALILEO: Have I? Then welcome to my gutter, dear colleague in science and brother in treason: I sold out, you are a buyer. The first sight of the book! His mouth watered and his scoldings were drowned. Blessed be our bargaining, whitewashing, deathfearing community!

ANDREA: The fear of death is human.

GALILEO: Even the church will teach you that to be weak is not human. It is just evil.

ANDREA: The church, yes! But science is not concerned with our weaknesses.

GALILEO: No? My dear Sarti, in spite of my present convictions, I may be able to give you a few pointers as to the concerns of your chosen profession.

(Enter Virginia with a platter)

In my spare time, I happen to have gone over this case. I have spare time.—Even a man who sells wool, however good he is at buying wool cheap and selling it dear, must be concerned with the standing of the wool trade. The practice of science would seem to call for valor. She trades in knowledge, which is the product of doubt. And this new art of doubt has enchanted the public. The plight of the multitude is old as the rocks, and is believed to be basic as the rocks. But now they have learned to doubt. They snatched the telescopes out of our hands and had them trained on their tormentors: prince, official, public moralist. The mechanism of the heavens was clearer, the mechanism of their courts was still murky. The battle to measure the heavens is won by doubt; by credulity the Roman housewife's battle for milk will always be lost. Word is passed down that this is of no concern to the scientist who is told he will only release such of his findings as do not disturb the peace, that is, the peace of mind of the well-to-do. Threats and bribes fill the air. Can the scientist hold out on the numbers?—For what reason do you labor? I take it the intent of science is to ease human existence. If you give way to coercion, science can be crippled, and your new machines may simply suggest new drudgeries. Should you then, in time, discover all there is to be discovered, your progress must then become a progress away from the bulk of humanity. The gulf might even grow so wide that the sound of your cheering at some new achievement would be echoed by a universal howl of horror.—As a scientist I had an almost unique opportunity. In my day astronomy emerged into the market place. At that particular time, had one man put up a fight, it could have had wide repercussions. I have come to believe that I was never in real danger; for some years I was as strong as the authorities, and I surrendered my knowledge to the powers that be, to use it, no, not *use* it, *abuse* it, as it suits their ends. I have betrayed my profession. Any man who does what I have done must not be tolerated in the ranks of science.

(Virginia, who has stood motionless, puts the platter on the table.)

VIRGINIA: You are accepted in the ranks of the faithful, father.

GALILEO *(sees her)*: Correct. *(He goes over to the table.)* I have to eat now.

VIRGINIA We lock up at eight.

ANDREA: I am glad I came. *(He extends his hand. Galileo ignores it and goes over to his meal.)*

GALILEO *(examining the plate; to Andrea)*: Somebody who knows me sent me a goose. I still enjoy eating.

ANDREA: And your opinion is now that the "new age" was an illusion?

GALILEO: Well.—This age of ours turned out to be a whore, spattered with blood. Maybe, new ages look like blood-spattered whores. Take care of yourself.

ANDREA: Yes. *(Unable to go)* With reference to your evaluation of the author in question—I do not know the answer. But I cannot think that your savage analysis is the last word.

GALILEO: Thank you, sir.

(Official knocks at the door)

VIRGINIA: *(showing Andrea out)* I don't like visitors from the past, they excite him.

(She lets him out. The official closes the iron door. Virginia returns.)

GALILEO *(eating)*: Did you try and think who sent the goose?

VIRGINIA: Not Andrea.

GALILEO: Maybe not. I gave Redhead his first lesson; when he held out his hand, I had to remind myself he is teaching now.—How is the sky tonight?

VIRGINIA *(at the window)*: Bright.

(Galileo continues eating.)

Scene Fourteen

The great book o'er the border went
And, good folk, that was the end.
But we hope you'll keep in mind
You and I were left behind.

Before a little Italian customs house early in the morning. Andrea sits upon one of his traveling trunks at the barrier and reads Galileo's book. The window of a small house is still lit, and a big grotesque shadow, like an old witch and her cauldron, falls upon the house wall beyond. Barefoot children in rags see it and point to the little house.

CHILDREN (*singing*):
  One, two, three, four, five, six,
  Old Marina is a witch.
  At night, on a broomstick she sits
  And on the church steeple she spits.

CUSTOMS OFFICER (*to Andrea*): Why are you making this journey?

ANDREA: I am a scholar.

CUSTOMS OFFICER (*to his Clerk*): Put down under "reason for leaving the country": Scholar. (*He points to the baggage*) Books! Anything dangerous in these books?

ANDREA: What is dangerous?

CUSTOMS OFFICER: Religion. Politics.

ANDREA: These are nothing but mathematical formulas.

CUSTOMS OFFICER: What's that?

ANDREA: Figures.

CUSTOMS OFFICER: Oh, figures. No harm in figures. Just wait a minute, sir, we will soon have your papers stamped. (*He exits with Clerk.*)
  (*Meanwhile, a little council of war among the Children has taken place. Andrea quietly watches. One of the Boys, pushed forward by the others, creeps up to the little house from which the shadow comes, and takes the jug of milk on the doorstep.*)

ANDREA (*quietly*): What are you doing with that milk?

BOY (*stopping in mid-movement*): She is a witch.
  (*The other Children run away behind the Custom House. One of them shouts*) "*Run, Paolo!*"

ANDREA: Hmm!—And because she is a witch she mustn't have milk. Is that the idea?

BOY: Yes.

ANDREA: And how do you know she is a witch?

BOY (*points to shadow on house wall*): Look!

ANDREA: Oh! I see.

BOY: And she rides on a broomstick at night—and she bewitches the coachman's horses. My cousin Luigi looked through the hole in the stable roof, that the snow storm made, and heard the horses coughing something terrible.

ANDREA: Oh!—How big was the hole in the stable roof?

BOY: Luigi didn't tell. Why?

ANDREA: I was asking because maybe the horses got sick because it was cold in the stable. You had better ask Luigi how big that hole is.

BOY: You are not going to say Old Marina isn't a witch, because you can't.

ANDREA: No, I can't say she isn't a witch. I haven't looked into it. A man can't know about a thing he hasn't looked into, or can he?

BOY: No!—But THAT! (*He points to the shadow.*) She is stirring hell-broth.

ANDREA: Let's see. Do you want to take a look? I can lift you up.

BOY: You lift me to the window, mister! (*He takes a sling shot out of his pocket.*) I can really bash her from there.

ANDREA: Hadn't we better make sure she is a witch before we shoot? I'll hold that.
  (*The Boy puts the milk jug down and follows him reluctantly to the window. Andrea lifts the boy up so that he can look in.*)

ANDREA: What do you see?

BOY (*slowly*): Just an old girl cooking porridge.

ANDREA: Oh! Nothing to it then. Now look at her shadow, Paolo.
  (*The Boy looks over his shoulder and back and compares the reality and the shadow.*)

BOY: The big thing is a soup ladle.

ANDREA: Ah! A ladle! You see, I would have taken it for a broomstick, but I haven't looked into the matter as you have, Paolo. Here is your sling.

CUSTOMS OFFICER (*returning with the Clerk and handing Andrea his papers*): All present and correct. Good luck, sir.
  (*Andrea goes, reading Galileo's book. The Clerk starts to bring his*

baggage after him. The barrier rises. Andrea passes through, still reading the book. The Boy kicks over the milk jug)

BOY *(shouting after Andrea)*: She *is* a witch! She *is* a witch!

ANDREA: You saw with your own eyes: think it over!

(The Boy joins the others. They sing.)

One, two, three, four, five, six,
Old Marina is a witch.
At night, on a broomstick she sits
And on the church steeple she spits.

(The Customs Officers laugh. Andrea goes.)

THE STORY OF PENGUIN CLASSICS

Before 1946 . . . "Classics" are mainly the domain of academics and students; readable editions for everyone else are almost unheard of. This all changes when a little-known classicist, E. V. Rieu, presents Penguin founder Allen Lane with the translation of Homer's *Odyssey* that he has been working on in his spare time.

1946 Penguin Classics debuts with *The Odyssey*, which promptly sells three million copies. Suddenly, classics are no longer for the privileged few.

1950s Rieu, now series editor, turns to professional writers for the best modern, readable translations, including Dorothy L. Sayers's *Inferno* and Robert Graves's unexpurgated *Twelve Caesars*.

1960s The Classics are given the distinctive black covers that have remained a constant throughout the life of the series. Rieu retires in 1964, hailing the Penguin Classics list as "the greatest educative force of the twentieth century."

1970s A new generation of translators swells the Penguin Classics ranks, introducing readers of English to classics of world literature from more than twenty languages. The list grows to encompass more history, philosophy, science, religion, and politics.

1980s The Penguin American Library launches with titles such as *Uncle Tom's Cabin* and joins forces with Penguin Classics to provide the most comprehensive library of world literature available from any paperback publisher.

1990s The launch of Penguin Audiobooks brings the classics to a listening audience for the first time, and in 1999 the worldwide launch of the Penguin Classics Web site extends their reach to the global online community.

The 21st Century Penguin Classics are completely redesigned for the first time in nearly twenty years. This world-famous series now consists of more than 1,300 titles, making the widest range of the best books ever written available to millions—and constantly redefining what makes a "classic."

The Odyssey continues . . .

The best books ever written

PENGUIN ⓟ CLASSICS

SINCE 1946

Find out more at www.penguinclassics.com

Visit www.vpbookclub.com

CLICK ON A CLASSIC
www.penguinclassics.com

The world's greatest literature at your fingertips

Constantly updated information on more than a thousand titles,
from Icelandic sagas to ancient Indian epics, Russian drama to
Italian romance, American greats to African masterpieces

•

The latest news on recent additions to the list, updated
editions, and specially commissioned translations

•

Original essays by leading writers

•

A wealth of background material, including biographies
of every classic author from Aristotle to Zamyatin, plot
synopses, readers' and teachers' guides, useful Web links

•

Online desk and examination copy assistance for academics

•

Trivia quizzes, competitions, giveaways, news on
forthcoming screen adaptations